C-3596   CAREER EXAMINATION SERIES

This is your
PASSBOOK for...

National Police Selection Test (POST)

Test Preparation Study Guide
Questions & Answers

COPYRIGHT NOTICE

This book is SOLELY intended for, is sold ONLY to, and its use is RESTRICTED to individual, bona fide applicants or candidates who qualify by virtue of having seriously filed applications for appropriate license, certificate, professional and/or promotional advancement, higher school matriculation, scholarship, or other legitimate requirements of education and/or governmental authorities.

This book is NOT intended for use, class instruction, tutoring, training, duplication, copying, reprinting, excerption, or adaptation, etc., by:

1) Other publishers
2) Proprietors and/or Instructors of "Coaching" and/or Preparatory Courses
3) Personnel and/or Training Divisions of commercial, industrial, and governmental organizations
4) Schools, colleges, or universities and/or their departments and staffs, including teachers and other personnel
5) Testing Agencies or Bureaus
6) Study groups which seek by the purchase of a single volume to copy and/or duplicate and/or adapt this material for use by the group as a whole without having purchased individual volumes for each of the members of the group
7) Et al.

Such persons would be in violation of appropriate Federal and State statutes.

PROVISION OF LICENSING AGREEMENTS – Recognized educational, commercial, industrial, and governmental institutions and organizations, and others legitimately engaged in educational pursuits, including training, testing, and measurement activities, may address request for a licensing agreement to the copyright owners, who will determine whether, and under what conditions, including fees and charges, the materials in this book may be used them. In other words, a licensing facility exists for the legitimate use of the material in this book on other than an individual basis. However, it is asseverated and affirmed here that the material in this book CANNOT be used without the receipt of the express permission of such a licensing agreement from the Publishers. Inquiries re licensing should be addressed to the company, attention rights and permissions department.

All rights reserved, including the right of reproduction in whole or in part, in any form or by any means, electronic or mechanical, including photocopying, recording, or by any information storage and retrieval system, without permission in writing from the Publisher.

Copyright © 2024 by
National Learning Corporation

212 Michael Drive, Syosset, NY 11791
(516) 921-8888 • www.passbooks.com
E-mail: info@passbooks.com

PUBLISHED IN THE UNITED STATES OF AMERICA

PASSBOOK® SERIES

THE *PASSBOOK® SERIES* has been created to prepare applicants and candidates for the ultimate academic battlefield – the examination room.

At some time in our lives, each and every one of us may be required to take an examination – for validation, matriculation, admission, qualification, registration, certification, or licensure.

Based on the assumption that every applicant or candidate has met the basic formal educational standards, has taken the required number of courses, and read the necessary texts, the *PASSBOOK® SERIES* furnishes the one special preparation which may assure passing with confidence, instead of failing with insecurity. Examination questions – together with answers – are furnished as the basic vehicle for study so that the mysteries of the examination and its compounding difficulties may be eliminated or diminished by a sure method.

This book is meant to help you pass your examination provided that you qualify and are serious in your objective.

The entire field is reviewed through the huge store of content information which is succinctly presented through a provocative and challenging approach – the question-and-answer method.

A climate of success is established by furnishing the correct answers at the end of each test.

You soon learn to recognize types of questions, forms of questions, and patterns of questioning. You may even begin to anticipate expected outcomes.

You perceive that many questions are repeated or adapted so that you can gain acute insights, which may enable you to score many sure points.

You learn how to confront new questions, or types of questions, and to attack them confidently and work out the correct answers.

You note objectives and emphases, and recognize pitfalls and dangers, so that you may make positive educational adjustments.

Moreover, you are kept fully informed in relation to new concepts, methods, practices, and directions in the field.

You discover that you are actually taking the examination all the time: you are preparing for the examination by "taking" an examination, not by reading extraneous and/or supererogatory textbooks.

In short, this PASSBOOK®, used directedly, should be an important factor in helping you to pass your test.

NATIONAL POLICE SELECTION TEST (POST)

DUTIES
This test is administered nationally to screen and select candidates for local police departments.

SCOPE OF THE EXAMINATION
The written test will cover knowledge, skills and/or abilities in such areas as:

1. Police knowledge, skills, and judgment in and for law enforcement situations;
2. Learning and applying police information;
3. Observation and memory;
4. Problem solving; and
5. Understanding and interpreting written material;

HOW TO TAKE A TEST

I. YOU MUST PASS AN EXAMINATION

A. WHAT EVERY CANDIDATE SHOULD KNOW

Examination applicants often ask us for help in preparing for the written test. What can I study in advance? What kinds of questions will be asked? How will the test be given? How will the papers be graded?

As an applicant for a civil service examination, you may be wondering about some of these things. Our purpose here is to suggest effective methods of advance study and to describe civil service examinations.

Your chances for success on this examination can be increased if you know how to prepare. Those "pre-examination jitters" can be reduced if you know what to expect. You can even experience an adventure in good citizenship if you know why civil service exams are given.

B. WHY ARE CIVIL SERVICE EXAMINATIONS GIVEN?

Civil service examinations are important to you in two ways. As a citizen, you want public jobs filled by employees who know how to do their work. As a job seeker, you want a fair chance to compete for that job on an equal footing with other candidates. The best-known means of accomplishing this two-fold goal is the competitive examination.

Exams are widely publicized throughout the nation. They may be administered for jobs in federal, state, city, municipal, town or village governments or agencies.

Any citizen may apply, with some limitations, such as the age or residence of applicants. Your experience and education may be reviewed to see whether you meet the requirements for the particular examination. When these requirements exist, they are reasonable and applied consistently to all applicants. Thus, a competitive examination may cause you some uneasiness now, but it is your privilege and safeguard.

C. HOW ARE CIVIL SERVICE EXAMS DEVELOPED?

Examinations are carefully written by trained technicians who are specialists in the field known as "psychological measurement," in consultation with recognized authorities in the field of work that the test will cover. These experts recommend the subject matter areas or skills to be tested; only those knowledges or skills important to your success on the job are included. The most reliable books and source materials available are used as references. Together, the experts and technicians judge the difficulty level of the questions.

Test technicians know how to phrase questions so that the problem is clearly stated. Their ethics do not permit "trick" or "catch" questions. Questions may have been tried out on sample groups, or subjected to statistical analysis, to determine their usefulness.

Written tests are often used in combination with performance tests, ratings of training and experience, and oral interviews. All of these measures combine to form the best-known means of finding the right person for the right job.

II. HOW TO PASS THE WRITTEN TEST

A. NATURE OF THE EXAMINATION

To prepare intelligently for civil service examinations, you should know how they differ from school examinations you have taken. In school you were assigned certain definite pages to read or subjects to cover. The examination questions were quite detailed and usually emphasized memory. Civil service exams, on the other hand, try to discover your present ability to perform the duties of a position, plus your potentiality to learn these duties. In other words, a civil service exam attempts to predict how successful you will be. Questions cover such a broad area that they cannot be as minute and detailed as school exam questions.

In the public service similar kinds of work, or positions, are grouped together in one "class." This process is known as *position-classification*. All the positions in a class are paid according to the salary range for that class. One class title covers all of these positions, and they are all tested by the same examination.

B. FOUR BASIC STEPS

1) Study the announcement

How, then, can you know what subjects to study? Our best answer is: "Learn as much as possible about the class of positions for which you've applied." The exam will test the knowledge, skills and abilities needed to do the work.

Your most valuable source of information about the position you want is the official exam announcement. This announcement lists the training and experience qualifications. Check these standards and apply only if you come reasonably close to meeting them.

The brief description of the position in the examination announcement offers some clues to the subjects which will be tested. Think about the job itself. Review the duties in your mind. Can you perform them, or are there some in which you are rusty? Fill in the blank spots in your preparation.

Many jurisdictions preview the written test in the exam announcement by including a section called "Knowledge and Abilities Required," "Scope of the Examination," or some similar heading. Here you will find out specifically what fields will be tested.

2) Review your own background

Once you learn in general what the position is all about, and what you need to know to do the work, ask yourself which subjects you already know fairly well and which need improvement. You may wonder whether to concentrate on improving your strong areas or on building some background in your fields of weakness. When the announcement has specified "some knowledge" or "considerable knowledge," or has used adjectives like "beginning principles of..." or "advanced ... methods," you can get a clue as to the number and difficulty of questions to be asked in any given field. More questions, and hence broader coverage, would be included for those subjects which are more important in the work. Now weigh your strengths and weaknesses against the job requirements and prepare accordingly.

3) Determine the level of the position

Another way to tell how intensively you should prepare is to understand the level of the job for which you are applying. Is it the entering level? In other words, is this the position in which beginners in a field of work are hired? Or is it an intermediate or advanced level? Sometimes this is indicated by such words as "Junior" or "Senior" in the class title. Other jurisdictions use Roman numerals to designate the level – Clerk I, Clerk II, for example. The word "Supervisor" sometimes appears in the title. If the level is not indicated by the title, check the description of duties. Will you be working under very close supervision, or will you have responsibility for independent decisions in this work?

4) Choose appropriate study materials

Now that you know the subjects to be examined and the relative amount of each subject to be covered, you can choose suitable study materials. For beginning level jobs, or even advanced ones, if you have a pronounced weakness in some aspect of your training, read a modern, standard textbook in that field. Be sure it is up to date and has general coverage. Such books are normally available at your library, and the librarian will be glad to help you locate one. For entry-level positions, questions of appropriate difficulty are chosen – neither highly advanced questions, nor those too simple. Such questions require careful thought but not advanced training.

If the position for which you are applying is technical or advanced, you will read more advanced, specialized material. If you are already familiar with the basic principles of your field, elementary textbooks would waste your time. Concentrate on advanced textbooks and technical periodicals. Think through the concepts and review difficult problems in your field.

These are all general sources. You can get more ideas on your own initiative, following these leads. For example, training manuals and publications of the government agency which employs workers in your field can be useful, particularly for technical and professional positions. A letter or visit to the government department involved may result in more specific study suggestions, and certainly will provide you with a more definite idea of the exact nature of the position you are seeking.

III. KINDS OF TESTS

Tests are used for purposes other than measuring knowledge and ability to perform specified duties. For some positions, it is equally important to test ability to make adjustments to new situations or to profit from training. In others, basic mental abilities not dependent on information are essential. Questions which test these things may not appear as pertinent to the duties of the position as those which test for knowledge and information. Yet they are often highly important parts of a fair examination. For very general questions, it is almost impossible to help you direct your study efforts. What we can do is to point out some of the more common of these general abilities needed in public service positions and describe some typical questions.

1) General information

Broad, general information has been found useful for predicting job success in some kinds of work. This is tested in a variety of ways, from vocabulary lists to questions about current events. Basic background in some field of work, such as sociology or economics, may be sampled in a group of questions. Often these are principles which have become familiar to most persons through exposure rather than through formal training. It is difficult to advise you how to study for these questions; being alert to the world around you is our best suggestion.

2) Verbal ability

An example of an ability needed in many positions is verbal or language ability. Verbal ability is, in brief, the ability to use and understand words. Vocabulary and grammar tests are typical measures of this ability. Reading comprehension or paragraph interpretation questions are common in many kinds of civil service tests. You are given a paragraph of written material and asked to find its central meaning.

3) Numerical ability

Number skills can be tested by the familiar arithmetic problem, by checking paired lists of numbers to see which are alike and which are different, or by interpreting charts and graphs. In the latter test, a graph may be printed in the test booklet which you are asked to use as the basis for answering questions.

4) Observation

A popular test for law-enforcement positions is the observation test. A picture is shown to you for several minutes, then taken away. Questions about the picture test your ability to observe both details and larger elements.

5) Following directions

In many positions in the public service, the employee must be able to carry out written instructions dependably and accurately. You may be given a chart with several columns, each column listing a variety of information. The questions require you to carry out directions involving the information given in the chart.

6) Skills and aptitudes

Performance tests effectively measure some manual skills and aptitudes. When the skill is one in which you are trained, such as typing or shorthand, you can practice. These tests are often very much like those given in business school or high school courses. For many of the other skills and aptitudes, however, no short-time preparation can be made. Skills and abilities natural to you or that you have developed throughout your lifetime are being tested.

Many of the general questions just described provide all the data needed to answer the questions and ask you to use your reasoning ability to find the answers. Your best preparation for these tests, as well as for tests of facts and ideas, is to be at your physical and mental best. You, no doubt, have your own methods of getting into an exam-taking mood and keeping "in shape." The next section lists some ideas on this subject.

IV. KINDS OF QUESTIONS

Only rarely is the "essay" question, which you answer in narrative form, used in civil service tests. Civil service tests are usually of the short-answer type. Full instructions for answering these questions will be given to you at the examination. But in case this is your first experience with short-answer questions and separate answer sheets, here is what you need to know:

1) Multiple-choice Questions

Most popular of the short-answer questions is the "multiple choice" or "best answer" question. It can be used, for example, to test for factual knowledge, ability to solve problems or judgment in meeting situations found at work.

A multiple-choice question is normally one of three types—
- It can begin with an incomplete statement followed by several possible endings. You are to find the one ending which *best* completes the statement, although some of the others may not be entirely wrong.
- It can also be a complete statement in the form of a question which is answered by choosing one of the statements listed.

- It can be in the form of a problem – again you select the best answer.

Here is an example of a multiple-choice question with a discussion which should give you some clues as to the method for choosing the right answer:

When an employee has a complaint about his assignment, the action which will *best* help him overcome his difficulty is to
- A. discuss his difficulty with his coworkers
- B. take the problem to the head of the organization
- C. take the problem to the person who gave him the assignment
- D. say nothing to anyone about his complaint

In answering this question, you should study each of the choices to find which is best. Consider choice "A" – Certainly an employee may discuss his complaint with fellow employees, but no change or improvement can result, and the complaint remains unresolved. Choice "B" is a poor choice since the head of the organization probably does not know what assignment you have been given, and taking your problem to him is known as "going over the head" of the supervisor. The supervisor, or person who made the assignment, is the person who can clarify it or correct any injustice. Choice "C" is, therefore, correct. To say nothing, as in choice "D," is unwise. Supervisors have and interest in knowing the problems employees are facing, and the employee is seeking a solution to his problem.

2) True/False Questions

The "true/false" or "right/wrong" form of question is sometimes used. Here a complete statement is given. Your job is to decide whether the statement is right or wrong.

SAMPLE: A roaming cell-phone call to a nearby city costs less than a non-roaming call to a distant city.

This statement is wrong, or false, since roaming calls are more expensive.

This is not a complete list of all possible question forms, although most of the others are variations of these common types. You will always get complete directions for answering questions. Be sure you understand *how* to mark your answers – ask questions until you do.

V. RECORDING YOUR ANSWERS

Computer terminals are used more and more today for many different kinds of exams.

For an examination with very few applicants, you may be told to record your answers in the test booklet itself. Separate answer sheets are much more common. If this separate answer sheet is to be scored by machine – and this is often the case – it is highly important that you mark your answers correctly in order to get credit.

An electronic scoring machine is often used in civil service offices because of the speed with which papers can be scored. Machine-scored answer sheets must be marked with a pencil, which will be given to you. This pencil has a high graphite content which responds to the electronic scoring machine. As a matter of fact, stray dots may register as answers, so do not let your pencil rest on the answer sheet while you are pondering the correct answer. Also, if your pencil lead breaks or is otherwise defective, ask for another.

Since the answer sheet will be dropped in a slot in the scoring machine, be careful not to bend the corners or get the paper crumpled.

The answer sheet normally has five vertical columns of numbers, with 30 numbers to a column. These numbers correspond to the question numbers in your test booklet. After each number, going across the page are four or five pairs of dotted lines. These short dotted lines have small letters or numbers above them. The first two pairs may also have a "T" or "F" above the letters. This indicates that the first two pairs only are to be used if the questions are of the true-false type. If the questions are multiple choice, disregard the "T" and "F" and pay attention only to the small letters or numbers.

Answer your questions in the manner of the sample that follows:

32. The largest city in the United States is
    A. Washington, D.C.
    B. New York City
    C. Chicago
    D. Detroit
    E. San Francisco

1) Choose the answer you think is best. (New York City is the largest, so "B" is correct.)
2) Find the row of dotted lines numbered the same as the question you are answering. (Find row number 32)
3) Find the pair of dotted lines corresponding to the answer. (Find the pair of lines under the mark "B.")
4) Make a solid black mark between the dotted lines.

VI. BEFORE THE TEST

Common sense will help you find procedures to follow to get ready for an examination. Too many of us, however, overlook these sensible measures. Indeed, nervousness and fatigue have been found to be the most serious reasons why applicants fail to do their best on civil service tests. Here is a list of reminders:

- Begin your preparation early – Don't wait until the last minute to go scurrying around for books and materials or to find out what the position is all about.
- Prepare continuously – An hour a night for a week is better than an all-night cram session. This has been definitely established. What is more, a night a week for a month will return better dividends than crowding your study into a shorter period of time.
- Locate the place of the exam – You have been sent a notice telling you when and where to report for the examination. If the location is in a different town or otherwise unfamiliar to you, it would be well to inquire the best route and learn something about the building.
- Relax the night before the test – Allow your mind to rest. Do not study at all that night. Plan some mild recreation or diversion; then go to bed early and get a good night's sleep.
- Get up early enough to make a leisurely trip to the place for the test – This way unforeseen events, traffic snarls, unfamiliar buildings, etc. will not upset you.
- Dress comfortably – A written test is not a fashion show. You will be known by number and not by name, so wear something comfortable.

- Leave excess paraphernalia at home – Shopping bags and odd bundles will get in your way. You need bring only the items mentioned in the official notice you received; usually everything you need is provided. Do not bring reference books to the exam. They will only confuse those last minutes and be taken away from you when in the test room.
- Arrive somewhat ahead of time – If because of transportation schedules you must get there very early, bring a newspaper or magazine to take your mind off yourself while waiting.
- Locate the examination room – When you have found the proper room, you will be directed to the seat or part of the room where you will sit. Sometimes you are given a sheet of instructions to read while you are waiting. Do not fill out any forms until you are told to do so; just read them and be prepared.
- Relax and prepare to listen to the instructions
- If you have any physical problem that may keep you from doing your best, be sure to tell the test administrator. If you are sick or in poor health, you really cannot do your best on the exam. You can come back and take the test some other time.

VII. AT THE TEST

The day of the test is here and you have the test booklet in your hand. The temptation to get going is very strong. Caution! There is more to success than knowing the right answers. You must know how to identify your papers and understand variations in the type of short-answer question used in this particular examination. Follow these suggestions for maximum results from your efforts:

1) Cooperate with the monitor

The test administrator has a duty to create a situation in which you can be as much at ease as possible. He will give instructions, tell you when to begin, check to see that you are marking your answer sheet correctly, and so on. He is not there to guard you, although he will see that your competitors do not take unfair advantage. He wants to help you do your best.

2) Listen to all instructions

Don't jump the gun! Wait until you understand all directions. In most civil service tests you get more time than you need to answer the questions. So don't be in a hurry. Read each word of instructions until you clearly understand the meaning. Study the examples, listen to all announcements and follow directions. Ask questions if you do not understand what to do.

3) Identify your papers

Civil service exams are usually identified by number only. You will be assigned a number; you must not put your name on your test papers. Be sure to copy your number correctly. Since more than one exam may be given, copy your exact examination title.

4) Plan your time

Unless you are told that a test is a "speed" or "rate of work" test, speed itself is usually not important. Time enough to answer all the questions will be provided, but this does not mean that you have all day. An overall time limit has been set. Divide the total time (in minutes) by the number of questions to determine the approximate time you have for each question.

5) Do not linger over difficult questions

If you come across a difficult question, mark it with a paper clip (useful to have along) and come back to it when you have been through the booklet. One caution if you do this – be sure to skip a number on your answer sheet as well. Check often to be sure that you have not lost your place and that you are marking in the row numbered the same as the question you are answering.

6) Read the questions

Be sure you know what the question asks! Many capable people are unsuccessful because they failed to *read* the questions correctly.

7) Answer all questions

Unless you have been instructed that a penalty will be deducted for incorrect answers, it is better to guess than to omit a question.

8) Speed tests

It is often better NOT to guess on speed tests. It has been found that on timed tests people are tempted to spend the last few seconds before time is called in marking answers at random – without even reading them – in the hope of picking up a few extra points. To discourage this practice, the instructions may warn you that your score will be "corrected" for guessing. That is, a penalty will be applied. The incorrect answers will be deducted from the correct ones, or some other penalty formula will be used.

9) Review your answers

If you finish before time is called, go back to the questions you guessed or omitted to give them further thought. Review other answers if you have time.

10) Return your test materials

If you are ready to leave before others have finished or time is called, take ALL your materials to the monitor and leave quietly. Never take any test material with you. The monitor can discover whose papers are not complete, and taking a test booklet may be grounds for disqualification.

VIII. EXAMINATION TECHNIQUES

1) Read the general instructions carefully. These are usually printed on the first page of the exam booklet. As a rule, these instructions refer to the timing of the examination; the fact that you should not start work until the signal and must stop work at a signal, etc. If there are any *special* instructions, such as a choice of questions to be answered, make sure that you note this instruction carefully.

2) When you are ready to start work on the examination, that is as soon as the signal has been given, read the instructions to each question booklet, underline any key words or phrases, such as *least, best, outline, describe* and the like. In this way you will tend to answer as requested rather than discover on reviewing your paper that you *listed without describing*, that you selected the *worst* choice rather than the *best* choice, etc.

3) If the examination is of the objective or multiple-choice type – that is, each question will also give a series of possible answers: A, B, C or D, and you are called upon to select the best answer and write the letter next to that answer on your answer paper – it is advisable to start answering each question in turn. There may be anywhere from 50 to 100 such questions in the three or four hours allotted and you can see how much time would be taken if you read through all the questions before beginning to answer any. Furthermore, if you come across a question or group of questions which you know would be difficult to answer, it would undoubtedly affect your handling of all the other questions.

4) If the examination is of the essay type and contains but a few questions, it is a moot point as to whether you should read all the questions before starting to answer any one. Of course, if you are given a choice – say five out of seven and the like – then it is essential to read all the questions so you can eliminate the two that are most difficult. If, however, you are asked to answer all the questions, there may be danger in trying to answer the easiest one first because you may find that you will spend too much time on it. The best technique is to answer the first question, then proceed to the second, etc.

5) Time your answers. Before the exam begins, write down the time it started, then add the time allowed for the examination and write down the time it must be completed, then divide the time available somewhat as follows:
    - If 3-1/2 hours are allowed, that would be 210 minutes. If you have 80 objective-type questions, that would be an average of 2-1/2 minutes per question. Allow yourself no more than 2 minutes per question, or a total of 160 minutes, which will permit about 50 minutes to review.
    - If for the time allotment of 210 minutes there are 7 essay questions to answer, that would average about 30 minutes a question. Give yourself only 25 minutes per question so that you have about 35 minutes to review.

6) The most important instruction is to *read each question* and make sure you know what is wanted. The second most important instruction is to *time yourself properly* so that you answer every question. The third most important instruction is to *answer every question*. Guess if you have to but include something for each question. Remember that you will receive no credit for a blank and will probably receive some credit if you write something in answer to an essay question. If you guess a letter – say "B" for a multiple-choice question – you may have guessed right. If you leave a blank as an answer to a multiple-choice question, the examiners may respect your feelings but it will not add a point to your score. Some exams may penalize you for wrong answers, so in such cases *only*, you may not want to guess unless you have some basis for your answer.

7) Suggestions
    a. Objective-type questions
        1. Examine the question booklet for proper sequence of pages and questions
        2. Read all instructions carefully
        3. Skip any question which seems too difficult; return to it after all other questions have been answered
        4. Apportion your time properly; do not spend too much time on any single question or group of questions

5. Note and underline key words – *all, most, fewest, least, best, worst, same, opposite*, etc.
6. Pay particular attention to negatives
7. Note unusual option, e.g., unduly long, short, complex, different or similar in content to the body of the question
8. Observe the use of "hedging" words – *probably, may, most likely*, etc.
9. Make sure that your answer is put next to the same number as the question
10. Do not second-guess unless you have good reason to believe the second answer is definitely more correct
11. Cross out original answer if you decide another answer is more accurate; do not erase until you are ready to hand your paper in
12. Answer all questions; guess unless instructed otherwise
13. Leave time for review

  b. Essay questions
   1. Read each question carefully
   2. Determine exactly what is wanted. Underline key words or phrases.
   3. Decide on outline or paragraph answer
   4. Include many different points and elements unless asked to develop any one or two points or elements
   5. Show impartiality by giving pros and cons unless directed to select one side only
   6. Make and write down any assumptions you find necessary to answer the questions
   7. Watch your English, grammar, punctuation and choice of words
   8. Time your answers; don't crowd material

8) Answering the essay question

Most essay questions can be answered by framing the specific response around several key words or ideas. Here are a few such key words or ideas:

M's: manpower, materials, methods, money, management
P's: purpose, program, policy, plan, procedure, practice, problems, pitfalls, personnel, public relations
  a. Six basic steps in handling problems:
   1. Preliminary plan and background development
   2. Collect information, data and facts
   3. Analyze and interpret information, data and facts
   4. Analyze and develop solutions as well as make recommendations
   5. Prepare report and sell recommendations
   6. Install recommendations and follow up effectiveness

  b. Pitfalls to avoid
   1. *Taking things for granted* – A statement of the situation does not necessarily imply that each of the elements is necessarily true; for example, a complaint may be invalid and biased so that all that can be taken for granted is that a complaint has been registered

2. *Considering only one side of a situation* – Wherever possible, indicate several alternatives and then point out the reasons you selected the best one
3. *Failing to indicate follow up* – Whenever your answer indicates action on your part, make certain that you will take proper follow-up action to see how successful your recommendations, procedures or actions turn out to be
4. *Taking too long in answering any single question* – Remember to time your answers properly

IX. AFTER THE TEST

Scoring procedures differ in detail among civil service jurisdictions although the general principles are the same. Whether the papers are hand-scored or graded by machine we have described, they are nearly always graded by number. That is, the person who marks the paper knows only the number – never the name – of the applicant. Not until all the papers have been graded will they be matched with names. If other tests, such as training and experience or oral interview ratings have been given, scores will be combined. Different parts of the examination usually have different weights. For example, the written test might count 60 percent of the final grade, and a rating of training and experience 40 percent. In many jurisdictions, veterans will have a certain number of points added to their grades.

After the final grade has been determined, the names are placed in grade order and an eligible list is established. There are various methods for resolving ties between those who get the same final grade – probably the most common is to place first the name of the person whose application was received first. Job offers are made from the eligible list in the order the names appear on it. You will be notified of your grade and your rank as soon as all these computations have been made. This will be done as rapidly as possible.

People who are found to meet the requirements in the announcement are called "eligibles." Their names are put on a list of eligible candidates. An eligible's chances of getting a job depend on how high he stands on this list and how fast agencies are filling jobs from the list.

When a job is to be filled from a list of eligibles, the agency asks for the names of people on the list of eligibles for that job. When the civil service commission receives this request, it sends to the agency the names of the three people highest on this list. Or, if the job to be filled has specialized requirements, the office sends the agency the names of the top three persons who meet these requirements from the general list.

The appointing officer makes a choice from among the three people whose names were sent to him. If the selected person accepts the appointment, the names of the others are put back on the list to be considered for future openings.

That is the rule in hiring from all kinds of eligible lists, whether they are for typist, carpenter, chemist, or something else. For every vacancy, the appointing officer has his choice of any one of the top three eligibles on the list. This explains why the person whose name is on top of the list sometimes does not get an appointment when some of the persons lower on the list do. If the appointing officer chooses the second or third eligible, the No. 1 eligible does not get a job at once, but stays on the list until he is appointed or the list is terminated.

X. HOW TO PASS THE INTERVIEW TEST

The examination for which you applied requires an oral interview test. You have already taken the written test and you are now being called for the interview test – the final part of the formal examination.

You may think that it is not possible to prepare for an interview test and that there are no procedures to follow during an interview. Our purpose is to point out some things you can do in advance that will help you and some good rules to follow and pitfalls to avoid while you are being interviewed.

What is an interview supposed to test?

The written examination is designed to test the technical knowledge and competence of the candidate; the oral is designed to evaluate intangible qualities, not readily measured otherwise, and to establish a list showing the relative fitness of each candidate – as measured against his competitors – for the position sought. Scoring is not on the basis of "right" and "wrong," but on a sliding scale of values ranging from "not passable" to "outstanding." As a matter of fact, it is possible to achieve a relatively low score without a single "incorrect" answer because of evident weakness in the qualities being measured.

Occasionally, an examination may consist entirely of an oral test – either an individual or a group oral. In such cases, information is sought concerning the technical knowledges and abilities of the candidate, since there has been no written examination for this purpose. More commonly, however, an oral test is used to supplement a written examination.

Who conducts interviews?

The composition of oral boards varies among different jurisdictions. In nearly all, a representative of the personnel department serves as chairman. One of the members of the board may be a representative of the department in which the candidate would work. In some cases, "outside experts" are used, and, frequently, a businessman or some other representative of the general public is asked to serve. Labor and management or other special groups may be represented. The aim is to secure the services of experts in the appropriate field.

However the board is composed, it is a good idea (and not at all improper or unethical) to ascertain in advance of the interview who the members are and what groups they represent. When you are introduced to them, you will have some idea of their backgrounds and interests, and at least you will not stutter and stammer over their names.

What should be done before the interview?

While knowledge about the board members is useful and takes some of the surprise element out of the interview, there is other preparation which is more substantive. It *is* possible to prepare for an oral interview – in several ways:

1) Keep a copy of your application and review it carefully before the interview

This may be the only document before the oral board, and the starting point of the interview. Know what education and experience you have listed there, and the sequence and dates of all of it. Sometimes the board will ask you to review the highlights of your experience for them; you should not have to hem and haw doing it.

2) Study the class specification and the examination announcement

Usually, the oral board has one or both of these to guide them. The qualities, characteristics or knowledges required by the position sought are stated in these documents. They offer valuable clues as to the nature of the oral interview. For example, if the job involves supervisory responsibilities, the announcement will usually indicate that knowledge of modern supervisory methods and the qualifications of the candidate as a supervisor will be tested. If so, you can expect such questions, frequently in the form of a hypothetical situation which you are expected to solve. NEVER go into an oral without knowledge of the duties and responsibilities of the job you seek.

3) Think through each qualification required

Try to visualize the kind of questions you would ask if you were a board member. How well could you answer them? Try especially to appraise your own knowledge and background in each area, *measured against the job sought*, and identify any areas in which you are weak. Be critical and realistic – do not flatter yourself.

4) Do some general reading in areas in which you feel you may be weak

For example, if the job involves supervision and your past experience has NOT, some general reading in supervisory methods and practices, particularly in the field of human relations, might be useful. Do NOT study agency procedures or detailed manuals. The oral board will be testing your understanding and capacity, not your memory.

5) Get a good night's sleep and watch your general health and mental attitude

You will want a clear head at the interview. Take care of a cold or any other minor ailment, and of course, no hangovers.

What should be done on the day of the interview?

Now comes the day of the interview itself. Give yourself plenty of time to get there. Plan to arrive somewhat ahead of the scheduled time, particularly if your appointment is in the fore part of the day. If a previous candidate fails to appear, the board might be ready for you a bit early. By early afternoon an oral board is almost invariably behind schedule if there are many candidates, and you may have to wait. Take along a book or magazine to read, or your application to review, but leave any extraneous material in the waiting room when you go in for your interview. In any event, relax and compose yourself.

The matter of dress is important. The board is forming impressions about you – from your experience, your manners, your attitude, and your appearance. Give your personal appearance careful attention. Dress your best, but not your flashiest. Choose conservative, appropriate clothing, and be sure it is immaculate. This is a business interview, and your appearance should indicate that you regard it as such. Besides, being well groomed and properly dressed will help boost your confidence.

Sooner or later, someone will call your name and escort you into the interview room. *This is it.* From here on you are on your own. It is too late for any more preparation. But remember, you asked for this opportunity to prove your fitness, and you are here because your request was granted.

What happens when you go in?

The usual sequence of events will be as follows: The clerk (who is often the board stenographer) will introduce you to the chairman of the oral board, who will introduce you to the other members of the board. Acknowledge the introductions before you sit down. Do not be surprised if you find a microphone facing you or a stenotypist sitting by. Oral interviews are usually recorded in the event of an appeal or other review.

Usually the chairman of the board will open the interview by reviewing the highlights of your education and work experience from your application – primarily for the benefit of the other members of the board, as well as to get the material into the record. Do not interrupt or comment unless there is an error or significant misinterpretation; if that is the case, do not hesitate. But do not quibble about insignificant matters. Also, he will usually ask you some question about your education, experience or your present job – partly to get you to start talking and to establish the interviewing "rapport." He may start the actual questioning, or turn it over to one of the other members. Frequently, each member undertakes the questioning on a particular area, one in which he is perhaps most competent, so you can expect each member to participate in the examination. Because time is limited, you may also expect some rather abrupt switches in the direction the questioning takes, so do not be upset by it. Normally, a board member will not pursue a single line of questioning unless he discovers a particular strength or weakness.

After each member has participated, the chairman will usually ask whether any member has any further questions, then will ask you if you have anything you wish to add. Unless you are expecting this question, it may floor you. Worse, it may start you off on an extended, extemporaneous speech. The board is not usually seeking more information. The question is principally to offer you a last opportunity to present further qualifications or to indicate that you have nothing to add. So, if you feel that a significant qualification or characteristic has been overlooked, it is proper to point it out in a sentence or so. Do not compliment the board on the thoroughness of their examination – they have been sketchy, and you know it. If you wish, merely say, "No thank you, I have nothing further to add." This is a point where you can "talk yourself out" of a good impression or fail to present an important bit of information. Remember, *you close the interview yourself.*

The chairman will then say, "That is all, Mr. _____, thank you." Do not be startled; the interview is over, and quicker than you think. Thank him, gather your belongings and take your leave. Save your sigh of relief for the other side of the door.

How to put your best foot forward

Throughout this entire process, you may feel that the board individually and collectively is trying to pierce your defenses, seek out your hidden weaknesses and embarrass and confuse you. Actually, this is not true. They are obliged to make an appraisal of your qualifications for the job you are seeking, and they want to see you in your best light. Remember, they must interview all candidates and a non-cooperative candidate may become a failure in spite of their best efforts to bring out his qualifications. Here are 15 suggestions that will help you:

1) **Be natural – Keep your attitude confident, not cocky**

If you are not confident that you can do the job, do not expect the board to be. Do not apologize for your weaknesses, try to bring out your strong points. The board is interested in a positive, not negative, presentation. Cockiness will antagonize any board member and make him wonder if you are covering up a weakness by a false show of strength.

2) **Get comfortable, but don't lounge or sprawl**

Sit erectly but not stiffly. A careless posture may lead the board to conclude that you are careless in other things, or at least that you are not impressed by the importance of the occasion. Either conclusion is natural, even if incorrect. Do not fuss with your clothing, a pencil or an ashtray. Your hands may occasionally be useful to emphasize a point; do not let them become a point of distraction.

3) **Do not wisecrack or make small talk**

This is a serious situation, and your attitude should show that you consider it as such. Further, the time of the board is limited – they do not want to waste it, and neither should you.

4) Do not exaggerate your experience or abilities

In the first place, from information in the application or other interviews and sources, the board may know more about you than you think. Secondly, you probably will not get away with it. An experienced board is rather adept at spotting such a situation, so do not take the chance.

5) If you know a board member, do not make a point of it, yet do not hide it

Certainly you are not fooling him, and probably not the other members of the board. Do not try to take advantage of your acquaintanceship – it will probably do you little good.

6) Do not dominate the interview

Let the board do that. They will give you the clues – do not assume that you have to do all the talking. Realize that the board has a number of questions to ask you, and do not try to take up all the interview time by showing off your extensive knowledge of the answer to the first one.

7) Be attentive

You only have 20 minutes or so, and you should keep your attention at its sharpest throughout. When a member is addressing a problem or question to you, give him your undivided attention. Address your reply principally to him, but do not exclude the other board members.

8) Do not interrupt

A board member may be stating a problem for you to analyze. He will ask you a question when the time comes. Let him state the problem, and wait for the question.

9) Make sure you understand the question

Do not try to answer until you are sure what the question is. If it is not clear, restate it in your own words or ask the board member to clarify it for you. However, do not haggle about minor elements.

10) Reply promptly but not hastily

A common entry on oral board rating sheets is "candidate responded readily," or "candidate hesitated in replies." Respond as promptly and quickly as you can, but do not jump to a hasty, ill-considered answer.

11) Do not be peremptory in your answers

A brief answer is proper – but do not fire your answer back. That is a losing game from your point of view. The board member can probably ask questions much faster than you can answer them.

12) Do not try to create the answer you think the board member wants

He is interested in what kind of mind you have and how it works – not in playing games. Furthermore, he can usually spot this practice and will actually grade you down on it.

13) Do not switch sides in your reply merely to agree with a board member

Frequently, a member will take a contrary position merely to draw you out and to see if you are willing and able to defend your point of view. Do not start a debate, yet do not surrender a good position. If a position is worth taking, it is worth defending.

14) Do not be afraid to admit an error in judgment if you are shown to be wrong

The board knows that you are forced to reply without any opportunity for careful consideration. Your answer may be demonstrably wrong. If so, admit it and get on with the interview.

15) Do not dwell at length on your present job

The opening question may relate to your present assignment. Answer the question but do not go into an extended discussion. You are being examined for a *new* job, not your present one. As a matter of fact, try to phrase ALL your answers in terms of the job for which you are being examined.

Basis of Rating

Probably you will forget most of these "do's" and "don'ts" when you walk into the oral interview room. Even remembering them all will not ensure you a passing grade. Perhaps you did not have the qualifications in the first place. But remembering them will help you to put your best foot forward, without treading on the toes of the board members.

Rumor and popular opinion to the contrary notwithstanding, an oral board wants you to make the best appearance possible. They know you are under pressure – but they also want to see how you respond to it as a guide to what your reaction would be under the pressures of the job you seek. They will be influenced by the degree of poise you display, the personal traits you show and the manner in which you respond.

ABOUT THIS BOOK

This book contains tests divided into Examination Sections. Go through each test, answering every question in the margin. We have also attached a sample answer sheet at the back of the book that can be removed and used. At the end of each test look at the answer key and check your answers. On the ones you got wrong, look at the right answer choice and learn. Do not fill in the answers first. Do not memorize the questions and answers, but understand the answer and principles involved. On your test, the questions will likely be different from the samples. Questions are changed and new ones added. If you understand these past questions you should have success with any changes that arise. Tests may consist of several types of questions. We have additional books on each subject should more study be advisable or necessary for you. Finally, the more you study, the better prepared you will be. This book is intended to be the last thing you study before you walk into the examination room. Prior study of relevant texts is also recommended. NLC publishes some of these in our Fundamental Series. Knowledge and good sense are important factors in passing your exam. Good luck also helps. So now study this Passbook, absorb the material contained within and take that knowledge into the examination. Then do your best to pass that exam.

EXAMINATION SECTION

VISUAL RECALL
EXAMINATION SECTION

PICTURE BOOKLET

DIRECTIONS: You will have five minutes to memorize as much as possible of all the details in the pictures. The pictures include a street scene and various faces. You may not write or make any notes while studying the pictures. The test will be based on these pictures.

After five minutes, close the Picture Booklet and do not look at the pictures again. Then, answer the questions that follow.

Street Scene

While on foot-patrol, you receive a call on your portable police radio that a robbery may be in progress at a watch repair shop. It so happens that the shop is across the street from where you are standing. What you see at this moment will help you decide what to do, and remembering what you see may be very important later on.

Study this scene carefully. You will be asked questions about it in this examination.

Faces

Below are twelve photographs taken from FBI files. Study the twelve faces carefully. Your ability to remember these faces will be tested in this examination.

RECALL OF DETAILS

DIRECTIONS: Questions 1 through 5 test your ability to remember the details of the street scene at the beginning of this examination. Each question is followed by four choices. Choose the one BEST answer (A, B, C, or D). *PRINT THE LETTER OF THE CORRECT ANSWER IN THE SPACE AT THE RIGHT.*

1. The boy by the dark-colored car
    A. had on dark glasses
    B. was a lookout
    C. had on a jacket
    D. wore an 'Afro' haircut

    1._____

2. The group of men on the sidewalk were
    A. facing one another
    B. looking at the watch repair shop
    C. all African-American
    D. talking and laughing

    2._____

3. Nearest to the watch repair shop was a
    A. boy standing by a dark-colored car
    B. woman in a doorway
    C. group of men on the sidewalk
    D. man next to a light-colored car

    3._____

4. The dark-colored car
    A. was a four-door sedan
    B. carried New York State plates
    C. was headed uptown
    D. had a man in the driver's seat

    4._____

5. A woman on the sidewalk appeared to be
    A. looking at the apartment windows directly above her
    B. looking toward the watch repair shop
    C. watching the boy by the dark-colored car
    D. coming out of a store

    5._____

RECOGNITION OF FACES

DIRECTIONS: Questions 6 through 15 test your ability to recognize faces that you have seen before. Each test number is followed by three faces. If one of the three faces was among the FBI photographs that you studied at the beginning of the examination, select its letter (A, B or C). If *none* of the three faces was among the FBI photographs, select the letter D. (Do not forget that every question has a fourth choice.) *PRINT THE LETTER OF THE CORRECT ANSWER IN THE SPACE AT THE RIGHT.*

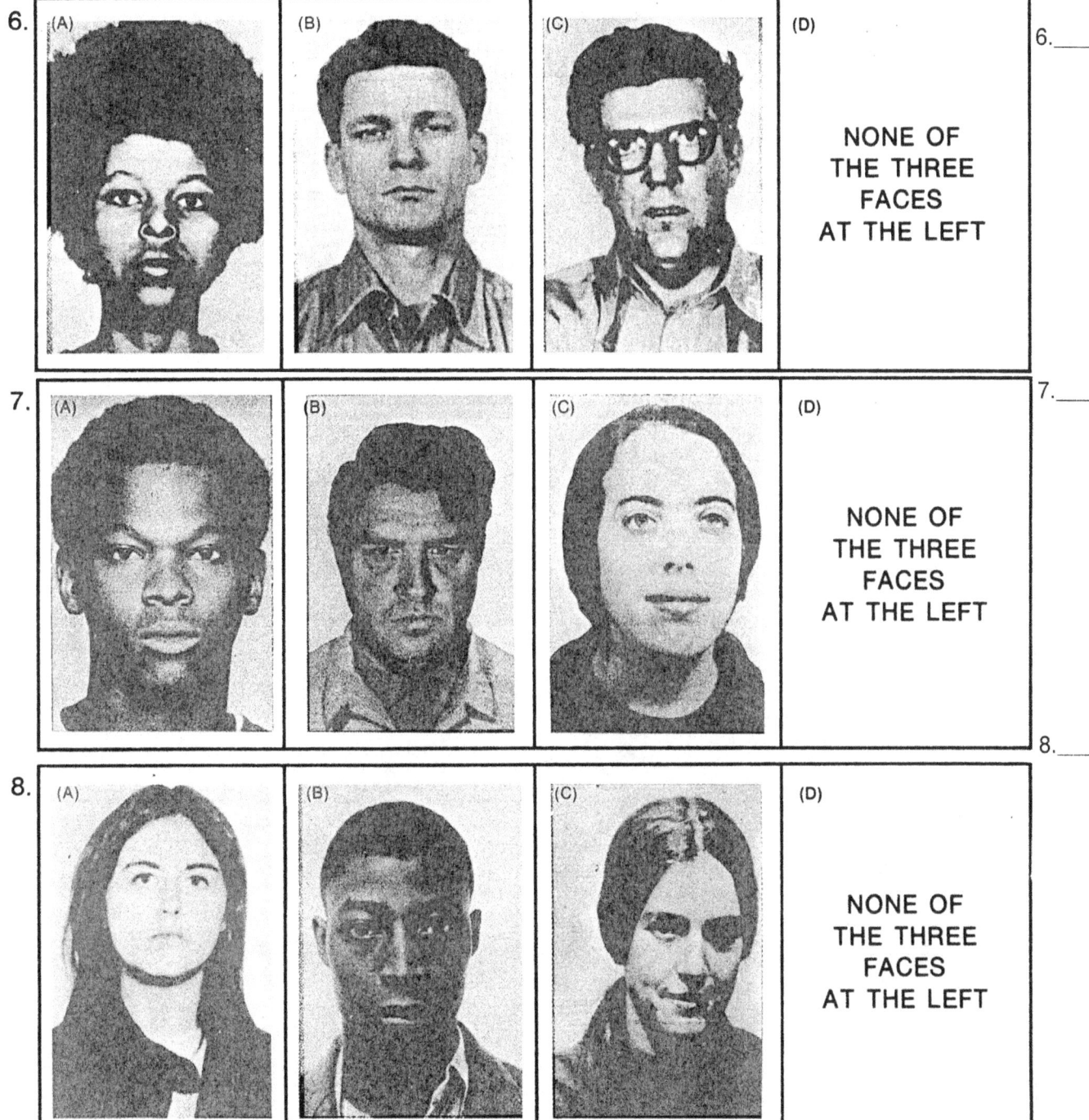

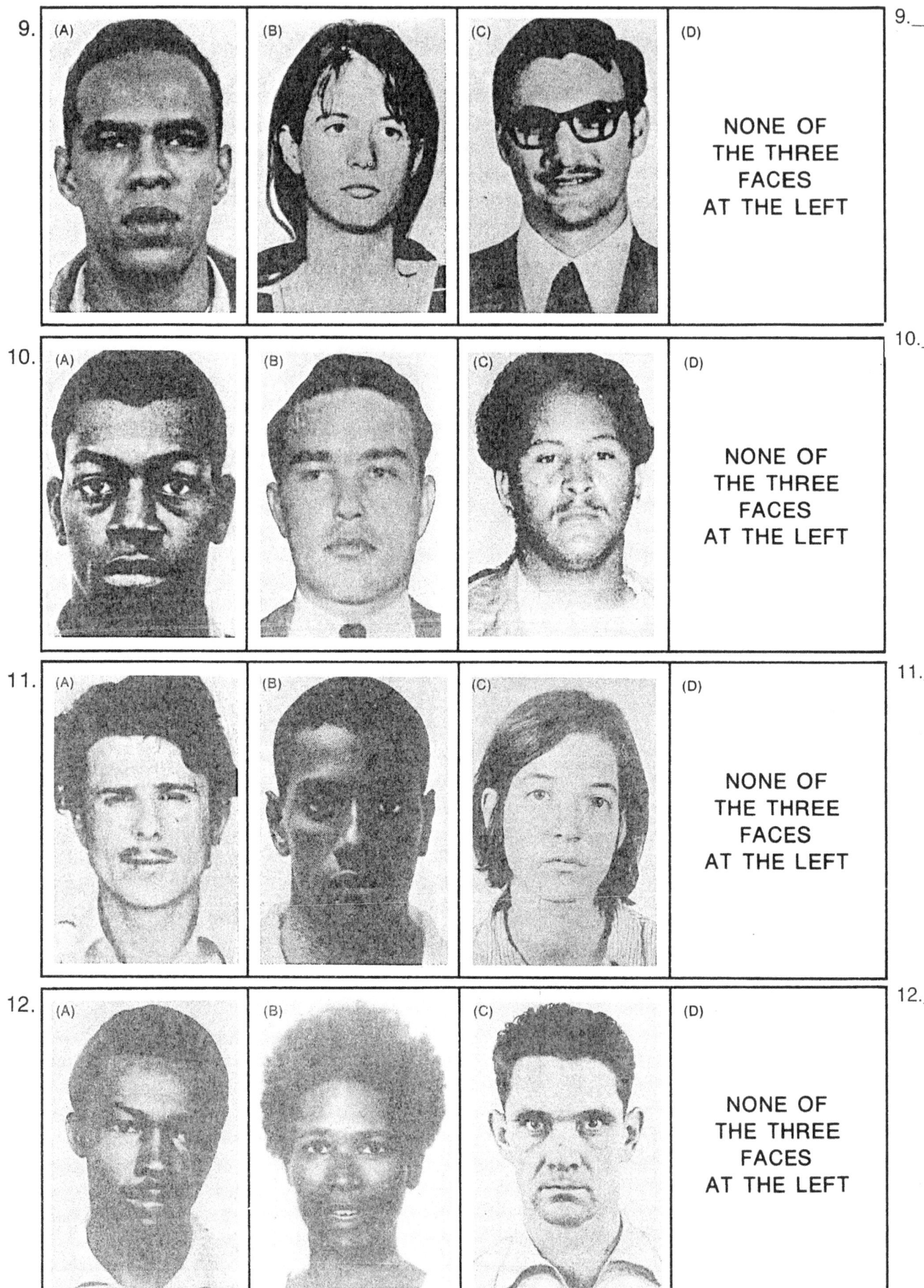

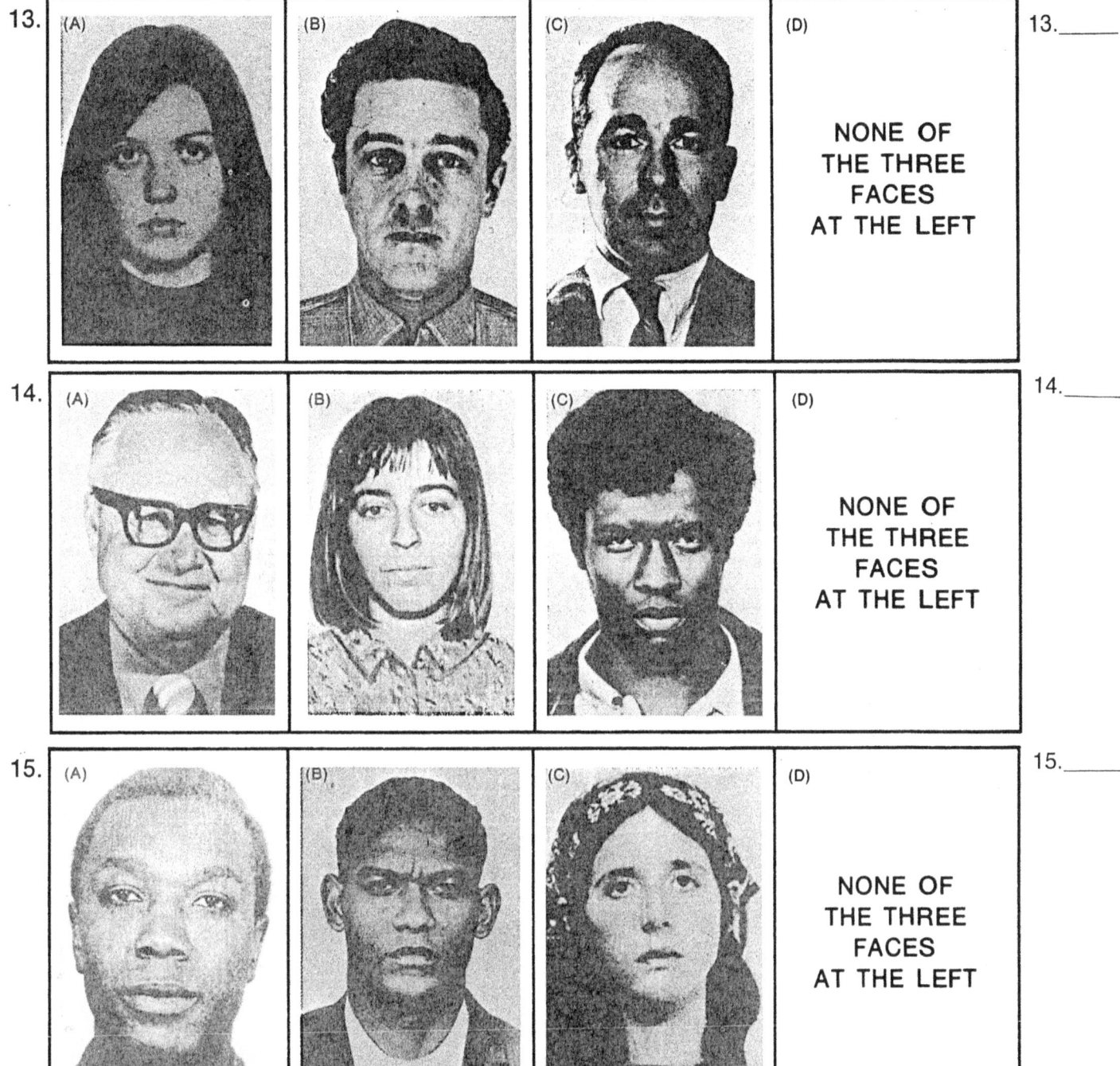

KEY (CORRECT ANSWERS)

1. C	6. B	11. B
2. A	7. D	12. B
3. D	8. D	13. A
4. A	9. B	14. C
5. B	10. C	15. B

EXAMINATION SECTION
TEST 1

DIRECTIONS: Each question or incomplete statement is followed by several suggested answers or completions. Select the one that BEST answers the question or completes the statement. *PRINT THE LETTER OF THE CORRECT ANSWER IN THE SPACE AT THE RIGHT.*

Questions 1-3.

DIRECTIONS: Questions 1 to 3 measure your ability to fill out forms correctly and to remember information and ideas. Below and on the following two pages are directions for completing two kinds of forms, a correctly completed sample of each form, and a section from a procedures manual. You should memorize the sets of directions and the section from the procedures manual.

In the test, you will be (1) asked questions about the information and ideas in the manual and (2) presented with completed forms and asked to identify entries that are INCORRECT (contain wrong information, incomplete information, information in wrong order, etc.).

DIRECTIONS FOR COMPLETING CASE REPORT FORM

A case report form (see completed sample) is to be filled out by each officer at the time of the preliminary investigation. The entry for each numbered box is as follows:

Box 1 - The time the assignment was received.

Box 2 - The day, date, and time of the occurrence, in that order. Names of months and days may be abbreviated.

Box 3 - The manner in which the report was received. Use P = person, TOC = Through Official Channels (911 or other emergency numbers), M = mail, or T = telephone.

Box 4 - Name of the person notifying the department.

Box 5 - The address of the occurrence. include number, street, and village, and name of establishment, if appropriate. Do NOT abbreviate the name of a street, village, or establishment. If no street address is available, supply directions.

Box 6 - Victim's name, last name first.

Box 7 - Victim's birthdate - month, day, and year. Use the style shown in the completed sample.

Box 8 - Victim's sex and race: F = female, M = male, B = black, W = white, Y = yellow, O = other.

Box 9 - Relationship of victim to the offender (be as specific as possible):
HU = husband, WI = wife, MO = mother, FA = father,

SO = son, DA = daughter, BR = brother, SI = sister,
AQ = acquaintance, ST = stranger, UN = unknown.

SAMPLE OF COMPLETED CASE REPORT FORM

1. Time Received 5:57 PM		2. Date and Time of Occurrence Wed., Oct. 17, 2017, 1:00 PM	
3. Original Complaint Received TOC		4. Reported by Jeffrey Greene	
5. Place of Occurrence Sam's Stationery Shop, 130 Main St., Brooketown			
6. Victim's Name Silver, Sam	7. Date of Birth 3/17/72		8. Sex and Race M - W
7. Relationship to the Offender ST			

DIRECTIONS FOR COMPLETING
AUTOMOBILE FIELD INTERVIEW FORM

An automobile field interview form (see completed sample on the following page) is to be filled out when a car is stopped under suspicious circumstances, but no arrests are made. The entry for each numbered box is as follows:

Box 1 - Driver's name, last name first.

Box 2 - Village of residence, if within the county

Box 3 - Type of vehicle: S = sedan, C = convertible, SW = station wagon, V = van, T = truck.

Box 4 - Vehicle registration number.

Box 5 - Time and place of interview: location (street address only), time (per 24-hour clock), date, in that order.

Box 6 - Type of area: C = commercial, H = highway, R = residential, I = industrial, S = school

Box 7 - Patrol post number: precinct number is first digit; sector number is last two digits.

Box 8 - Officer's name and shield number, in that order.

SAMPLE OF COMPLETED AUTOMOBILE FIELD INTERVIEW FORM

1. Operator Robbins, Susan		2. Village Shady Brook	
3. Type of Vehicle C		4. Registration C 7237	
5. Time and Place of Interview Merry Road at Elm Street, 1428, 2/7/17			
6. Type of Area R	7. Post No. 221		8. Officer Sally Dodd, 2212

CASE REPORT MANUAL
Section 1 - Solvability Factors

A solvability factor can be defined as any information about a crime that can provide a means to determine who committed it. In other words, a solvability factor is a useful clue to the identity of the perpetrator.

Based on national-level research, the following twelve universal factors have been identified:

1. Existence of witnesses to the crime
2. Knowledge of a perpetrator's name
3. Knowledge of a perpetrator's whereabouts
4. Description of a perpetrator
5. Identification of a perpetrator
6. Property that has traceable characteristics such as a registration number
7. Existence of a distinctive MO
8. Presence of significant physical evidence such as a set of burglar's tools
9. Description of a perpetrator's automobile
10. Positive results from a crime scene evidence search, such as fingerprints or footprints
11. Belief that a crime may be solved with publicity and/or reasonable investigative effort
12. Opportunity for only one person to have committed the crime

The presence of at least one of these solvability factors is necessary for there to be a reasonable chance for a solution to the crime. When there is no solvability factor, the chance of crime solution is limited. Therefore, the police officer who arrives at the scene of a crime first must make the greatest possible effort to identify solvability factors. This effort should include identification of witnesses and a thorough search of the crime scene.

DIRECTIONS: After you have memorized the directions and manual section, try to answer the following questions without referring to the study materials.

1. Which of the following crimes is *most likely* to have a solvability factor?   1.____

    A. A pickpocket takes several wallets on a crowded bus.
    B. Two muggers take money from a blind man in an alley.
    C. A hospital drug cabinet is broken into during a major emergency.
    D. A kidnapper escapes in a van decorated with pink, yellow, and avocado-green paint.

2. At 7:30 AM on Wednesday, February 6, 2017, Patrol Officer Alex White was assigned to investigate a suspected child-beating. The boy had been brought to the hospital, and Dr. Paul Cohen called the local station house at 7:20 AM. David Pepson, a White boy born on June 27, 2015, was brought from his home by his mother, who claims that her husband had punished David an hour earlier for making loud noises. David resides with his parents at 86 Whitewood Lane in Middletown.   2.____

4 (#1)

CASE REPORT FORM			
1. Time Received 7:30 AM		2. Date and Time of Occurrence Wed., February 6, 2017, 5:00 AM	
3. Original Complaint Received T		4. Reported by Dr. Paul Cohen	
5. Place of Occurrence 86 Whitewood Lane, Middletown			
6. Victim's Name David Pepson	7. Date of Birth 6/27/15		8. Sex and Race M - W
9. Relationship to the Offender FA			

Of the following, the box in the form above which is filled out INCORRECTLY is Box
   A. 3   B. 4   C. 8   D. 9

3. Officer Steven Brown, 7234, stopped a station wagon in the business section of Westville. He talked to the driver, John Caseman, on Rocky Road near South Bend and the western boundary of section 16 of precinct 2 at 8:20 PM on 3/8/17. The vehicle, registration number 2729H belongs to Mr. Caseman, who resides in Silverton.

AUTOMOBILE FIELD INTERVIEW FORM

1. Operator Caseman, John		2. Village Westville
3. Type of Vehicle V		4. Registration 2729H
5. Time and Place of Interview Rocky Road near South Bend, 2020, 3/8/17		
6. Type of Area C	7. Post No. 216	8. Officer Steven Brown, 7234

Of the following, the box in the form above which is filled out INCORRECTLY is Box
   A. 1   B. 3   C. 5   D. 7

Questions 4-6.

DIRECTIONS: Questions 4 to 6 measure your ability to recall information in a set of bulletins. To do well in the test, you must memorize both the pictorial and the written portions of each of the following eight bulletins.

Date of Issuance 5/13/17

INFORMATION WANTED

by

Police Department, County of Allamin
Hooblertown, Indiana 43102

The Allamin County Police Department homicide squad requests all auto repair shops, dealers and General Motors parts dealers in the precinct be contacted and questioned relative to the below described vehicle which is wanted for a felony - leaving the scene of a fatality. If vehicle is located, contact the homicide squad, (731) 624-1372. Refer to Homicide Case 130.

Place of Occurrence:	Midway State Road, South Strata, Indiana
Time of Occurrence:	0240 hours on March 3, 2017
Vehicle Wanted:	1980 Oldsmobile Cutlass Supreme, color green
Damage:	The Vehicle will have damage to the plastic grill located in the vicinity of the right front headlights. The chrome strip which is affixed to the center of the hood was recovered at the scene.
Parts:	The following parts will be needed to repair the vehicle: 1. Hood - GM Part No. 557547 or 557557 2. Plastic Grill - GM Part No. 22503156

6 (#1)

WANTED
by
Police Department. County of Paradise
Cobbs Cove, Louisiana 41723
for
MURDER

BULLETIN NO. 9-17

No. FJ110M

Note
Seiko watch with Gold Face and three section band is not a standard import into this area.

Occurrence:	Blue Jay Way and Nickel Drive, Yellowbird, 0530 hours on April 12, 2017.
Modus Operandi:	The deceased returned to his home at 2 Blue Jay Way, Yellowbird, at about 0530 hours, April 12, 2017. Four male whites were waiting in the vicinity of his garage and robbed him of U.S. currency and the above watch. They ran to the intersection of Blue Jay Way and Nickel Drive and got into a late model, shiny dark color, four door sedan with large tail-lights. The deceased chased them to the corner. One shot was fired causing his death.
Subjects:	Four Male Whites, dark hair.
Property:	One Seiko Quartz - Sports 100 - wrist watch, yellow metal face and crystal retainer. The band is an expandable three-section, white, yellow, white metal.
Note:	Anyone with information is requested to contact the Paradise County Homicide Squad.

WANTED
by
Police Department. County of Whitewall
Short Hills, Kentucky 27135

for
MURDER

BULLETIN NO. 15-17

RC-550JW/C

Occurrence:	Public street, Brown Avenue, 60 ft. north of Camino Street, South Hill, KY, at 2340 hours, 6/25/17.
Modus Operandi:	The victim of the murder was walking south on Brown Avenue when he was accosted by the suspect and shot in the head by the suspect.
Subject:	Male, Black, 25-28 years, 5'9"-6' tall, thin build, short dark hair, medium dark skin, wearing a dark waist-length jacket, sneakers - armed with a gun.
Property:	The above property, a JVC AM-FM cassette radio, Model RC 550JW/C made of black plastic with chrome trim was stolen during the commission of a murder on Brown Avenue in South Hill. The battery compartment door is missing from the radio.
Note:	Anyone with information concerning the murder or the radio is asked to call the Whitewall Homicide Squad.

8 (#1)

WANTED
by
Police Department, County of Larinda
Blue Ridge. CA 97235

for
BURGLARY

BULLETIN NO. 6-17

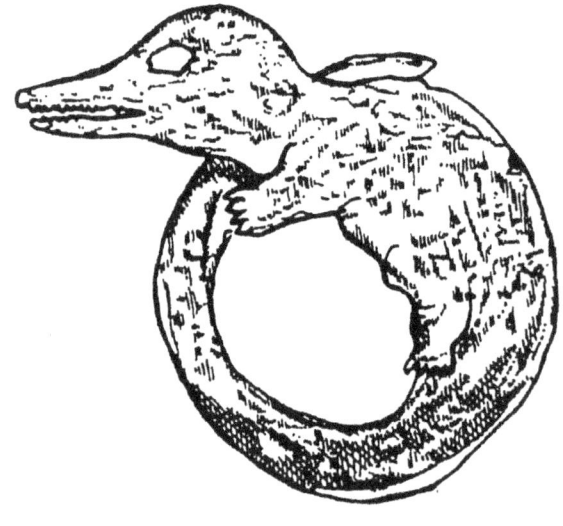

#1

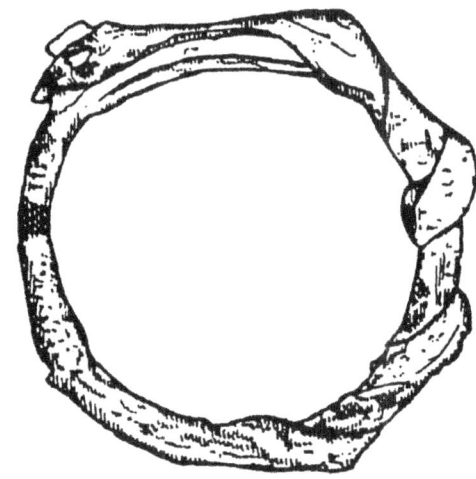

#2

Date of Occurrence:	August 17, 2017 - 1930 to 2230 hours.
Place of Occurrence:	Private home, 37 Cliffmount Dr., Palasino, CA
Property:	Two distinctive, original designer rings taken.

1. Ladies, yellow gold, 18K ring, size 8, an alligator with green emerald eye.
2. Mans, yellow gold ring, a snake with 1/4 carat white diamond head and white diamond chips for eyes.

Value: 1. $5,000   2. $7,500
Note: Any information - contact Burglary Squad, Refer to DD 4-25.

9 (#1)

WANTED
by

BULLETIN NO. 12-17

Police Department, County of Canton
Midship. Texas 84290

for
BURGLARY

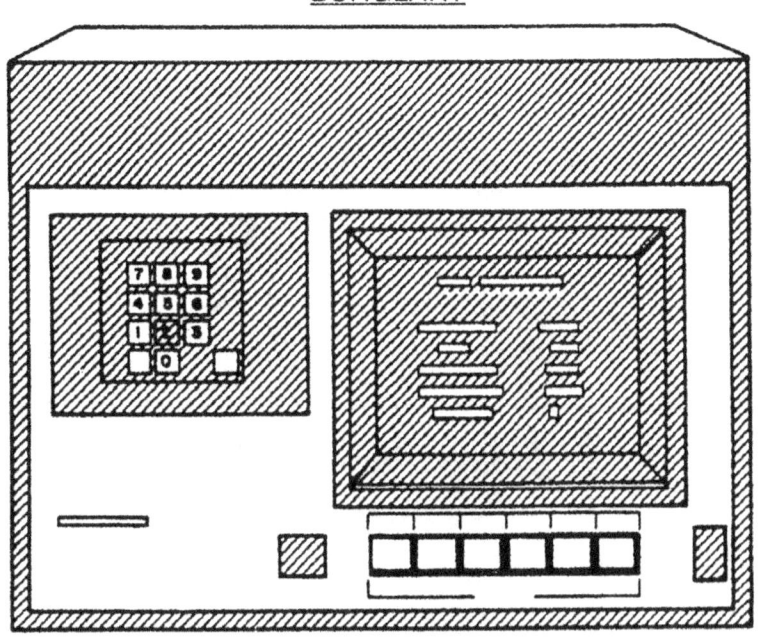

Date of Occurrence: July 31, 2017 - 1640 hours to August 1 - 0720 hours.
Place of Occurrence: 606 Hillmont Drive, Alston, TX Freemont Testing Systems
Property: Three engine analysers, color red, measuring 14" x 20" x 19"
Serial Numbers: 1. AN-0059 2. BP-0079 3. CR-0099
Value: $6,666.00 each.
Note: Request officers on patrol check service stations on post for the above items. Any information contact Detective Bryant, Third Squad, and refer to DD 3-52.

10 (#1)

WANTED by

BULLETIN NO. 5-17

Police Department, County of Marina
Waterford, CT 03612

for
ROBBERY

2014 PHOTO

Occurrences:	Robberies of gas stations and boutiques in North End precincts of Marina County.
Modus Operandi:	Subject enters store and uses telephone or shops. He then produces sawed-off shotgun or revolver from under his coat and announces robbery.
Subject:	Harry Hamilton, Male, White, DOB 6/22/73, 5'10", 180 lbs., medium complexion, severely pockmarked face.
Further Details:	Contact Robbery Squad at (203) 832-7663. Refer to Robbery Case 782. Robbery Squad has warrant for subject. IF THIS PERSON ENTERS YOUR STORE DIAL 911 OR THE ABOVE NUMBER

11 (#1)

WANTED
by

BULLETIN NO.
30-17

Police Department, County of Panfield
Lanser, South Carolina 30012

for
ROBBERY

#1

2014 PHOTO
#2

Occurrence:	3 North Avenue, Anita, South Carolina, on 11/26/17 at 2310 hours.
Modus Operandi:	The above subjects forced their way into the private residence of a rug dealer, accosted the dealer, his wife, and brother, demanding jewelry, currency, escaped on foot after binding victims.
Subjects:	No. 1 - Male, White, 40-45 years, 200 lbs., heavy build, bald shaved head, fair complexion, mustache, goatee, large hooked nose, black leather jacket, armed with a knife. No. 2 - Male, White, 6'1" tall, medium build, brown hair, subject identified as Mark Nine, DOB 4/16/78, last known address 1275 East 61st Street, Brooklyn, NY in 2011, hard drug user, armed with a hand gun, subject has been indicted for residence robbery. See Wanted Bulletin 21-12.
Possible 3rd Suspect:	Male, Hispanic, 30-35 years, 5'6", thin build, collar-length black wavy hair, eyes close together, with a large Doberman. Subject observed in the area before robbery talking to bald, stocky male. Also seen entering a vehicle containing 3 or 4 males after the robbery.
Loss:	U.S. currency and jewelry valued at $3,000 to $4,000.

Further Details: Contact Robbery Squad.

12 (#1)

<table>
<tr><td>WANTED
by
Police Department, County of Fantail
Sweet Waters, Vermont 04610

for
HI-JACKING</td><td>BULLETIN NO.
1-17</td></tr>
</table>

Occurrence:	Vicinity of Nikon Plaza, off Jewel Avenue & Brook Bubble Road, Sweet Waters, VT at 1820 hours, 2/6/17.
Modus Operandi:	Subjects accosted the driver of a United Parcel tractor/trailer, forcing him into a pale yellow van-type vehicle, make and year unknown. Vehicle contained a black and yellow leopard rug. Driver released after two (2) hours, in the vicinity of West Lake, VT. Tractor/trailer recovered in White River, New Hampshire.
Subjects:	Four (4) male Whites, one possibly named Joe, armed with hand guns. No further description.
Loss:	Photo of above item: one (1) of four (4) broadcasting TV zoom lenses made by Nikon, valued at $7,000. Also included in the Nikon loss were current models of cameras, lenses, calculators, valued at $196,000. Medical supplies, mfg. by True Tell Inc., value $49,000. High quality medical examination scopes, industrial fiberscopes, cassette recorders and cameras, all mgf. by Canon Inc. valued at over $250,000. Sweaters, young mens, vee-neck design, mfg. Milford, Inc., labeled Dimension, Robt. Klein, J.C. Penney. Valued at over $20,450. Above items bearing serial numbers have been entered in NCIC.

Further Details: Contact Robbery Squad.

DIRECTIONS: After you have memorized both the pictorial and written portions of the bulletins, try to answer the following questions WITHOUT referring to the study materials.

4. Which of the following statements about the contents of the *Information Wanted* bulletin is or are true?
   I. The subject vehicle is involved in a felony.
   II. The subject vehicle is green-colored.
   The CORRECT answer is:

   A. I *only*
   B. II *only*
   C. Both I and II
   D. Neither I nor II

5.

   Which of the following statements about the object above is or are true?
   I. It was taken in the robbery of a residence.
   II. Its value is between $1,000 and $2,000.
   The CORRECT answer is:

   A. I *only*
   B. II *only*
   C. Both I and II
   D. Neither I nor II

6. Which of the following, if any, fits the description of the individual who is wanted for the robbery of several gas stations?

   A.
   B.

C.

D. None of these

Questions 7-10.

DIRECTIONS: Questions 7 to 10 measure your ability to memorize and recall addresses, identification numbers and codes, and similar data.
In the test, you will be asked questions about the following body of information. You will NOT have the information in front of you when you take the test.

RADIO SIGNALS
01 - Back in Service
02 - Acknowledgement(OK)
06 - On Coffee
08 - Off Meal, Coffee, Personal
27 - Valid License
33 - Clear Channel (Any Emergency Request)
41 - One-Car Assistance Request
63 - Responding to Command
78 - Police Officer in Danger
99 - Possible Emergency Situation, Respond Quietly

TRUCK-TRACTOR IDENTIFICATION NUMBERS
VIN* Plate

Make	Location
Autocar	8
Brockway	2
Diamond Reo	9
Ford	10
GMC	4
Kenworth	1
Peterbuilt	7
White	5

*Vehicle Identification Number

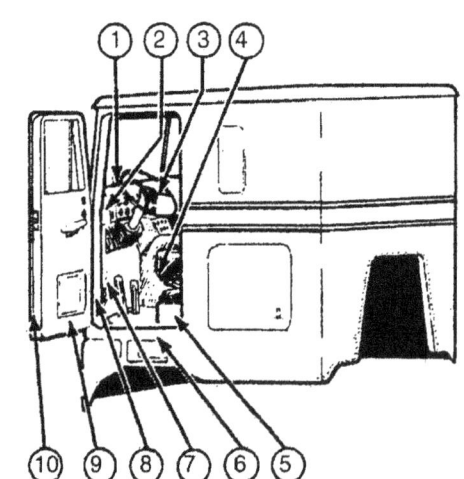

15 (#1)

Location of County Precinct Houses

First -   In H,* on S side of Merrick Rd., just E of Grand Avenue.
Second - In OB,* 1/8 mi. E of Seaford-Oyster Bay Expressway, 1/8 mi.S. of Jericho Trnpk.
Third -   In NH,* 1/8 mi. N of Hillside Ave., 1/8 mi. W of Willis Avenue
Fourth -   In H, on E side of Broadway, just N of Rockaway Avenue
Fifth -   In H, on S side of Dutch Broadway, 1/4 mi. N of Exit 14 of Southern State Parkway
Six -   In NH, just E of Community Drive, and just S of Whitney Pond Park. Seventh - In H,
           on side of Merrick Rd., just W of Seaford-Oyster Bay Expressway
Eighth -   In H, on E side of Wantagh Ave., just N of Hempstead Farmingdale Trnpk.

Location of Universities, Colleges, and Institutes
Adelphi U. -   In H,* 1/4 mi. E of Nassau Blvd., 1/4 mi. S of Stewart Ave.
Hofstra U. -   In H, at Oak and Fulton Streets.
Molloy College -   In H, on Hempstead Ave., just S of Southern State Pkway., and midway
                    between Exits 19 and 20.
C. W. Post College - In OB,* on Northern Blvd., 1 1/2 mi. W of Massapequa-Glen Cove Rd.
Nassau Community College - In H, on Stewart Ave., 1/2 mi. E of Clinton Rd.
Long Island Agri. & Tech. Institute - In OB, 1/2 mi. E of Round Swamp Rd., between Bethpage
       State Park and Old Bethpage Village Restoration.
N.Y. Inst. of Technology - In OB, on Northern Blvd., just E of line dividing OB and NH.
U.S. Merchant Marine Acad. - In NH,* at NW end of Elm Point Rd.

---
*H - Town of Hempstead; NH - Town of North Hempstead; OB - Town of Oyster Bay.

DIRECTIONS: After you have memorized the listed data, try to answer the following questions
              WITHOUT referring to the list.

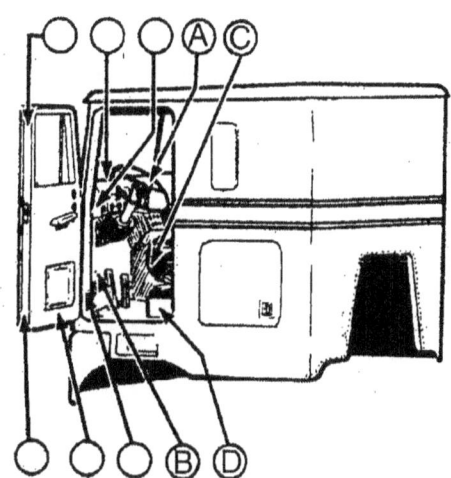

7. On a GMC truck-tractor, above, the VIN is located at   7.____

    A. A   B. B   C. C   D. D

8. The radio signal for *back in service* is   8.____

    A. 01   B. 04   C. 08   D. none of these

9. The Third Precinct House is located in 9._____
   A. NH, 1/8 mi. N of Hillside Ave., 1/8 mi. W of Willis Ave.
   B. NH, 1/4 mi. S of I.U. Willets Rd., 1/4 mi. E of Herricks Rd.
   C. Williston Park, on Willis Ave., 1/4 mi. S of Northern State Parkway
   D. Mineola, on Mineola Blvd., 1/2 mi. N of Jericho Trnpk.

10. The U.S. Merchant Marine Academy is at the NW end of _____ Rd. 10._____
    A. Sands Point   B. Mill Neck
    C. Kings Point   D. Elm Point

KEY (CORRECT ANSWERS)

1. D
2. D
3. B
4. C
5. A

6. D
7. C
8. A
9. A
10. D

EXAMINATION SECTION
TEST 1

DIRECTIONS: Each question or incomplete statement is followed by several suggested answers or completions. Select the one that BEST answers the question or completes the statement. *PRINT THE LETTER OF THE CORRECT ANSWER IN THE SPACE AT THE RIGHT.*

1. Which of the following events would typically cause the GREATEST amount of stress in a person's life?
    A. A major change in financial status
    B. Vacation
    C. Pregnancy
    D Marital separation

    1.____

2. A local shopping center has experienced a recent rash of shoplifting. Officer Jones is patrolling the mall parking lot frequently.
   Which situation below should Officer Jones regard as MOST suspicious?
    A. A man running out a store entrance with a shopping bag from the store under his arm
    B. A car parked for a long time near the front entrance of the store
    C. A woman loading a pile of clothes, some with plastic security tags still attached, into the trunk of her car
    D. A young man walking around looking in through the windows of various parked cars

    2.____

3. An officer is faced with the responsibility of telling a woman her husband has been murdered. While the officers should phrase the news as gently as possible, he or she should also demonstrate empathy nonverbally.
   The BEST way to do this is to
    A. stand with arms crossed
    B. hold the woman closely
    C. maintain eye contact
    D. tell the woman you understand her pain

    3.____

4. Cognitive symptoms of anxiety include
    A. rapid heart rate
    B. feelings of fear of helplessness
    C. poor social functioning
    D. euphoria

    4.____

5. Which of the following is MOST likely to help a person to improve her attitude?
    A. Avoiding people who make her feel bad about herself
    B. Learning to become more goal-oriented
    C. Learning to look more clearly at her own faults
    D. Taking charge of an unruly situation

    5.____

6. A suspect has been handcuffed, but refuses to take a seat in the patrol car after several requests.
   The arresting officer should
   A. tap the suspect behind the knees with the baton, just hard enough so that the suspect's legs will fold and he can be inserted into the car
   B. tighten the handcuffs until the pain compel compliance
   C. try to frighten the suspect with threats
   D. inform the suspect of the consequences for resisting arrest

7. Each of the following is likely to be a cause of stress on the job, EXCEPT
   A. work overload
   B. differences in organizational and personal values
   C. a narrowly-defined role
   D. time pressures

8. In communicating with people, especially in stressful or high-conflict situations, nonverbal communication is
   A. more important than the verbal message
   B. less important than the verbal message
   C. universal across all cultures
   D. typically contradictory to the verbal message

9. Problem-oriented police work does NOT
   A. help officers get to the roots of a crime problem
   B. offer a proactive model for policing
   C. focus on responding to calls for service
   D. have any impact on preventing or reducing crime

10. The difference between assertiveness and aggressiveness is that
    A. assertiveness is not potentially harmful to others
    B. aggressiveness involves strangers
    C. aggressiveness has to do with achieving goals
    D. assertiveness is always negative

11. As an officer and his partner arrive to investigate a reported domestic disturbance, the husband and wife are still arguing. In the presence of the officers, each spouse makes a verbal threat of physical harm against the other. In resolving this conflict, the FINAL step that should be taken by the officers is to
    A. indicate the consequences if this behavior continues
    B. empathize with each of the spouses
    C. present the spouses with problem-solving strategies
    D. describe the behaviors that appeared to cause the disturbance

12. Elements of community policing include
    I. the police   II. the business community
    III. the media   IV. religious institutions
    The CORRECT ANSWER IS:
    A. I, II   B. I, II, III   C. I, III   D. I, II, III, IV

13. In a grocery store parking lot, a pair of officers arrest both the buyer and seller in an alleged drug transaction in a grocery store parking lot. After the suspects have been handcuffed and placed in a patrol car, one of the officers notices a wad of bills on the ground where the transaction took place. The officer pockets the money and decides to keep it, telling herself that the money is "dirty" and that she has more of a right to it than either of the criminal suspects. Legally, the officer has committed a crime; ethically, she has committed a(n)
    A. rationalization B. kickback   C. stereotyping   D. deviance

14. Probably the MOST effective way to deal with on-the-job stress is to
    A. find alternative employment
    B. take early retirement
    C. participate in a personal wellness program
    D. acquire assertiveness skills that will help confront the people responsible for the stress

Questions 15-16.

DIRECTIONS: Questions 15 and 16 deal with the following situation.

A pharmacist has complained to the police department that several drug addicts in his neighborhood have been attempting to obtain drugs legally, usually by passing fake prescriptions.

15. Which of the following people should arouse the MOST suspicion when approaching the prescription counter?
    A. A middle-aged woman who appears homeless and is poorly groomed
    B. A young African-American male in a hooded sweatshirt on a hot day
    C. A man in his thirties who glances around furtively and brings a large amount of nonprescription items to the counter for purchase
    D. None of the above should be regarded as suspicious on the basis of their appearance alone

16. After refusing to fill several prescriptions, the pharmacist describes or gives each of the prescriptions to an investigating officer.
    Which of the following MOST warrants investigation?
    A. A written investigation that is covered with several coffee rings
    B. A prescription written on a Post-It note
    C. A written prescription for pain killers with a date indicating it was written more than a week ago
    D. A prescription that is phoned in by a doctor

17. An individual's personality, whether normal or deviant, will ALWAYS
    A. refer to the person's deep inner self, rather than just superficial aspects
    B. involve unique characteristics that are all different from another person's
    C. be a product of social and cultural environments, with no biological foundation
    D. be organized into patterns that are observable and measurable to some degree

18. Change in a person's life that is due to personal growth is almost always 18.____
    A. negative   B. dramatic   C. positive   D. minor

19. Residents in an urban neighborhood have complained of a recent increase in gang-related graffiti in their community. 19.____
    Which of the following should be regarded as MOST suspicious by an officer on patrol?
    A. One young man walking down the street and flashing gang signs at passing cars
    B. A pair of teenagers riding their bicycles in a tenement parking lot late at night
    C. A group of teenagers hanging out in a convenience store parking lot, leaning against a wall that is covered with graffiti
    D. A group of teenagers hanging out in a convenience store parking lot. One of the teenagers has a spray paint can.

20. Common symptoms of stress include each of the following EXCEPT 20.____
    A. digestive problem   B. sluggishness
    C. sleep problems   D. emotional instability

21. The general goal of community policing is 21.____
    A. a lower overall crime rate
    B. conviction of criminals who are caught in the community
    C. fewer violent crimes
    D. a higher quality of life in the community

22. In most settings, the simplest and most effective method of stopping sexual harassment is to 22.____
    A. threaten the person with legal or administrative consequences
    B. ignore it
    C. avoid the person as much as possible
    D. ask or tell the person to stop

23. Of the following types of crime, the one MOST likely to have a widespread impact on a victims community is 23.____
    A. hate or bias crime   B. workplace violence
    C. theft   D. sexual assault

24. Functional roles of the police include: 24.____
    I. Crime prevention   II. Order maintenance
    III. Public service   IV. Criminal prosecution
    The CORRECT answer is:
    A. I only   B. I, II   C. I, II, III   D. I, II, III, IV

25. A pre-existing thought or belief that people have about members of a given group—whether the belief is positive, negative, or neutral—is 25.____
    A. ethnocentrism   B. a stereotype
    C. self-centeredness   D. discrimination

KEY (CORRECT ANSWERS)

1. D
2. C
3. C
4. B
5. B

6. D
7. C
8. A
9. C
10. A

11. A
12. D
13. A
14. C
15. D

16. B
17. D
18. B
19. D
20. B

21. D
22. D
23. A
24. C
25. B

TEST 2

DIRECTIONS: Each question or incomplete statement is followed by several suggested answers or completions. Select the one that BEST answers the question or completes the statement. *PRINT THE LETTER OF THE CORRECT ANSWER IN THE SPACE AT THE RIGHT.*

1. Role expectations for police officers generally 1.____
   A. are consistent across the country, with a strong focus on peacekeeping
   B. change from community to community, depending on the local culture
   C. direct them to be more lenient with juvenile offenders
   D. direct them to be self-reliant in both preventing and investigating crime

2. Officer Shinjo takes a complaint from a woman who says she is being 2.____
   stalked by a man who is a classmate in one of her night business courses. The man has sent her unwanted gifts and left numerous unanswered telephone messages, but she did not become concerned until last night, when she noticed the man following her home from class. She asks Officer Shinjo what to do about the situation.
   At least part of Officer Shinjo's advice to the woman should include the suggestion that she
   A. immediately apply for a restraining order
   B. create a logbook to document each of the stalking incidents in as much detail as possible
   C. answer one of the man's telephone calls and try to explain that the unwanted attention is making her uncomfortable
   D. call the man herself and threaten legal action if he doesn't stop bothering her

3. Which of the following is an element of self-direction? 3.____
   A. Knowing when to seek help from others
   B. Being able to get from one geographic location to another without a map
   C. Establishing and reaching both short- and long-term goals
   D. Adopting healthier lifestyle habits

4. Each of the following factors is typically associated with ethnicity, EXCEPT 4.____
   A. culture   B. language
   C. economic status D. physical characteristics

5. Among the communication skills necessary for effective communication with 5.____
   people, the foundation upon which all others are based is considered to be
   A. confrontation   B. authoritativeness
   C. attending behavior D. observation

6. Which of the following offers the BEST definition of the word "ethics"? 6.____
   A. An individual's means of obtaining what he wants from and for other people in a society
   B. Standards of conduct that express a society's concept of right and wrong

C. A formal code of conduct that delineates a strict set of rules and framework for punishment
D. Morality and the consequences of behaviors

7. Which of the following is a measurement of a rate? 7.____
   A. The ratio of the number of new African-American arrestees for drug-related crimes in the 35-49 age bracket during a specific year, compared to the number of African-Americans in the same age group in the entire community
   B. The number of white females, aged 18-25, who are arrested each year on child endangerment charges
   C. The percentage change in the number of property crimes in a given year, compared to the previous year
   D. The ratio of the number of persons currently under prosecution for violent crimes to the number of people, aged 14-55, in the entire community

8. In recent weeks, several patrons at a local restaurant have had their cars broken 8.____
   into by having a window smashed in, and then having valuable items taken from the car. Officer Jackson is patrolling the restaurant parking lot.
   Which situation below should she regard as MOST suspicious?
   A. A young man in a hooded sweatshirt walking around the parking lot at lunchtime, carrying a long, heavy flashlight
   B. A car parked so as to partially block other cars from exiting the parking lot
   C. A man's voice raised in anger coming from the parking lot
   D. Several young men leaning against the outside of the parking lot fence in the early evening, bouncing a basketball and apparently waiting for the arrival of another person

9. Among the skills important to effective communication with people, the MOST 9.____
   complex and difficult to master are those that help to
   A. encourage   B. confront   C. influence   D. summarize

10. The FIRST step in dealing with an alcohol or drug addiction is to 10.____
    A. admit there is a problem
    B. talk to a counselor or close friend
    C. stop taking the drug or drinking alcohol
    D. join a support group or enter a rehabilitation center

11. Key elements of police professionalism include: 11.____
    I. an advanced education
    II. a clearly stated code of ethics
    III. accountability through peer review
    IV. demonstrated understanding of the field's core body of knowledge
    The CORRECT answer is:
    A. I, II   B. I, III, IV   C. II, III, IV   D. I, II, III, IV

12. A factor that makes a police officer susceptible to corruption is that the officer
    A. is typically different from most members of society
    B. can be sure that if a suspect is arrested, the suspect will be prosecuted and punished
    C. is usually better off financially than most of the people she interacts with in carrying out her duties
    D. has the professional discretion not to enforce the law

13. In resolving an ethical dilemma, a police officer's FIRST step should generally be to
    A. identify the ethical issues that are in conflict
    B. identify the people and organizations likely to be affected by the decision
    C. consult with colleagues and appropriate experts
    D. examine the reasons in favor of and opposed to each possible course of action

14. During a lengthy interview with a witness, an officer decides to use "reflection of meaning" strategies in order to clarify the information he's being given.
    This strategy would involve each of the following EXCEPT
    A. trying to paraphrase longer statements offered by the witness
    B. closing with a check on the witness's words, such as "So do I understand this correctly?"
    C. beginning sentences with phrases such as "You mean….." or "Sounds as if you saw….."
    D. offering an interpretation of the witness's words

15. Officer McGee is meeting with several community members to determine a course of action for reducing gang-related activities in the area.
    Each of the following is a guideline to be used by an officer in building a constructive relationship with community members, EXCEPT
    A. viewing community members as equals
    B. adopting a completely neutral tone of voice when speaking with people
    C. using a shared vocabulary of easily understood, nonoffensive words
    D. asking for the input of community members before making any suggestions

16. In solving a complex problem, the FIRST step is always to
    A. develop a plan
    B. gather information
    C. define the problem
    D. envision contingencies

17. Role conflict can occur when an officer encounters two sets of expectations that are inconsistent with each other. Role strain can occur when an officer's role is limited by what he or she is authorized to do.
    The MAIN difference between these two is that role
    A. conflict is relatively rare among police officers
    B. conflict can be resolved; role strain cannot
    C. strain creates stressful situations for officers
    D. strain has a greater influence on the officer's exercise of discretion

18. Generally, police community relations differs from public relations in that they
    A. consider the needs of the community first
    B. are much more successful in reducing social problems
    C. are without inherent spheres of interest
    D. encourage two-way communications

19. Factors that place a man at risk as a potential batterer include each of the following, EXCEPT
    A. poverty
    B. drug or alcohol use
    C. 30-45 years of age
    D. witnessing spousal abuse between parents

20. The four major categories of commonly abused substances include
    A. stimulants   B. alcohol   C. nicotine   D. caffeine

21. After receiving their monthly assistance payments from the local social services agency, some members of the homeless community immediately use the money to carry out drug transactions.
    In his patrol of the area around the agency, which situation below should Officer Garcia regard as MOST suspicious?
    A. A group of several homeless people who meet every day in a local park, where they sit together for about three hours and then move on
    B. A homeless woman who walks up and down the entire length of a busy city street all day long, endlessly smoking cigarettes
    C. An abandoned car that sits on a privately-owned lot and is used as a sleeping place by several homeless people throughout the day
    D. A single man remaining in the same area for several hours at a time, during which many homeless people approach him and greet him with handshakes

22. The MOST significant factor that requires police to perform functions other than law enforcement is
    A. greater public trust relative to other agencies or institutions
    B. a broader resource base
    C. round-the-clock availability
    D. the level of police interaction with community members

23. A "minority" group is a group that is discriminated against on the basis of
    A. physical or cultural characteristics
    B. the size of the group relative to the majority
    C. race
    D. the group's degree of conformity to the norms of the majority

24. An officer is talking with a resident of a high-crime urban neighborhood about a recent increase in drug-related activities. Because of the active police presence in the area, some residents are suspicious of the police.
    Each of the following nonverbal cues is a likely indicator of distrust on the part of a listener, EXCEPT

A. holding arms crossed over one's chest
B. steady eye contact
C. clenched jaw
D. shoulders angled away from speaker

25. Personality characteristics necessary for the successful performance of police duties include 25._____
    I. dependent style in problem-solving
    II. emotional expressiveness in interpersonal communication
    III. cohesiveness in group performance
    IV. emotional restraint
    The CORRECT answer is:
    A. I, III   B. I, II, IV   C. II, III, IV   D. I, II, III, IV

KEY (CORRECT ANSWERS)

1. B
2. B
3. C
4. C
5. C

6. B
7. B
8. A
9. C
10. A

11. D
12. D
13. A
14. D
15. B

16. C
17. B
18. D
19. C
20. A

21. D
22. C
23. A
24. B
25. C

EXAMINATION SECTION
TEST 1

DIRECTIONS: Each question or incomplete statement is followed by several suggested answers or completions. Select the one that BEST answers the question or completes the statement. *PRINT THE LETTER OF THE CORRECT ANSWER IN THE SPACE AT THE RIGHT.*

1. Officer Hayes has arrived at the scene of an automobile accident to find the two drivers arguing heatedly in the middle of the intersection, where their two cars remain entangled by their front bumpers. Traffic has backed up on all four sides of the intersection. As Officer Hayes approaches, the two drivers each begin to tell their side of the story at the same time. As they grow more agitated and begin to call each other names, one of the drivers threatens the other with physical harm.
Officer Hayes' FIRST action should be to
   A. ask each driver to stand on an opposite corner of the intersection and wait for him to begin documenting the accident
   B. call a tow truck to clear the accident from the intersection
   C. arrest the driver who made the threat
   D. ask the drivers to pull their cars out of the intersection and off to the side of the road

2. Probably the MOST important thing a police officer can do to build and strengthen a trusting relationship with community members is to
   A. patrol the area often and conspicuously
   B. listen to them in a respectful and nonjudgmental way
   C. make sure people understand his background and qualifications
   D. establish clear, reachable goals for improving the community

3. Which of the following is NOT a factor that should influence an officer's exercise of discretion?
   A. Clear statutes and protocols
   B. Informal expectations of legislatures and the public
   C. Use of force
   D. Limited resources

4. The term for the policing style which emphasizes order maintenance is _____ style.
   A. service   B. coercive   C. watchman   D. legalistic

5. Officer Torres, a community service law enforcement officer, approaches the home of recent Vietnamese immigrants to speak to several community members gathered there. He notices several pairs of shoes on the front porch.

It is reasonable for Officer Torres too assume that
- A. the people in the home are superstitious
- B. the house must have some religious significance
- C. if he removes his own shoes before entering, it will be perceived as a sign of respect
- D. the homeowners are having their carpets cleaned

6. Ethical issues are
   - A. usually a problem only in individual behaviors
   - B. relevant to all aspects of police work
   - C. usually referred to a board or committee for decision-making
   - D. the same as legal issues

   6._____

7. In using the "reflection of meaning" technique in a client interview, a social worker should do each of the following, EXCEPT
   - A. begin with a sentence stem such as "You mean..." or "Sounds like you believe..."
   - B. offer an interpretation of the client's words
   - C. add paraphrasing of longer client statements
   - D. close with a "check-out" such as, "Am I hearing you right?"

   7._____

8. A police officer is speaking with a victim who is hearing-impaired. The police officer should try to do each of the following, EXCEPT
   - A. speak slowly and clearly
   - B. gradually increase the volume of his voice
   - C. face the victim squarely
   - D. reduce or eliminate any background or ambient noise

   8._____

9. An officer is interviewing a witness who is a recent immigrant from China. In general, the officer should avoid
   - A. verbal tracking or requests for clarification
   - B. open-ended questions
   - C. sustained eye contact
   - D. attentive body language

   9._____

10. Which of the following statements about rape is FALSE?
    - A. The use of alcohol and drugs can reduce sexual inhibitions.
    - B. Rape is a crime of violence.
    - C. Rape is a crime that can only be committed against women.
    - D. It is not a sustainable legal charge if the partner has already consented to sex in the past.

    10._____

11. A person's individual code of ethics is typically determined by each of the following factors, EXCEPT
    - A. reason
    - B. religion
    - C. emotion
    - D. law

    11._____

12. Officer Long, new to the urban precinct where he is assigned patrol, has received a pair of complaints from two customers about the owner of a local convenience store, who works the cash register on most days. According to one customer, the owner became angry and ordered her out of the store after she had asked the price of a certain item. The other customer claims that on another occasion, the owner pulled a handgun from behind the counter and trained it on him as he walked slowly out of the store with his hands up. Each of the customers has lived in the neighborhood for many years and has never before seen or heard of any strange behavior on the owner's part.
    In investigating these complaints, Officer Long should suspect that
    A. the owner should be considered armed and dangerous and any entry into the store should be made with weapons drawn
    B. the cause of the problem is most likely the onset of a serious psychological disturbance
    C. the customers may have reasons to be untruthful about the convenience store owner
    D. the store owner has probably experienced a recent trauma, such as a robber attempt or a personal loss

13. Typical signs and symptoms of stress include
    I. weakened immune system   II. prolonged, vivid daydreams
    III. insomnia   IV. depression
    The CORRECT answer is:
    A. I only   B. I, III, IV   C. III, IV   D. I, II, III, IV

14. Other than solid, ethical police work, an officer's BEST defense against a lawsuit or complaint is usually
    A. detailed case records
    B. a capable advocate
    C. a vigorous counterclaim against the plaintiff
    D. the testimony of professional character witnesses

15. Assertive people
    A. avoid stating feelings, opinions, or desires
    B. appear passive, but behave aggressively
    C. state their views and needs directly
    D. appear aggressive, but behave passively

16. In the non-verbal communication process, meaning is MOST commonly provided by
    A. body language   B. touch
    C. tone of voice   D. context

17. The MOST obvious practical benefit that deviance has on a society is the
    A. advancement of the status quo
    B. vindication of new laws
    C. inducement to reach cultural goals
    D. promotion of social unity

18. What is the term for policing that focuses on providing a wider and more thorough array of social services to defeat the social problems that cause crime?
    A. Reflecting policing
    B. Order maintenance
    C. Social engineering
    D. Holistic policing

19. The term "active listening" MOSTLY refers to a person's ability to
    A. both listen and accomplish other tasks at the same time
    B. take an active role in determining which information is provided by the speaker
    C. concentrate on what is being said
    D. indicate with numerous physical cues that he/she is listening

20. Police officers in any jurisdiction are MOST likely to receive calls about
    A. threats
    B. suspicious persons
    C. petty theft or property crime
    D. disturbances, such as family arguments

21. Which of the following is NOT a physiological explanation for rape?
    A. Uncontrollable sex drive
    B. Lack of available partners
    C. Reaction to repressed desires
    D. Consequence of the natural selection process

22. Which of the following is an element of self-discipline?
    A. Establishing and reaching short-term goals
    B. Establishing and reaching long-term goals
    C. Taking an honest look at one's lifestyle and making conscious changes toward improvement
    D. Taking an honest look at one's personality and revealing traits, both good and bad, to others

23. Most of the events in a person's life are the result of
    A. chance events
    B. a sense of intuition
    C. individual choices and decisions
    D. the decisions of one's parents or other authority figures

24. Which of the following is the MOST effective way for a department to limit the discretion exercised by police officers?
    A. Open and flexible departmental directives
    B. Close supervision by departmental management
    C. Broadening role definitions for officers
    D. Statutory protection from civil liability lawsuits

25. Police officers who demonstrate critical thinking skills are also more likely to demonstrate each of the following, EXCEPT   25.____
   A. the ability to empathize
   B. the tendency to criticize
   C. self-awareness
   D. reflective thinking

KEY (CORRECT ANSWERS)

1.	A	11.	D
2.	B	12.	D
3.	A	13.	B
4.	C	14.	A
5.	C	15.	C
6.	B	16.	A
7.	B	17.	D
8.	B	18.	D
9.	C	19.	C
10.	D	20.	D

21.	C
22.	C
23.	C
24.	B
25.	B

TEST 2

DIRECTIONS: Each question or incomplete statement is followed by several suggested answers or completions. Select the one that BEST answers the question or completes the statement. *PRINT THE LETTER OF THE CORRECT ANSWER IN THE SPACE AT THE RIGHT.*

1. Officer Park responds to a domestic disturbance call to find a mother and her two young children huddled together in the living room, all of them crying. The mother explains that her husband is no longer there; he flew into a fit of rage and then stormed out to join his friends for a night of drinking.
Officer Park's FIRST action would MOST likely be to
   A. determine the location of the husband
   B. contact the appropriate social services agency to arrange a consultation
   C. try to calm the family down and ask the mother to explain what happened
   D. refer the mother to a local battered-spouse shelter

1.____

2. Most commonly, the reason for crimes involving stranger violence is
   A. anger   B. retaliation   C. hate   D. robbery

2.____

3. For a police officer, "burst stress" is MOST likely to be caused by
   A. a shootout   B. financial troubles
   C. departmental politics   D. substance abuse

3.____

4. The MOST significant factor in whether a person achieves success in his/her personal life, school, and career is
   A. intelligence   B. a positive attitude
   C. existing financial resources   D. innate ability

4.____

5. Typically, a professional code of ethics
   A. embodies a broad picture of expected moral conduct
   B. is voluntary
   C. provides specific guidance for performance in situations
   D. are decided by objective ethicists outside of the profession

5.____

6. Components recognized by contemporary society as elements of sexual harassment include
   I. abuse of power   II. immature behavior
   III. sexual desire   IV. hormonal imbalance
   The CORRECT answer is:
   A. I only   B. I, III   C. II, III   D. I, II, III, IV

6.____

7. The phrase "substance abuse" is typically defined as
   A. an addiction to an illegal substance
   B. the continued use of a psychoactive substance even after it creates problems in a person's life
   C. the overuse of an illegal substance
   D. a situation in which a person craves a drug and organizes his or her life around obtaining it

7.____

8. The humanist perspective of behavior holds that people who commit crimes or otherwise act badly are 8.____
    A. willfully disregarding societal norms
    B. reacting to the deprivation of basic needs
    C. suffering from a psychological illness
    D. experiencing a moral lapse

9. Which of the following is NOT involved in the process of empathic listening? 9.____
    A. Actually hearing exactly what the other person is saying
    B. Searching for the "hidden meanings" behind statements
    C. Listening without judgment
    D. Communicating that you're hearing what the other person is saying, both verbally and nonverbally

10. Which of the following is NOT a component in developing a stress-resistant lifestyle? 10.____
    A. Finding leisure time
    B. Eating nutritious foods
    C. Getting enough sleep
    D. Seeking financial independence

11. Which of the following was NOT a factor that led to the expansion of a community policing model? 11.____
    A. Information obtained at a crime scene during a preliminary investigation was the most important factor determining the probability of an arrest.
    B. Police response times typically had little to do with the probability of making an arrest.
    C. Traditional "preventive patrols" generally failed to reduce crime.
    D. People who knew police officers personally often tried to take advantage of them.

12. Most of the correspondence in a pyramid scheme that has defrauded several elderly victims has been traced to a post office box in a rural area. 12.____
    Probably the simplest and most efficient way of arresting the suspect(s) in this case would be to
    A. use an elderly man as a "victim" to lure the suspects into an attempt to defraud him
    B. address a letter to the post office box asking the user to come in for questioning
    C. check Postal Service records to see who is leasing the post office box
    D. physically observe the post office box for a while, to see who is using it

13. The process of hiring a police officer typically involves each of the following, EXCEPT 13.____
    A. technical preparation
    B. medical examination
    C. background checks
    D. physical ability test

14. The MOST common form of rape is _____ rape. 14.____
    A. stranger
    B. acquaintance
    C. sadistic
    D. spousal

15. Officer Stevens and his partner respond to a domestic disturbance call involving a father and his teenage daughter. As the officers arrive at their home, the two are still arguing heatedly, but when the officers enter, the daughter retreats to the kitchen, where she continues crying. The father explains that his wife, the daughter's mother, died last year, and the daughter's behavior and school performance have suffered as a result. The father is afraid that the daughter is falling in with the wrong crowd, and may be getting involved with drugs. He is afraid for her and doesn't know what to do.
Within the scope of his police role, the MOST appropriate action for Officer Stevens to take in this case would be to
   A. warn both the father and the daughter of the potential consequences of conviction on a charge of disturbing the peace
   B. refer the father and the daughter to a social services or counseling agency
   C. inform the daughter of the drug statutes that may apply in her case as a way to influence her choices
   D. question the daughter about her feelings surrounding the death of her mother

16. During an interview, a suspect confesses to the rape of a co-worker that occurred in the office after the rest of the employees had left for the day. The suspect says he was tormented by the seductive behavior of the co-worker until he could no longer stand it. He was himself a victim, he says.
In this case, the suspect is making use of the psychological defense mechanism known as
   A. projection   B. regression   C. denial   D. sublimation

17. Which of the following is NOT a good stress-reduction strategy?
   A. Spend some time each day doing absolutely nothing
   B. Become more assertive
   C. Develop a hobby
   D. Have a sense of humor

18. The term for the policing style which emphasizes problem-solving is _____ style.
   A. watchman   B. order maintenance
   C. service   D. legalistic

19. According to current rules and statutes, any employer
   A. may inquire as to a job applicant's age or date of birth
   B. may keep on file information regarding an employee's race, color, religion, sex, or national origin
   C. may refuse employment to someone without a car
   D. must give a woman who has taken time off for maternity leave her same job and salary when she is read to return to work

20. During a conversation with the mother of a teenage boy who has been arrested twice for shoplifting, an officer attempts to be an active listener as the mother explains why she thinks the boy is having so much trouble.
Being an active listener includes each of the following strategies, EXCEPT
    A. putting the speaker at ease
    B. interrupting with questions to clarify meaning
    C. summarizing the speaker's major ideas and feelings
    D. withholding criticism

21. Which of the following is NOT a characteristic of the typical poverty-class family?
    A. Female-headed, single-parent families
    B. Unwed parents
    C. Isolated from neighbors and relatives
    D. High divorce rates

22. When speaking with community members about improving the quality of life in the neighborhood, an officer should look for signs of social desirability bias among the people with whom he's talking.
Social desirability bias often causes people to
    A. judge other people based on their social role rather than inner character
    B. attribute their successes to skill, while blaming external factors for failures
    C. modify their interactions or behaviors based on what they think is acceptable to others
    D. contend for leadership positions

23. For a number of reasons, Officer Stone thinks a fellow officer might have a drinking problem, and decides to talk to her about it. The officer says she doesn't have a drinking problem; she doesn't even take a drink until after it gets dark.
Her answer indicates that she
    A. doesn't have a drinking problem
    B. is probably a social drinker
    C. drinks more during the winter months
    D. is in denial

24. Factors which shape the police role include each of the following, EXCEPT
    A. individual goals   B. role expectations
    C. role acquisition   D. multiple-role phenomenon

25. "Deviance" is a social term denoting
    A. any violation of norms
    B. any serious violation of norms
    C. a type of nonconforming behavior recognizable in all cultures
    D. a specific set of crime statistics

KEY (CORRECT ANSWERS)

1.	C	11.	D
2.	D	12.	D
3.	A	13.	A
4.	B	14.	B
5.	A	15.	B
6.	A	16.	A
7.	B	17.	A
8.	B	18.	C
9.	B	19.	B
10.	D	20.	B

21. C
22. C
23. D
24. A
25. A

EXAMINATION SECTION
TEST 1

DIRECTIONS: Each question or incomplete statement is followed by several suggested answers or completions. Select the one that BEST answers the question or completes the statement. *PRINT THE LETTER OF THE CORRECT ANSWER IN THE SPACE AT THE RIGHT.*

1. Upon arriving at the scene of an accident in which a pedestrian was struck and killed by an automobile, an officer's first action was to clear the scene of spectators.
   Of the following, the PRINCIPAL reason for this action is that
   A. important evidence may be inadvertently destroyed by the crowd
   B. this is a fundamental procedure in first aid work
   C. the operator of the vehicle may escape in the crowd
   D. witnesses will speak more freely if other persons are not present

   1.____

2. In questioning witnesses, an officer is instructed to avoid leading questions or questions that will suggest the answer.
   Accordingly, when questioning a witness about the appearance of a suspect, it would be BEST for him to ask:
   A. What kind of hat did he wear?
   B. Did he wear a felt hat?
   C. What did he wear?
   D. Didn't he wear a hat?

   2.____

3. The only personal description the police have of a particular criminal was made several years ago.
   Of the following, the item in the description that will be MOST useful in identifying him at the present time is the
   A. color of his eyes
   B. color of his hair
   C. number of teeth
   D. weight

   3.____

4. Crime statistics indicate that property crimes such as larceny, burglary, and robbery are more numerous during winter months than in summer.
   The one of the following explanations that MOST adequately accounts for this situation is that
   A. human needs, such as clothing, food, heat, and shelter, are greater in winter
   B. criminal tendencies are aggravated by climatic changes
   C. there are more hours of darkness in winter and such crimes are usually committed under cover of darkness
   D. urban areas are more densely populated during winter months, affording greater opportunity for such crimes

   4.____

5. When automobile tire tracks are to be used as evidence, a plaster cast is made of them.
   Of the following, the MOST probable reason for taking a photograph is that
   A. photographs can be duplicated more easily than castings
   B. less skill is required for photographing than casting
   C. the tracks may be damaged in the casting process
   D. photographs are more easily transported than castings

6. It is generally recommended that an officer, in lifting a revolver that is to be sent to the police laboratory for ballistics tests and fingerprint examination, do so by insetting a pencil through the trigger guard rather than into the barrel of the weapon.
   The reason for preferring this procedure is that
   A. every precaution must be taken not to eliminate fingerprints on the weapon
   B. there is a danger of accidentally discharging the weapon by placing the pencil in the barrel
   C. the pencil may make scratches inside the barrel that will interfere with the ballistics tests
   D. a weapon can more easily be lifted by the trigger guard

7. PHYSICIAN is to PATIENT as ATTORNEY is to
   A. court   B. client   C. counsel   D. judge

8. JUDGE is to SENTENCE as JURY is to
   A. court   B. foreman   C. defendant   D. verdict

9. REVERSAL is to AFFIRMANCE as CONVICTION is to
   A. appeal   B. acquittal   C. error   D. mistrial

10. GENUINE is to TRUE as SPURIOUS is to
    A. correct   B. conceived   C. false   D. speculative

11. ALLEGIANCE is to LOYALTY as TREASON is to
    A. felony   B. faithful   C. obedience   D. rebellion

12. CONCUR is to AGREE as DIFFER is to
    A. coincide   B. dispute   C. join   D. repeal

13. A person who has an uncontrollable desire to steal without need is called a
    A. dipsomaniac   B. kleptomaniac
    C. monomaniac   D. pyromaniac

14. In the sentence, "The placing of any inflammable substance in any building or the placing of any device or contrivence capable of producing fire, for the purpose of causing a fire is an attempt to burn," the MISSPELLED word is
    A. inflammable   B. substance   C. device   D. contrivence

15. In the sentence, "The word 'break' also means obtaining an entrance into a building by any artifice used for that purpose, or by colussion with any person therein," the MISSPELLED word is
    A. obtaining   B. entrance   C. artifice   D. colussion

    15.____

16. In the sentence, "Any person who with intent to provoke a breech of the peace causes a disturbance or is offensive to others may be deemed to have committed disorderly conduct," the MISSPELLED word is
    A. breech   B. disturbance   C. offensive   D. committed

    16.____

17. In the sentence, "When the offender inflicts a grevious harm upon the person from whose possession, or in his presence, property is taken, he is guilty of robbery, the MISSPELLED word is
    A. offender   B. grevious   C. possession   D. presence

    17.____

18. In the sentence, "A person who wilfully encourages or advises another person in attempting to take the latter's life is guilty of a felony," the MISSPELLED word is
    A. wilfully   B. encourages   C. advises   D. attempting

    18.____

19. The treatment to be given the offender cannot alter the fact of his offense; but we can take measures to reduce the chances of similar acts in the future. We should banish the criminal, not in order to exact revenge nor directly to encourage reform, but to deter him and others from further illegal attacks on society.
    According to this paragraph, the PRINCIPAL reason for punishing criminals is to
    A. prevent the commission of future crimes
    B. remove them safely from society
    C. avenge society
    D. teach them that crime does not pay

    19.____

20. Even the most comprehensive and best substantiated summaries of the total volume of criminal acts would not contribute greatly to an understanding of the varied social and biological factors which are sometimes assumed to enter into crime causation, nor would they indicate with any degree of precision the needs of police forces in combating crime.
    According to this statement,
    A. crime statistics alone do not determine the needs of police forces in combating crime
    B. crime statistics are essential to a proper understanding of the social factors of crime
    C. social and biological factor which enter the crime causation have little bearing on police needs
    D. a knowledge of the social and biological factors of crime is essential to a proper understanding of crime statistics

    20.____

21. The police officer's art consists in applying and enforcing a multitude of laws and ordinances in such degree or proportion and in such manner that the greatest degree of social protection will be secured. The degree of enforcement and the method of application will vary with each neighborhood and community.
According to the foregoing paragraph,
   A. each neighborhood or community must judge for itself to what extent the law is to be enforced
   B. a police officer should only enforce those laws which are designed to give the greatest degree of social protection
   C. the manner and intensity of law enforcement is not necessarily the same in all communities
   D. all laws and ordinances must be enforced in a community with the same degree of intensity

22. Police control in the sense of regulating the details of police operations involves such matters as the technical means for so organizing the available personnel that competent police leadership, when secured, can operate effectively. It is concerned not so much with the extent to which popular controls can be trusted to guide and direct the course of police protection a with the administrative relationships which should exist between the component parts of the police organism.
According to the foregoing statement, police control is
   A. solely a matter of proper personnel assignment
   B. the means employed to guide and direct the course of police protection
   C. principally concerned with the administrative relationships between units of a police organization
   D. the sum total of means employed in rendering police protection

23. Two patrol cars hurry to the scene of an accident from different directions. The first proceeds at the rate of 45 miles per hour and arrives in four minutes. Although the second car travels over a route which is three-fourths of a mile longer, it arrives at the scene only a half-minute later.
The speed of the second car, expressed in miles per hour, is
   A. 50   B. 55   C. 60   D. 65

24. A motorcycle officer issued 72 traffic summonses in January, 60 in February and 83 in March.
In order to average 75 summonses per month for the four months of January, February, March, and April, during April he will have to issue _____ summonses.
   A. 80   B. 85   C. 90   D. 95

25. In a unit of the Police Department to which 40 officers are assigned, the sick report record during 2022 was as follows: 1 was absent 8 days, 5 were absent 3 days each, 4 were absent 5 days each, 10 were absent 2 days each, 8 were absent 4 days each, 5 were absent 1 day each.
The average number of days on sick report for all the members of this unit is MOST NEARLY
   A. ½   B. 1   C. 2 ½   D. 3

Questions 26-30.

DIRECTIONS: Column I lists various statements of fact. Column II is a list of crimes. Next to the numbers corresponding to the number preceding the statements of fact in Column I, place the letter preceding the crime listed in Column II with which Jones should be charged. In answering these questions, the following definitions of crimes should be applied, bearing in mind that ALL elements contained in the definitions must be present in order to charge a person with that crime.

BURGLARY is breaking and entering a building with intent to commit some crime therein. EMBEZZLEMENT is the appropriation to one's use of another's property which has been entrusted to one's care or which has come lawfully into one's possession. EXTORTION is taking or obtaining property from another with his consent, induced by a wrongful use of force or fear. LARCENY is taking and carrying away the personal property of another with intent to deprive or defraud the true owner of the use and benefit of such property. ROBBERY is the unlawful taking of the personal property of another from his person or in his presence by force or violence, or fear of injury.

COLUMN I

26. Jones, believing Smith had induced his wife to leave him, went to Smith's home armed with a knife with which he intended to assault Smith. When his knock was unanswered, he forced open the door of Smith's home and entered but, finding the house empty, he threw away the knife and left.

27. Jones was employed as a collection agent by Smith. When Smith refused to reimburse him for certain expenses he claimed to have incurred in connection with his work, Jones deducted this amount from sums he had collected for Smith.

28. Jones spent the night in a hotel. During the night he left his room, went downstairs to the desk, stole money and returned to his room.

29. Jones, a building inspector, found that the elevators in Smith's building were being operated without a permit. He threatened to report the matter and have the elevators shut down unless Smith paid him a sum of money. Smith paid the amount demanded

30. Jones held-up Smith on the street and, pointing a revolve at him, demanded his money. Smith, without resisting, handed Jones his money. When Jones was apprehended, it was discovered that the revolver was a toy.

COLUMN II

A. burglary
B. embezzlement
C. extortion
D. larceny
E. robbery
F. no crime

26._____
27._____
28._____
29._____
30._____

Questions 31-40.

DIRECTIONS: Questions 31 through 40 consist of statements from which a term is missing. Each of these statements can be completed correctly with one of the terms in the following list. In the space opposite the number corresponding to the number of the question, place the LETTER preceding the term in the following list which MOST accurately completes the statement.

A. affidavit
B. appeal
C. arraignment
D. arrest
E. bench warrant
F. habeas corpus
G. indictment
H. injunction
I. sentence
J. subpoena

31. A _____ is a writ calling witnesses to court. 31._____

32. _____ is a method used to obtain a review of a case in court of superior jurisdiction. 32._____

33. A judgment passed by a court on a person on trial as a criminal offender is called a _____. 33._____

34. _____ is a writ or order requiring a person to refrain from a particular act. 34._____

35. _____ is the name given to a writ commanding the bringing of the body of a certain person before a certain court. 35._____

36. A _____ is a court order directing that an offender be brought into court. 36._____

37. The calling of a defendant before the court to answer an accusation is called _____. 37._____

38. The accusation in writing, presented by the grand jury to a competent court charging a person with a public offense is an _____. 38._____

39. A sworn declaration in writing is an _____. 39._____

40. _____ is the taking of a person into custody for the purpose of holding him to answer a criminal charge. 40._____

Questions 41-55.

DIRECTIONS: Questions 41 through 55 consist of statements from which a term is missing. Each of these statements can be completed correctly with one of the terms in the following list. In the space opposite the number corresponding to the number of the question, place the LETTER preceding the term in the following list which MOST accurately completes the statement.

A. accessory   B. accomplice   C. alibi
D. autopsy   E. ballistics   F. capital
G. confidence man   H. commission   I. conspiracy
J. corroborated   K. grand jury   L. homicide
M. misdemeanors   N. penology   O. perjury

41. _____ is the dissection of a dead human body to determine the cause of death.   41._____

42. The general term which mean the killing of one person by another is _____.   42._____

43. _____ is the science of the punishment of crime.   43._____

44. False swearing constitutes the crime of _____.   44._____

45. A combination of two or more persons to accomplish a criminal or unlawful act is called _____.   45._____

46. By _____ is meant evidence showing that a defendant was in another place when the crime was committed.   46._____

47. _____ is a term frequently used to describe a person engaged in a kind of swindling operation.   47._____

48. A _____ offense is one for which a life sentence or death penalty is prescribed by law.   48._____

49. A violation of a law may be either an act of omission or an act of _____.   49._____

50. An _____ is a person who is liable to prosecution for the identical offense charged against a defendant on trial.   50._____

51. A person would be an _____ who after the commission of a crime aided in the escape of one he knew to be an offender.   51._____

52. An official body called to hear complaints and to determine whether there is ground for criminal prosecution is known as the _____.   52._____

53. Crimes are generally divided into two classes, namely felonies and _____.   53._____

54. _____ is the science of the motion of projectiles.   54._____

55. Testimony of a witness which is confirmed by another witness is _____.   55._____

Questions 56-60.

DIRECTIONS: Next to the question number which corresponds with the number of each item in Column I, place the letter preceding the adjective in Column II which BEST describes the persons in Column I.

COLUMN I	COLUMN II	
56. A talkative woman	A. abstemious	56.____
	B. pompous	
57. A person on a reducing diet	C. erudite	57.____
	D. benevolent	
58. A scholarly professor	E. docile	58.____
	F. loquacious	
59. A man who seldom speaks	G. indefatigable	59.____
	H. taciturn	
60. A charitable person		60.____

Questions 61-65.

DIRECTIONS: Next to the question number which corresponds with the number preceding each profession in Column I, place the letter preceding the word in Column II which BEST explains the subject of that profession.

COLUMN I	COLUMN II	
61. Geologist	A. animals	61.____
	B. eyes	
62. Oculist	C. feet	62.____
	D. fortune-telling	
63. Podiatrist	E. language	63.____
	F. rocks	
64. Palmist	G. stamps	64.____
	H. woman	
65. Zoologist		65.____

Questions 66-70.

DIRECTIONS: Next to the question number corresponding to the number of each of the words in Column I, place the letter preceding the word in Column II that is MOST NEARLY OPPOSITE to it in meaning.

COLUMN I	COLUMN II	
66. comely	A. beautiful	66.____
	B. cowardly	
67. eminent	C. kind	67.____
	D. sedate	
68. frugal	E. shrewd	68.____
	F. ugly	
69. gullible	G. unknown	69.____
	H. wasteful	
70. valiant		70.____

KEY (CORRECT ANSWERS)

1. A	16. A	31. J	46. C	61. F
2. C	17. B	32. B	47. G	62. B
3. A	18. A	33. I	48. F	63. C
4. C	19. A	34. H	49. H	64. D
5. C	20. A	35. F	50. B	65. A
6. C	21. C	36. E	51. A	66. F
7. B	22. C	37. C	52. L	67. G
8. D	23. A	38. G	53. N	68. H
9. B	24. B	39. A	54. E	69. E
10. C	25. C	40. D	55. K	70. B
11. D	26. A	41. D	56. F	
12. B	27. B	42. M	57. A	
13. B	28. D	43. O	58. C	
14. D	29. C	44. P	59. H	
15. D	30. E	45. J	60. D	

EXAMINATION SECTION
TEST 1

DIRECTIONS: Each question or incomplete statement is followed by several suggested answers or completions. Select the one that BEST answers the question or completes the statement. *PRINT THE LETTER OF THE CORRECT ANSWER IN THE SPACE AT THE RIGHT.*

1. The delivery of an arrested person to his sureties, upon their giving security for his appearance at the time and place designated to submit to the jurisdiction and judgment of the court, is known as
    A. bail
    B. habeas corpus
    C. parole
    D. probation

    1._____

2. Jones was charged with the murder of Smith. Brown, Jones' landlord, testified at the trial that Jones had in his home a well-equipped laboratory which contained all the necessary chemical for producing the poison which an autopsy showed caused Smith's death.
    Brown's testimony constitutes what is called _____ evidence.
    A. corroborative   B. opinion   C. hearsay   D. circumstantial

    2._____

3. In addressing a class of recruits, a police lieutenant remarked: "Carelessness and failure are twins."
    The one of the following that MOST NEARLY expresses his meaning is
    A. negligence seldom accompanies success
    B. incomplete work is careless work
    C. conscientious work is never attended by failure
    D. a conscientious person never makes mistakes

    3._____

4. In taking a statement from a person who has been shot by an assailant and is not expected to live, police are instructed to ask the person: "Do you believe you are about to die?"
    Of the following, the MOST probable reason for this question is
    A. the theory that a person about to die will tell the truth
    B. to determine if the victim is conscious and capable of making a statement
    C. to put the victim mentally at ease and more willing to talk
    D. that the statement could not be used in court if his mind was distraught by the fear of impending death

    4._____

5. If, while you are on duty at a busy intersection, a pedestrian asks you for directions to a particular place, the BEST course of conduct is to
    A. ignore the question and continue directing operations
    B. tell the pedestrian to ask a patrolman on foot patrol
    C. answer the question in a brief, courteous manner
    D. leave your post only long enough to give clear and adequate directions

    5._____

6. In lecturing on the law of arrest, a lieutenant remarked: "To go beyond is as bad as to fall short."
   The one of the following which MOST NEARLY expresses his meaning is
   A. never undertake the impossible   B. extremes are not desirable
   C. look before you leap   D. too much success is dangerous

7. Suppose you are an officer assigned to a patrol precinct. While you are in the vicinity of a school, your attention is called to a man who is selling small packages to school children. You are told that this man distributes similar packages to these same children daily and that he is suspected of dealing in narcotics.
   Of the following, the BEST action for you to take is to
   A. pretend to be an addict and attempt to purchase narcotics from him
   B. observe the man's action yourself for several days in order to obtain grounds for arrest
   C. stop and question one or more of the children after they have transacted business with the man
   D. stop and question the man as he leaves the children

8. In the event of a poison gas attack, civil defense authorities advise civilians to _____ door and windows and go to _____.
   A. open; upper floors   B. close; upper floors
   C. open; the basement   D. close; the basement

9. The procedure whereby a defendant is brought before a magistrate, informed of the charge against him, and asked how he pleads thereto, is called
   A. arraignment   B. indictment   C. presentment   D. inquisition

10. A written accusation of a crime presented by a grand jury is called a(n)
    A. commitment   B. arraignment   C. indictment   D. demurrer

11. The one of the following statements made by a prisoner that is correctly called an alibi is:
    A. "He struck me first."
    B. "I didn't intend to hurt him."
    C. "I was miles away from there at the time."
    D. "I don't remember what happened."

12. A person who, after the commission of a crime, conceals the defender with the intent that the latter may escape from arrest and trial, is called a(n)
    A. accessory   B. accomplice   C. confederate   D. associate

13. A sworn statement of fact is called a(n)
    A. affidavit   B. oath
    C. acknowledgment   D. subpoena

14. The right of trial by jury in the courts of the state is PRIMARILY safeguarded by a provision of
    A. the United States Constitution   B. the constitution of the state
    C. a state statute   D. a Federal statute

15. The task of protecting the President and his family is entrusted PRIMARILY to the
    A. Federal Bureau of Investigation
    B. United States Secret Service
    C. Central Intelligence Agency
    D. District of Columbia Police Department

16. The coordinating organization for the various Federal agencies engaged in intelligence activities is the
    A. Federal Bureau of Investigation   B. Federal Security Agency
    C. Mutual Security Agency   D. Central Intelligence Agency

17. A drug addict whose arm shows many scars from the injection of a hypodermic needle is MOST apt to be addicted to
    A. heroin   B. cocaine   C. opium   D. marijuana

18. All of the following drugs are derived from opium EXCEPT
    A. cocaine   B. heroin   C. morphine   D. codeine

19. In addition to cases of submersion, artificial respiration is a recommended first aid procedure for
    A. sunstroke   B. chemical poisoning
    C. electric shock   D. apoplexy

20. An injury to a muscle or tendon brought about by severe exertion and resulting in pain and stiffness is called a
    A. strain   B. sprain   C. bruise   D. fracture

21. Of the following kinds of wounds, the one in which there is the LEAST danger of infection is a(n) _____ wound.
    A. abrasive   B. punctured   C. lacerated   D. incised

22. When a person is found injured on the street, it is generally advisable, pending arrival of a physician, to help prevent fainting or shock by keeping the patient
    A. in a sitting position   B. lying down with the head level
    C. lying down with the head raised   D. standing on his feet

23. When an injured person appears to be suffering from shock, of the following, it is MOST essential to
    A. loosen his clothing   B. keep him warm
    C. administer a stimulant   D. place him in a prone position

24. In the sentence, "Malice was immanent in all his remarks," the word "immanent" means MOST NEARLY
    A. elevated   B. inherent   C. threatening   D. foreign

25. In the sentence, "The extant copies of the document were found in the safe," the word "extant" means MOST NEARLY
    A. existing   B. original   C. forged   D. duplicate

26. In the sentence, "The recruit was more complaisant after the captain spoke to him," the word "complaisant" means MOST NEARLY
    A. calm   B. affable   C. irritable   D. confident

27. In the sentence, "The man was captured under highly creditable circumstances," the word "creditable" means MOST NEARLY
    A. doubtful   B. believable   C. praiseworthy   D. unexpected

28. In the sentence, "His superior officers were more sagacious than he," the word "sagacious" means MOST NEARLY
    A. shrewd   B. obtuse   C. absurd   D. verbose

29. In the sentence, "He spoke with impunity," the word "impunity" means MOST NEARLY
    A. rashness   B. caution   C. without fear   D. immunity

30. In the sentence, "The new patrolman displayed unusual temerity during the emergency," the word "temerity" means MOST NEARLY
    A. fear   B. rashness   C. calmness   D. anxiety

31. In the sentence, "The portions of food were parsimoniously served," the word "parsimoniously" means MOST NEARLY
    A. stingily   B. piously   C. elaborately   D. generously

32. In the sentence, "Generally the speaker's remarks were sententious," the word "sententious" means MOST NEARLY
    A. verbose
    B. witty
    C. argumentative
    D. pithy

33. In the sentence, "The prisoner was fractious when brought to the station house," the word "fractious" means MOST NEARLY
    A. penitent   B. talkative   C. irascible   D. broken-hearted

34. In the sentence, "The judge was implacable when the attorney pleaded for leniency," the word "implacable" means MOST NEARLY
    A. inexorable
    B. disinterested
    C. inattentive
    D. indifferent

35. In the sentence, "The court ordered the mendacious statements stricken from the record," the word "mendacious" means MOST NEARLY
    A. begging   B. lying   C. threatening   D. lengthy

36. In the sentence, "The district attorney spoke in a strident voice," the word "strident" means MOST NEARLY
    A. loud
    B. harsh-sounding
    C. sing-song
    D. low

37. In the sentence, "The speaker had a predilection for long sentences," the word "predilection" means MOST NEARLY
    A. aversion   B. talent   C. propensity   D. diffidence

38. In the sentence, "The candidate wants to file his application for preference before it is too late," the word "before" is used as a(n)
    A. preposition
    B. subordinating conjunction
    C. pronoun
    D. adverb

39. The one of the following sentences which is grammatically PREFERABLE to the others is:
    A. Our engineers will go over your blueprints so that you may have no problems in construction.
    B. For a long time he had been arguing that we, not he, are to blame for the confusion.
    C. I worked on this automobile for two hours and still cannot find out what is wrong with it.
    D. Accustomed to all kinds of hardships, fatigue seldom bothers veteran policemen.

40. The plural of
    A. turkey is turkies
    B. cargo is cargoes
    C. bankruptcy is bankruptcys
    D. son-in-law is son-in-laws

41. The abbreviation "viz." means MOST NEARLY
    A. namely   B. for example   C. the following   D. see

42. In the sentence, "A man in a light-grey suit waited thirty-five minutes in the ante-room for the all-important document," the word IMPROPERLY hyphenated is
    A. light-grey   B. thirty-five   C. ante-room   D. all-important

43. The MOST accurate of the following sentences is:
    A. The commissioner, as well as his deputy and various bureau heads, were present.
    B. A new organization of employers and employees have been formed.
    C. One or the other of these men have been selected.
    D. The number of pages in the book is enough to discourage a reader.

44. The MOST accurate of the following sentences is:
    A. Between you and me, I think he is the better man.
    B. He was believed to be me.
    C. Is it us that you wish to see?
    D. The winners are him and her.

45. In the sentence, "The committee favored submiting the amendment to the electorate," the MISSPELLED word is
    A. committee   B. submiting   C. amendment   D. electorate

46. In the sentence, "He maliciously demurred to an ajornment of the proceedings," the MISSPELLED word is
    A. maliciously   B. demurred   C. ajornment   D. proceedings

47. In the sentence, "His innocence at that time is irrelevent in view of his more recent villainous demeanor," the MISSPELLED word is
    A. innocence   B. irrelevent   C. villainous   D. demeanor

48. In the sentence, "The mischievous boys aggrevated the annoyance of their neighbor," the MISSPELLED word is
    A. mischievous   B. aggrevated   C. annoyance   D. neighbor

49. In the sentence, "While his persiverance was commendable, his judgment was debatable, the MISSPELLED word is
    A. persiverance
    B. commendable
    C. judgment
    D. debatable

50. In the sentence, "He was hoping the appeal would facilitate his aquittal," the MISSPELLED word is
    A. hoping   B. appeal   C. facilitate   D. aquittal

51. In the sentence, "It would be preferable for them to persue separate courses," the MISSPELLED word is
    A. preferable   B. persue   C. separate   D. courses

52. In the sentence, "The litigant was complimented on his persistance and achievement," the MISSPELLED word is
    A. litigant
    B. complimented
    C. persistance
    D. achievement

53. In the sentence, "Ocassionally there are discrepancies in the descriptions of miscellaneous items," the MISSPELLED word is
    A. ocassionally
    B. discrepancies
    C. descriptions
    D. miscellaneous

54. In the sentence, "The councilmanic seargent-at-arms enforced the prohibition," the MISSPELLED word is
    A. councilmanic
    B. seargent-at-arms
    C. enforced
    D. prohibition

55. In the sentence, "The teacher had an ingenious device for mantaining attendance," the MISSPELLED word is
    A. ingenious   B. device   C. mantaining   D. attendance

Questions 56-63.

DIRECTIONS: Questions 56 through 63 are to be answered on the basis of the following excerpt from a recorded annual report of the police department. This material should be read first and then referred to in answering these questions, which are to be answered SOLELY on the basis of the material herein contained.

LEGAL BUREAU

One of the more important functions of this bureau is to analyze and furnish the department with pertinent information concerning Federal and State statutes and Local Laws which affect the department, law enforcement or crime prevention. In addition, all measures introduced in the State Legislature and the City Council which may affect this department are carefully reviewed by members of the Legal Bureau and, where necessary, opinions and recommendations thereon are prepared.

Another important function of this office is the prosecution of cases in the Magistrate's Courts. This is accomplished by assignment of attorneys who are members of the Legal Bureau to appear in those cases which are deemed to raise issues of importance to the department or questions of law which require technical presentation to facilitate proper determination; and also in those cases where request is made for such appearances by a magistrate, some other official of the city, or a member of the force. Attorneys are regularly assigned to prosecute all cases in the Women's Court.

Proposed legislation was prepared and sponsored for introduction in the State Legislature and, at this writing, one of these proposals has already been enacted into law and five others are presently on the Governor's desk awaiting executive action. The new law prohibits the sale or possession of a hypodermic syringe or needle by an unauthorized person. The bureau's proposals awaiting executive action pertain to an amendment to the Code of Criminal Procedure prohibiting desk officers from taking bail in gambling cases or in cases mentioned in Section 552, Code of Criminal Procedure; including confidence men and swindlers as jostlers in the Penal Law; prohibiting the sale of switchblade knives of any size to children under 16 and bills extending the licensing period of gunsmiths.

The Legal Bureau has regularly cooperated with the Corporation Counsel and the District Attorneys in respect to matters affecting this department, and has continued to advise and represent the Police Athletic League, the Police Sports Association, the Police Relief Fund, and the Police Pension Fund.

The following is a statistical report of the activities of the bureau during the current year as compared with the previous year:

	Current Year	Previous Year
Memoranda of law prepared	68	83
Legal matters forwarded to corporation counsel	122	144
Letters requesting legal information	756	807
Letters requesting departmental records	139	111
Matters for publication	17	26
Court appearances of members of bureau	4,678	4,621
Conferences	94	103
Lectures at Police Academy	30	33
Reports on proposed legislation	194	255
Deciphering of codes	79	27
Expert testimony	31	16
Notices to court witnesses	55	81
Briefs prepared	22	18
Court papers prepared	258	--

56. One of the functions of the Legal Bureau is to
    A. review and make recommendations on proposed Federal laws affecting law enforcement
    B. prepare opinions on all measures introduced in the State Legislature and the City Council
    C. furnish the Police Department with pertinent information concerning all new Federal and State laws
    D. analyze all laws affecting the work of the Police Department

57. The one of the following that is NOT a function of the Legal Bureau is
    A. law enforcement and crime prevention
    B. prosecution of all cases in Women's Court
    C. advise and represent the Police Sports Association
    D. lecturing at the Police Academy

58. Members of the Legal Bureau frequently appear in Magistrate's Court for the purpose of
    A. defending members of the Police Force
    B. raising issues of importance to the Police Department
    C. prosecuting all offenders arrested by members of the Force
    D. facilitating proper determination of questions of law requiring technical presentation

59. The Legal Bureau sponsored a bill that would
    A. extend the licenses of gunsmiths
    B. prohibit the sale of switchblade knives to children of any size
    C. place confidence men and swindlers in the same category as jostlers in the Penal Law
    D. prohibit desk officers from admitting gamblers, confidence men, and swindlers to bail

60. From the report, it is NOT reasonable to infer that
    A. fewer bills affecting the Police Department were introduced in the current year
    B. the preparation of court papers was a new activity assumed in the current year
    C. the Code of Criminal Procedure authorizes desk officers to accept bail in certain cases
    D. the penalty for jostling and swindling is the same

61. According to the statistical report, the activity showing the GREATEST percentage of decrease in the current year as compared to the previous year was
    A. matters for publication
    B. reports on proposed legislation
    C. notices to court witnesses
    D. memoranda of law prepared

62. According to the statistical report, the activity showing the GREATEST percentage of increase in the current year as compare with the previous year was
    A. court appearances of members of the bureau
    B. giving expert testimony
    C. deciphering of codes
    D. letters requesting departmental records

63. According to the report, the percentage of bills prepared and sponsored by the Legal Bureau which were passed by the State Legislature and sent to the Governor for approval was APPROXIMATELY
    A. 3.1%
    B. 2.6%
    C. .5%
    D. not capable of determination from the data given

64. A squad of officers assigned to enforce a new parking regulation in a particular area issued tag summonses on a particular day as follows: four officers issued 16 summonses each; three issued 19 each; one issued 22; seven issued 25 each; eleven issued 28 each; ten issued 30 each; two issued 36 each; one issued 41; and three issued 45 each.
    The average number of summonses issued by a member of this squad was MOST NEARLY
    A. 6.2   B. 17.2   C. 21.0   D. 27.9

65. A water storage tank is 75 feet long and 30 feet wide and has a depth of 6½ feet. Each cubic foot of the tank holds 9½ gallons.
    The TOTAL capacity of the tank is _____ gallons.
    A. 73,125½   B. 131,625   C. 138,937½   D. 146,250

10 (#1)

66. The price of admission to a PAL entertainment were $2.50 each for adults and $1.00 for children; the turnstile at the entrance showed that 358 persons entered and the gate receipts were $626.50.
The number of children who attended was
    A. 170   B. 175   C. 179   D. 183

67. A patrol car travels six times as fast as a bicycle.
If the patrol car goes 168 miles in two hours less time than the bicycle requires to go 42 miles, their respective rates of speed are _____ miles per hour.
    A. 36 and 6   B. 42 and 7   C. 63 and 10½   D. 126 and 21

68. The radiator of an automobile already contains six quarts of a 10% solution of alcohol.
In order to make a mixture of 20% alcohol, it will be necessary to add _____ quarts of alcohol.
    A. ¾   B. 1¾   C. 2½   D. 3

69. A man received an inheritance of $80,000 and wanted to invest it so that it would produce an annual income sufficient to pay his rent of $400 a month. In order to do this, he will have to receive interest or dividends at the rate of _____% per annum.
    A. 3   B. 4   C. 5¾   D. 6

70. If the price of a bus ticket varies *directly* as the mileage involved, and a ticket to travel 135 miles costs $29.70, a ticket for a 30-mile trip will cost
    A. $15.20   B. $13.40   C. $6.60   D. $2.20

71. A man owed a debt of $5,800. After a first payment of $100, he agreed to pay the balance by monthly payments in which each payment after this first would be $20 more than that of the preceding month.
If no interest charge is made, he will have to make, including the first payment, a total of _____ monthly payments.
    A. 16   B. 20   C. 24   D. 28

72. The written test of a civil service examination has a weight of 30, the oral test a weight of 20, experience a weight of 20, and the physical test a weight of 30. A candidate received ratings of 76 on the written test, 84 on the oral, and 80 for experience.
In order to attain an average of 85 on the examination, his rating on the physical test must be
    A. 86   B. 90   C. 94   D. 98

73. A family has an income of $3,200 per month. It spends 22% of this amount for rent, 36% for food, 16% for clothing, and 12% for additional household expenses. After meeting these expenses, 50% of the balance is deposited in the bank.
The amount deposited monthly is
    A. $224.00   B. $366.00   C. $448.00   D. $520.00

74. Upon retirement last July, an officer bought a farm of 64 acres for $18,000 per acre. He made a down payment of $612,000 and agreed to pay the balance in installments of $7,500 a month commencing on August 1, 2022. Disregarding interest, he will make his LAST payment in
    A. July 2028
    B. August 2030
    C. January 2032
    D. April 2035

75. 40% of those who commit a particular crime are subsequently arrested and convicted. 75% of those committed receive sentences of 10 years or more. Assuming that those arrested for the first time serve less than 10 years, the percentage of those committing this crime who receive sentences of ten years or more is MOST NEARLY
    A. 20%   B. 30%   C. 40%   D. 50%

KEY (CORRECT ANSWERS)

1.	A	21.	D	41.	A	61.	A
2.	D	22.	B	42.	C	62.	C
3.	A	23.	B	43.	D	63.	D
4.	A	24.	B	44.	A	64.	D
5.	C	25.	A	45.	B	65.	C
6.	B	26.	B	46.	C	66.	C
7.	C	27.	C	47.	C	67.	B
8.	B	28.	A	48.	B	68.	A
9.	A	29.	D	49.	A	69.	D
10.	C	30.	B	50.	D	70.	C
11.	C	31.	A	51.	B	71.	B
12.	A	32.	D	52.	C	72.	D
13.	A	33.	C	53.	A	73.	A
14.	B	34.	A	54.	B	74.	A
15.	B	35.	B	55.	C	75.	B
16.	D	36.	B	56.	D		
17.	A	37.	C	57.	A		
18.	A	38.	B	58.	D		
19.	C	39.	A	59.	C		
20.	A	40.	B	60.	D		

EXAMINATION SECTION
TEST 1

DIRECTIONS: Each question or incomplete statement is followed by several suggested answers or completions. Select the one that BEST answers the question or completes the statement. *PRINT THE LETTER OF THE CORRECT ANSWER IN THE SPACE AT THE RIGHT.*

1. As an officer, you should know that, of the following, the one which is LEAST likely to be followed by an increase in crime is   1.____

    A. war
    B. depression
    C. poor housing
    D. prosperity

2. As an officer interested in the promotion of traffic safety, you should know that according to recent statistics, the one group which has the highest number of deaths as a result of being struck in traffic is   2.____

    A. adults over 55 years of age
    B. adults between 36 and 55 years of age
    C. adults between 22 and 35 years of age
    D. children up to 4 years old

3. As an officer having a knowledge of the various types of crimes, you should know that in recent years, the age group 16 through 25 showed the greatest number of arrests for   3.____

    A. grand larceny from highways and vehicles
    B. burglary
    C. rape
    D. homicide

4. Of the following groups, the GREATEST number of arrests made and summonses served is for   4.____

    A. offenses against property rights
    B. general criminality
    C. bestial criminality
    D. offenses against public health and safety

5. As an officer interested in the reduction of unnecessary traffic accidents, you should know that two of the chief sources of such accidents to pedestrians in recent years were for crossing a street   5.____

    A. against the light, and crossing past a parked car
    B. at a point other than the crossing, and crossing against the light
    C. at a point other than the crossing, and running off the sidewalk
    D. against the light, and failing to observe whether cars were making right or left turns

6. A "modus operandi" file will be MOST valuable to an officer as a means of showing the   6.____

    A. methods used by criminals
    B. various bureaus and divisions of the police department
    C. number and nature of vehicular accidents
    D. forms used by the police department

7. An officer is frequently advised to lie down before returning fire, if a person is shooting at him.
   This is *primarily* for the reason that

   A. a smaller target will thus be presented to the assailant
   B. he can return fire more quickly while in the prone position
   C. the assailant will think he has struck the officer and cease firing
   D. it will indicate that the officer is not the aggressor

8. In making arrests during a large riot, it is the practice of the police to take the ringleaders into custody as soon as possible.
   This is *primarily* because

   A. the police can obtain valuable information from them
   B. they deserve punishment more than the other rioters
   C. rioters need leadership and, without it, will disperse more quickly
   D. arrests of wrongdoers should always be in order of their importance

9. You observe two men running toward a parked automobile in which a driver is seated. You question the three men and you note the license number.
   You should

   A. let them go if you see nothing suspicious
   B. warn them not to be caught litering again
   C. arrest them because they have probably committed a crime
   D. take them back with you to the place from which the two men came

10. You find a flashlight and a screw-driver lying near a closed bar and grill. You notice further some jimmy marks on the door.
    You should

    A. note in your memorandum book what you have seen
    B. arrest any persons standing in the vicinity
    C. try to enter the bar and grill to investigate whether it has been robbed
    D. telephone the owner of the bar and grill to inform him of what you have seen outside the door

11. While you are patrolling your post, you notice that a peddler is vending merchandise. As you approach, he gathers up his wares and begins to run.
    You should

    A. shoot at him as he is a violator of the law
    B. blow your whistle to summon other patrolmen in order to apprehend him
    C. remain for some time at this place so as to be certain that he does not return
    D. disregard him and continue patrolling your post

12. You have been assigned to a patrol post in a park during winter months. You hear the cries of a boy who has fallen through the ice.
    The FIRST thing you should do is to

    A. rush to the nearest call telephone and summon paramedics
    B. call upon passersby to summon additional patrolmen

C. rush to the spot from which the cries came and try to save the boy
D. rush to the spot from which the cries came and question the boy concerning his identity so that you can summon his parents

13. You have been summoned about a robbery in a train station. Three men are grappling with each other. Two of the men are plainclothesmen, but their identity is not known to you.
The FIRST thing you should do is to

   A. advance with your nightstick and be ready to use it as soon as you know which one is the thief
   B. order the men to stop fighting
   C. ask any bystanders to identify the thief before you use your gun
   D. shoot the one who is most likely to be the thief, letting yourself be guided by your own experience as to the thief's identity

14. Assume that you are a police officer. A woman has complained to you about a man's indecent exposure in front of a house. As you approach the house, the man begins to run.
You should

   A. shoot to kill as the man may be a dangerous maniac
   B. fire a warning shot to try to halt the man
   C. summon other officers in order to apprehend him
   D. question the woman regarding the man's identity

15. You are patrolling a parkway in a radio car with another officer. A maroon car coming from the opposite direction signals you to stop and the driver informs you that he was robbed by three men speeding ahead of him in a black sedan. Your radio car cannot cross the center abutment.
Your should

   A. request the driver to make a report to the nearest precinct as your car cannot cross over to the other side
   B. make a U turn in your radio car and give chase on the wrong side of the parkway
   C. fire warning shots in the air to summon other patrolmen
   D. flash headquarters over your radio system

16. You are on patrol duty in a crowded part of the city.
You hear the traffic patrolman fire four shots in the air and cry, "Get out of his way. He's got a gun." You see a man tearing along the street dodging traffic.
You should

   A. fire several shots in the air to alert other patrolmen
   B. give chase to the man and shoot as it is possible that one of your shots may hit him
   C. wait for an opening in the crowds and then shoot at the man from one knee
   D. disperse the crowds and then shout at the man to stop

17. Assume that you have been assigned to a traffic post at a busy intersection. A car bearing out-of-town license plates is about to turn into a one-way street going in the opposite direction. You blow your whistle and stop the car.
You should then

A. hand out a summons to the driver in order to make an example of him, since out-of-town drivers notoriously disregard our traffic regulations
B. pay no attention to him and let him continue in the proper direction
C. ask him to pull over to the curb and advise him to drive to the nearest precinct to get a copy of the latest traffic regulations
D. call his attention to the fact that he was violating a traffic regulation and permit him to continue in the proper direction

18. A storekeeper has complained to you that every day at noon several peddlers congregate outside his store in order to sell their merchandise.
You should

    A. inform him that such complaints must be made directly to the Police Commissioner
    B. inform him that peddlers have a right to earn their living too
    C. make it your business to patrol that part of your post around noon
    D. pay no attention to him as this storekeeper is probably a crank inasmuch as nobody else has complained

19. You notice that a man is limping hurriedly, leaving a trail of blood behind him. You question him and his explanation is that he was hurt accidentally while he was watching a man clean a gun.
You should

    A. let him go as you have no proof that his story is not true
    B. have him sent to the nearest city hospital under police escort
    C. ask him whether the man had a license for his gun
    D. ask him to lead you to the man who cleaned his gun so that you may question him further about the accident

20. There have been a series of burglaries in a certain residential area consisting of one-family houses. You have been assigned to select a house in this area in which detectives can wait secretly for the attempt to burglarize that house so that the burglars can be apprehended in the act.
Which of the following would be the BEST house to select for this purpose?

    A. The house was recently burglarized and several thousand dollars worth of clothing and personal property were taken.
    B. The house whose owner reports that several times the telephone has rung but the person making the call hung up as soon as the telephone was answered.
    C. The house is smaller and looks much less pretentious than other houses in the same area.
    D. The house is occupied by a widower who works long hours but who lives with an invalid mother requiring constant nursing service.

21. The two detectives noticed the man climb a ladder to the roof of a loft building. The detectives followed the same route. They saw him break a skylight and lower himself into the building. Through the broken skylight, one of the detectives covered the man with his gun and told him to throw up his hands.
The action of the detectives in this situation was FAULTY chiefly because

    A. one of the detectives should have remained on the ladder
    B. criminals should be caught red-handed

C. the detectives should have made sure of the identity of the man before following him
D. the possibility of another means of escape from the building should have been foreseen

22. Suppose that, while you are patrolling your post, a middle-aged woman informs you that three men are holding up a nearby express office. You rush immediately to the scene of the holdup. While you are still about 75 feet away, you see the three men, revolvers in their hands, emerge from the office and make for what is apparently their getaway car, which is pointed in the opposite direction.
Of the following, your FIRST consideration in this situation should be to

22.____

A. enter the express office in order to find out what the men have taken
B. maneuver quickly so as to get the getaway car between you and the express office
C. make a mental note of the descriptions of the escaping men for immediate alarm
D. attempt to disable the car in which the holdup men seek to escape

23. Which of the following situations, if observed by you while on patrol, should you consider MOST suspicious and deserving of further investigation?

23.____

A. A shabbily dressed youth is driving a new Buick.
B. An old battered car has been parked without lights outside an apartment house for several hours.
C. A light is on in the rear of a one-family, luxurious residence.
D. Two well-dressed men are standing at a bus stop at 2 A.M. and arguing heatedly.

24. Suppose that, while on patrol late at night, you find a woman lying in the street, apparently the victim of a hit-and-run driver. She seems to be injured seriously but you wish to ask her one or two questions in order to help apprehend the hit-and-run car.
Of the following, the BEST question to ask is:

24.____

A. In what direction did the car go?
B. What time did it happen?
C. What kind of car was it?
D. How many persons were in the car?

25. Assume that you are driving a police car, equipped with a two-way radio, along an isolated section of the parkway at 3 A.M. You note that the headlights of a car are blinking rapidly. When you stop to investigate, the driver of the car informs you that he was just forded to the side of the road by two men in a green convertible, who robbed him of a large amount of cash and jewelry at the point of a gun and then sped away.
Your FIRST consideration in this situation should be to

25.____

A. drive rapidly along the parkway in the direction taken by the criminals in an effort to apprehend them before they escape
B. question the driver carefully, looking for inconsistencies indicating that he made up the whole story
C. obtain a complete listing and identification of all materials lost
D. notify your superior to have the parkway exits watched for a car answering the description of the getaway car

26. Suppose that you have been assigned to check the story of a witness in a holdup case. The witness states that, while sitting at her window, she observed the suspect loitering outside a cigar store. As she watched, the suspect entered a nearby liquor store. He remained there only a minute or two. Then she saw him walk out rapidly, hurry to the corner and hail a cab. Assume that Figure 1 is a scale drawing of the scene. All four corners of the intersection are occupied by tall buildings. W indicates the window at which the witness sat, C indicates the cigar store and L indicates the liquor store.

    On the basis of this sketch, the BEST reason for doubting the truthfulness of the witness is that
    A. the window is far removed from the cigar store
    B. the cigar store and the window are not on the same street
    C. distances may be distorted by a high angle of observation
    D. the liquor store cannot be seen from the window

    FIGURE 1

27. Assume that you are investigating a case of reported suicide. You find the deceased sitting in a chair, sprawled over his desk, a revolver still clutched in his right hand. In your examination of the room, you find that the window is partly open. Only one bullet has been fired from the revolver. The bullet has lodged in the wall. Assume that Figure 2 is a scale drawing of the scene. D indicates the desk, C indicates the chair, W indicates the window and B indicates the bullet.

    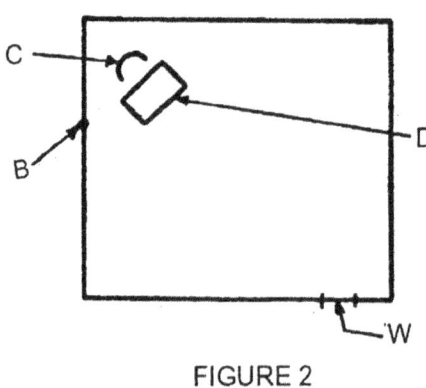

    FIGURE 2

    The one of the following features which indicates *most strongly* that the deceased did NOT commit suicide is the
    A. distance between the desk and the bullet hole
    B. relative position of the bullet hole and the chair
    C. fact that the window was partly open
    D. relative position of the desk and the window

28. "Driver 1 claimed that the collision occurred because, as he approached the intersection, Driver 2 started to make a left turn suddenly and at high speed, even though the light had been red against him for 15 or 20 seconds." Suppose that you have been assigned to make a report on this accident. The position of the vehicles after the accident is indicated in Figure 3, the point in each case indicating the front of the vehicle. On the basis of this sketch, the BEST reason for concluding that Driver 1's statement is *false* is that Driver

    A. 2's car is beyond the center of the intersection
    B. 2's car is making the turn on the proper side of the road
    C. 1's car is beyond the sidewalk line
    D. 1's car is on the right hand side of the road

    FIGURE 3

28.____

29. Suppose that, while you are on patrol, a teen-age boy dashes out of a dry cleaning store, his clothes afire.
    The BEST action for you to take in this situation is to

    A. stop the boy and roll him in a coat to smother the flames
    B. lead the boy quickly to the nearest store and douse him with large quantities of water
    C. remove all burning articles of clothing from the boy as quickly as possible
    D. take the boy back into the dry cleaning store, where a fire extinguisher will almost certainly be available to extinguish the flames quickly

29.____

30. A woman comes running towards you crying that her child was bitten by their pet dog.
    The FIRST action you should take is to

    A. summon a doctor so that he may treat the wounds
    B. shoot the dog to prevent it from biting others
    C. have the child put to bed
    D. apply ice packs to the wounds until the pain subsides

30.____

31. You are called to an apartment house to stop a quarrel between a husband and wife. When you arrive there, you find that the husband has left and that the woman is lying unconscious on the floor. In the meantime, a neighbor has telephoned for an ambulance. You note that the room temperature is about 50 degrees.
    The FIRST action you should take is to

    A. rub the hands of the woman to keep her blood circulating
    B. make her drink hot tea or coffee to try to revive her
    C. place a hot water bottle under her feet to keep them warm
    D. place one blanket underneath her and another one over her

31.____

32. As an officer who is well-informed in the fundamentals of giving first aid, you should know that the "Schaefer Method" is MOST helpful for

    A. stopping bleeding
    B. transporting injured persons

32.____

C. promoting respiration
D. stopping the spread of infection

33. While you are on traffic duty, a middle-aged man crossing the street cries out with pain, presses his hand to his chest and stands perfectly still. You suspect that he may have suffered a heart attack. You should FIRST

    A. ask him to cross the street quickly in order to prevent his being hit by moving traffic
    B. permit him to lie down flat in the street while you divert the traffic
    C. ask him for the name of his doctor so that you can summon him
    D. request a cab to take him to the nearest hospital for immediate treatment

34. A misdemeanor is

    A. any crime not punishable by death or imprisonment in a state prison
    B. only such offense as is so defined in the Penal Law
    C. any violation of a state law or municipal ordinance which does not amount to a crime
    D. an act for which no penalty is imposed by the Penal Law

35. A writing in which a grand jury charges a person with the commission of a crime is called

    A. a pleading
    B. a talesman
    C. a complaint
    D. an indictment

36. A statute of limitations is a law

    A. limiting the time within which a criminal prosecution or civil action must be commenced
    B. prohibiting a second prosecution for a crime for which a person has once been tried
    C. regulating the descent and distribution of the property of a person dying intestate
    D. limiting the sentence that may be imposed upon conviction for a particular crime

37. Strengthening or confirming evidence given in support of the truth of facts testified to by another witness is most accurately termed

    A. hearsay evidence
    B. corroborative evidence
    C. circumstantial evidence
    D. conclusive evidence

38. A writ or order directed to a person and requiring his attendance at a particular time and place to testify as a witness is properly termed a

    A. summons
    B. subpoena
    C. warrant
    D. mandamus

39. If A is accused of having caused the death of B, of the following, the factor which will weigh most heavily in determining whether A should be indicted for murder or manslaughter is

    A. his age
    B. his intent in committing the homicide

C. the nature of the weapon used
D. the existence of a corpus delicti

QUESTIONS 40-42.

Items 40-42 consist of four words each. One word in each item is incorrectly pronounced. The stress in each word is indicated in capital letters while the spelling is indicated in parentheses. For each item, print the letter preceding the word which is incorrectly pronounced in the space at the right.

40. A. vee-HIK-yoo-ler (vehicular)
    B. phe-DESS-tree-an (pedestrian)
    C. myoo-nih-SIH-p'1 (municipal)
    D. rih-SEET (receipt)

40.____

41. A. DEF (deaf)
    B. eye-TAL-yun (Italian)
    C. in-KLEM-'nt (inclement)
    D. awg-ZIL-yu-ree (auxiliary)

41.____

42. A. kog-NEYE-z'ns (cognizance)
    B. MAYN-tuh-nunss (maintenance)
    C. FEB-roo-er-ee (February)
    D. ROSS-ter (roster)

42.____

43. A section of the Penal Law provides, in part, that "whenever the punishment or penalty for an offense is mitigated by any provision of this chapter, such provision may be applied to any sentence or judgment imposed for the offense." The word "mitigated" as used in this statute means *most nearly*

43.____

    A. removed
    C. changed
    B. augmented
    D. decreased

44. A section of the Penal Law states that "a morbid propensity to commit prohibited acts....forms no defense to a prosecution therefor." The word "propensity" as used in this statute means *most nearly*

44.____

    A. capacity
    C. tendency
    B. ability
    D. aptitude

45. A police department rule provides that "a Chaplain shall have the assimilated rank of Inspector." The word "assimilated" as used in this rule means *most nearly*

45.____

    A. false
    C. comparable
    B. superior
    D. presumed

46. A police department rule provides that, "Pushcarts and derelict automobiles shall be delivered to the Bureau of Incumbrances." The word "derelict" as used in this rule means *most nearly*

46.____

    A. dilapidated
    C. delinquent
    B. abandoned
    D. contraband

47. A police department rule provides that "when the exigencies of the service shall so require, a captain may assign a patrolman from the outgoing platoon to house duty." The word "exigencies" as used in this rule means *most nearly*

   A. needs
   B. conveniences
   C. changes
   D. increases

48. A police department rule provides for the award of a Medal for Merit "for an act of outstanding bravery, performed in the line of duty, at imminent personal hazard of life." The word "imminent" as used in this rule means *most nearly*

   A. impending
   B. inherent
   C. certain
   D. great

49. A police department rule provides that "the Police Commissioner shall have cognizance and control of the government, administration, disposition and discipline of the Police Department." The word "cognizance" as used in this rule means *most nearly*

   A. responsibility for
   B. jurisdiction over
   C. knowledge of
   D. ability for

50. A police department rule provides that a member of the department shall not communicate with a railroad company "for the purpose of expediting the issue of a transportation pass." The word "expediting" as used in this rule means *most nearly*

   A. extorting
   B. procuring
   C. demanding
   D. hastening

51. A Police Department Manual of Procedure provides that a member of the force who comes into possession of a document containing scurrilous matter will take precautions to safeguard fingerprints thereon. The word "scurrilous" as used in this regulation means *most nearly*

   A. irrelevant
   B. offensive
   C. defamatory
   D. evidentiary

52. Under cases of "Mendicancy" should be listed cases of

   A. loitering
   B. begging
   C. carrying of weapons
   D. injury to property

53. A police department rule states that the Department Medal of Honor may be awarded to a member of the Force who distinguishes himself by an act of gallantry and intrepidity. The word "intrepidity" as used in this rule means *most nearly*

   A. chivalry
   B. virility
   C. fear
   D. courage

54. A person who, without lawful excuse, omits to perform a duty to furnish food, clothing, shelter or medical or surgical attendance to a minor, or to make such payments towards the maintenence of a minor as may have been required by a court, is guilty of a misdemeanor according to Section 482 of the Penal Law. In this sentence the word which is *misspelled s*

   A. lawful
   B. omits
   C. attendance
   D. maintenence

55. A section of the Penal Law provides that "a conviction under this article cannot be had on the uncorraborated testimony of the person with whom the offense is charged to have been committed." In this sentence the word which is *misspelled* is

   A. conviction
   B. uncorraborated
   C. offense
   D. committed

56. A section of the Penal Law provides, in part, that "a person who wilfully.... inflicts grievous bodily harm upon another is punishable by imprisonment in a penitentiary for a term not exceeding five years." In this sentence the word which is *misspelled* is

   A. wilfully
   B. grievous
   C. punishible
   D. exceeding

57. An article of the Penal Law provides that "moneys received by the Department of State persuant to this article may, within three months of the receipt thereof, be refunded to the person entitled thereto, on satisfactory proof that the applicant for the license has predeceased its issuance." In this sentence the word which is *misspelled* is

   A. persuant
   B. issuance
   C. satisfactory
   D. predeceased

58. "The Deputy Commissioner in charge is authorized to exercise all of the powers and duties of the Police Commissioner in connection with the granting, renewing, revoking, suspending, cancelling and transferring of the miscelaneous licenses and permits issued by the Division."
In this sentence the word which is *misspelled* is

   A. authorized
   B. cancelling
   C. transferring
   D. miscelaneous

59. A police department rule states that "a commanding officer is responsible for properly preparing, transmitting, filing, using and preserving official records, returns, forms and correspondance originating in or forwarded to his command." In this sentence the word which is *misspelled* is

   A. responsible
   B. transmitting
   C. filing
   D. correspondance

QUESTIONS 60-67.

The sentences numbered 60-67 deal with some phase of police activity. They may be classified most appropriately under one of the following four categories:

   A. Faulty because of incorrect grammar
   B. Faulty because of incorrect punctuation
   C. Faulty because of incorrect use of a word
   D. Correct

Examine each sentence carefully. Then, in the space at the right, print the capital letter preceding the option which is the BEST of the four suggested above. All incorrect sentences contain only one type of error. Consider a sentence correct if it contains none of the types of errors mentioned, even though there may be other correct ways of expressing the same thought.

60. The Department Medal of Honor is awarded to a member of the Police Force who distinguishes himself inconspicuously in the line of police duty by the performance of an act of gallantry. 60.___

61. Members of the Detective Division are charged with the prevention of crime, the detection and arrest of criminals and the recovery of lost or stolen property. 61.___

62. Detectives are selected from the uniformed patrol forces after they have indicated by conduct, aptitude and performance that they are qualified for the more intricate duties of a detective. 62.___

63. The patrolman, pursuing his assailant, exchanged shots with the gunman and immortaly wounded him as he fled into a nearby building. 63.___

64. The members of the Traffic Division has to enforce the Vehicle and Traffic Law, the Traffic Regulations and ordinances relating to vehicular and pedestrian traffic. 64.___

65. After firing a shot at the gunman, the crowd dispersed from the patrolman's line of fire. 65.___

66. The efficiency of the Missing Persons Bureau is maintained with a maximum of public personnel due to the specialized training given to its members. 66.___

67. Records of persons arrested for violations of Vehicle and Traffic Regulations are transmitted upon request to precincts, courts and other authorized agencies. 67.___

68. Assume that in 2008 there were 21,580 vehicular highway accidents resulting in 713 deaths. This represents a 17% decrease over the year 2001. If the year 2009 indicates a 6.5% decrease over 2001, the number of highway accidents taking place in 2009 is *most nearly* 68.___

    A. 23,846   B. 24,817   C. 24,310   D. 22,983

69. Of 35 police officers assigned to Precinct P, 69.___
    5 have 2 years of service,
    5 have 4 years of service,
    9 have 6 years of service,
    4 have 8 years of service,
    7 have 12 years of service and
    5 have 16 years of service.
The average number of years of service in the Police Department for the 35 police officers is *most nearly*

    A. 6   B. 8   C. 7   D. 9

70. An officer purchases a two-family house for $318,000 and immediately rents one apartment to a tenant for $1500 a month. At the end of two years, he sells the house for $352,000. Taxes, repairs, insurance, interest and other expenses cost him $31,840. His total gain from renting and selling, based on his original investment, is *most nearly* 70.___

    A. 6%   B. 8%   C. 10%   D. 12%

71. Precincts S, T, W and Y are located in the county. The total number of officers assigned to these precincts is 430.
Precinct S has 7 officers more than Precinct Y;
Precinct T has 7 officers less than Precinct Y;
Precinct W has twice as many patrolmen as Precinct Y. The number of officers assigned to Precinct Y is *most nearly*

    A. 82   B. 86   C. 92   D. 96

71.____

72. Two radio patrol cars, coming from different directions, are rushing to the scene of a crime. The first car proceeds at the rate of 45 miles an hour and arrives there in 4 minutes. Although the second car travels over a route which is longer by 3/4 of a mile, it arrives only 1/2 minute later.
The speed of the second patrol car, expressed in miles per hour, is *most nearly*.

    A. 50   B. 55   C. 60   D. 65

72.____

73. A police department rule reads as follows: A Deputy Commissioner acting as Police Commissioner shall carry out the orders of the Police Commissioner, previously given, and such orders shall not, except in cases of extreme emergency, be countermanded. This means *most nearly* that, except in case of extreme emergency,

    A. the orders given by a Deputy Commissioner acting as Police Commissioner may not be revoked
    B. a Deputy Commissioner acting as Police Commissioner should not revoke orders previously given by the Police Commissioner
    C. A Deputy Commissioner acting as Police Commissioner is vested with the same authority to issue orders as the Police Commissioner himself
    D. only a Deputy Commissioner acting as Police Commissioner may issue orders in the absence of the Police Commissioner himself

73.____

QUESTIONS 74-75.

Questions 74-75 pertain to the following section of the Penal Law:

A person who, after having been three times convicted within this state, of felonies or attempts to commit felonies, or under the law of any other state, government or country, of crimes which if committed within this state would be felonious, commits a felony, other than murder, first or second degree, or treason, within this state, shall be sentenced upon conviction of such fourth, or subsequent offense to imprisonment in a state prison for an indeterminate term the minimum of which shall be not less than the maximum term provided for first offenders for the crime for which the individual has been convicted, but, in any event, the minimum term upon conviction for a felony as the fourth or subsequent offense, shall be not less than fifteen years, and the maximum thereof shall be his natural life.

74. Under the terms of the above quoted portion of the section of the Penal Law, a person must receive the increased punishment therein provided, if

    A. he is convicted of a felony and has been three times previously convicted of felonies
    B. he has been three times previously convicted of felonies, regardless of the nature of his present conviction

74.____

C. his fourth conviction is for murder, first or second degree, or treason
D. he has previously been convicted three times of murder, first or second degree, or treason

75. Under the terms of the above quoted portion of the section of the Penal Law, a person convicted of a felony for which the penalty is imprisonment for a term not to exceed ten years, and who has been three times previously convicted of felonies in the state, shall be sentenced to a term the MINIMUM of which shall be

A. ten years
B. fifteen years
C. indeterminate
D. his natural life

QUESTIONS 76-80.
In answering questions 76-80, the following definitions of crime should be applied, bearing in mind that ALL elements contained in the definition must be present in order to charge a person with that crime:

BURGLARY is the breaking and entering a building with intent to commit some crime therein.
EXTORTION is the obtaining of property from another, with his consent, induced by a wrongful use of force or fear, or under color of official right.
LARCENY is the taking and carrying away of the personal property of another with intent to deprive or defraud the owner of the use and benefit of such property.
ROBBERY is the unlawful taking of the personal property of another from his person or his presence, by force or violence or by putting him in fear of injury, immediate or future, to his person or property.

76. If A entered B's store during business hours, tied B to a chair and then helped himself to the contents of B's cash register, A, upon arrest, should be charged with

A. burglary   B. extortion   C. larceny   D. robbery

77. If A broke the pane of glass in the window of B's store, stepped in and removed some merchandise from the window, he should, upon arrest, be charged with

A. burglary   B. extortion   C. larceny   D. robbery

78. If A, after B had left for the day, found the door of B's store open, walked in, took some merchandise and then left through the same open door, he should, upon arrest, be charged with

A. burglary   B. extortion   C. larceny   D. robbery

79. If A, by threatening to report B for failure to pay to the city the full amount of sales tax he had collected from various customers, induced B to give him the contents of his cash register, A should, upon arrest, be charged with

A. burglary   B. extortion   C. larceny   D. robbery

80. If A, in a crowded hockey game, put his hand into B's pocket and removed B's wallet without his knowledge, A should, upon arrest, be charged with

A. burglary   B. extortion   C. larceny   D. robbery

KEY (CORRECT ANSWERS)

1.	D	16.	D	31.	D	46.	B	61.	B
2.	A	17.	D	32.	C	47.	A	62.	D
3.	B	18.	C	33.	B	48.	A	63.	C
4.	D	19.	B	34.	A	49.	C	64.	A
5.	B	20.	B	35.	D	50.	D	65.	A
6.	A	21.	D	36.	A	51.	B	66.	C
7.	A	22.	D	37.	B	52.	B	67.	D
8.	C	23.	D	38.	B	53.	D	68.	C
9.	A	24.	C	39.	B	54.	D	69.	B
10.	C	25.	D	40.	C	55.	B	70.	D
11.	D	26.	D	41.	B	56.	C	71.	B
12.	C	27.	B	42.	A	57.	A	72.	A
13.	B	28.	C	43.	D	58.	D	73.	B
14.	D	29.	A	44.	C	59.	D	74.	A
15.	D	30.	A	45.	C	60.	C	75.	B

76.	D
77.	A
78.	C
79.	B
80.	C

EXAMINATION SECTION
TEST 1

DIRECTIONS: Each question or incomplete statement is followed by several suggested answers or completions. Select the one that BEST answers the question or completes the statement. *PRINT THE LETTER OF THE CORRECT ANSWER IN THE SPACE AT THE RIGHT.*

1. While a police officer is on his way to report for an urgent assignment at a fire in a school during school hours, he sees several teenage boys fighting.
   Under these circumstances, the BEST procedure for him to follow at this time is to
   A. find the police officer assigned to duty in the area and let him handle the situation
   B. telephone the station house to send someone to stop the fight
   C. ignore the fight
   D. stop the fight since it is his duty as a police officer to see that order is preserved on a public thoroughfare

1.____

2. There has been a series of burglaries on a street containing many small stores. A police officer has been assigned to select a store on this street in which to wait in hiding for an attempt to burglarize the store and thereby trap the burglars in the act.
   Of the following, the BEST store to be selected for this purpose would be the one
   A. which is operated by an elderly widower who keeps it open long past usual business hours
   B. which is larger and more expensive looking than the others
   C. whose owner reports that suspicious-looking people have been loitering nearby
   D. which was recently burglarized and from which $2,000 worth of clothing was taken

2.____

3. While investigating the theft of a new bicycle from a retail store, a police officer discovers that the bicycle is in the possession of a boy who appears heartbroken at the prospect of losing it.
   The FIRST action for the police officer to take is to
   A. return the bicycle to the storekeeper and asks him to withdraw the charge
   B. tell the boy he can keep the bicycle until it is needed as evidence
   C. arrest the boy since he probably stole the bicycle
   D. ask the boy how he got the bicycle

3.____

4. While on patrol of his post, a police officer discovers a man wandering about in a dazed manner, talking to himself, and making peculiar gestures. He seems to be mentally ill and is unable to answer any questions in a sensible manner. The station house is nearby.

4.____

For the police officer to take him to the station house would be
- A. *undesirable*; it is always quicker to summon an ambulance
- B. *desirable*; at the station house he may be kept from harm or harming others until he can be taken to a hospital
- C. *undesirable*; the man has committed no crime
- D. *desirable*; the police officer can question the man in private to determine his sanity

5. There is an old abandoned house in a run-down area on one of the streets of your patrol post. Late at night, you notice several suspicious-looking people entering the house from the rear.
Of the following, the BEST course of action for you to take FIRST is to
- A. inquire of the neighbors as to any suspicious occurrences
- B. get to the nearest telephone and call your superior officer at once for assistance
- C. continue on patrol since you do not know that a crime has been committed
- D. attempt to observe what is going on in the house

6. Police officers are instructed to give particular attention at night to all automobiles in business districts moving at a slow rate through the streets or parking with the motor running.
Of the following, the MOST likely reason for this order is that
- A. the ownership of suspicious cars can be confirmed
- B. some store robberies may be prevented
- C. dangerous weapons may be discovered
- D. traffic accidents may be averted

7. The police often follow the practice of returning a suspect to the scene of the crime.
Of the following, the LEAST valid reason for this action is that the
- A. suspect may more readily be able to remember certain events
- B. psychological effect on the suspect may produce additional valuable evidence
- C. suspect may be more readily confronted by witnesses to the crime
- D. statements made by the suspect may be clarified

8. When assigned to keep crowds in order at the scene of a fire, police officers are instructed to be alert for persons showing extreme interest in the progress of the fire.
Of the following, the MOST probable purpose of this instruction is to
- A. make certain that another fire is not started
- B. detect the person who may have caused the fire
- C. obtain the services of experts who can assist in stopping the fire
- D. enroll interested persons in the Civil Defense volunteer fire organization

9. While patrolling his regular post, a police officer observes a storekeeper sweeping the sidewalk in front of his store and pushing the refuse into the roadway. This is the first time it has happened. This practice is forbidden by law.
   Of the following, the BEST course of action for the police officer to follow is to
   A. warn the shopkeeper that he is violating the law
   B. ignore the storekeeper's action since this is a relatively minor offense
   C. arrest the storekeeper
   D. report the storekeeper to the Department of Sanitation

10. A man who has a history of several previous convictions for burglary is a suspect in a recent case of burglary.
    In examining a file on this person, the one of the following items which would be of LEAST value as an indication as to whether this suspect is likely to have committed this particular crime is a
    A. description of his usual method of breaking into a building
    B. list of members of the suspect's family who have criminal records
    C. statement of the time of the day or night during which he generally operates
    D. listing of the tools he favors using

11. Investigation of a reported theft from a private house reveals that part of the missing property consisted of some very heavy articles.
    Of the following, the MOST valid conclusion that may be made from this fact is that
    A. the stolen property was most likely carried away in a truck
    B. footprints will surely be found on the walk leading to the front or back door
    C. the stolen merchandise is probably nearby
    D. more than one person was probably involved

12. Police officers assigned to foot patrol shall proceed directly to their own posts so as to arrive there at the time designated. The practice of congregating in one area of the precinct preparatory to going to their posts shall cease.
    Of the following, the BEST reason for this order is to
    A. aid the supervisors in checking attendance at assigned posts
    B. avoid having too many men cover nearby posts while distant posts are neglected
    C. have the police officers on duty at their posts without undue delay
    D. have police officers while on the way to their posts observe conditions in the precinct

13. It is sometimes necessary for police officers to be assigned in the vicinity of a factory where employees are on strike. These assignments are in addition to police assignments at the factory itself.
    Of the following, the MOST valid reason for this precaution is that
    A. picket lines are illegal
    B. factory employees may meet and conduct their union activity on the street

C. disorder may occur between strikers and non-strikers at other places in the neighborhood
D. the employees probably live in the neighborhood of the factory

14. A fugitive from the police in a serious crime is known to be suffering from an illness which requires constant treatment and medication.
 Of the following, the BEST means of utilizing this fact in attempting to find the fugitive would be to
 A. check drugstores in the business sections of the city where he is thought to be living
 B. contact hospitals, clinics, and doctors in the city where he is thought to be living
 C. search the homes of relatives and friends for poisonous drugs
 D. station a police officer directly outside of each drugstore, hospital, clinic, and doctor's office in the city where he is thought to be living

14._____

15. It is customary for the police to keep records of lost or stolen automobile license plates.
 Of the following, the BEST reason for this practice is to
 A. permit the prompt issuance of new plates
 B. keep a record of all outstanding license plates in use
 C. prevent cars from being stolen
 D. capture or detain any person found using or attempting to use any of these plates

15._____

16. A police officer on duty observes a blind man going through the cars of a subway train playing a saxophone and soliciting money in violation of the law.
 Of the following, the BEST course of action for the police officer to take is to
 A. permit the blind man to continue since it is his means of livelihood
 B. warn the blind man that he is not permitted to solicit on the transit system
 C. inform the blind man that he must register with a recognized social agency caring for blind persons
 D. escort the blind man to his home and leave him there

16._____

17. While a police officer is on duty in a crowded subway station, a woman runs up to him and complains that a man, still standing nearby on the station, has just pushed her so that she fell down and was injured.
 Of the following, the FIRST thing for the police officer to do is to
 A. ask the man to produce some form of identification
 B. urge the woman to overlook the incident since the subways are so crowded
 C. question the woman to determine if the pushing was deliberate
 D. arrest the man

17._____

18. While a police officer is on post in a busy subway station, the clerk in the change booth calls him to eject two disorderly teenagers from the area near the change booth. These teenagers use this station every day, and this is one of a series of undesirable activities on their part.

18._____

Of the following, the MOST important concern of the police officer in such a situation is to
- A. administer sufficient punishment to make sure they will not do the same thing again
- B. record the identity of the teenagers so that preventive action may be taken
- C. avoid damaging transit system property
- D. be certain not to cause any injury to the teenagers

19. While on duty on a subway platform, a police officer is stopped by a passenger who asks for some travel directions. The man is drunk and has caused a few people to gather.
    Of the following, the BEST action for the police officer to take is to
    - A. give the directions to one of the bystanders so that the bystander may help the man get the proper train and then continue with his duties
    - B. ignore the man since he is incapable of understanding directions
    - C. arrest the man since he may create a disturbance
    - D. place the man on the proper train in the same car as the conductor if possible

20. It is the practice in the transit system to place lost property in bags provided for this purpose and also to give a receipt to the employee or other person who has turned in the property.
    Of the following, the BEST reason for this procedure is to
    - A. prevent breakage of glass items and check on employee honesty
    - B. keep the items in good condition and protect the claim of the finder if the owner does not appear
    - C. safeguard valuables from being stolen and prevent any accidental damage
    - D. record the names of employees who may be rewarded for their honesty

21. Generally, before making an arrest for a serious crime, the police officer must have facts to provide a reasonable basis for believing the person to be guilty.
    The BEST reason for this rule is to
    - A. reduce the number of arrests
    - B. protect himself against being charged with false arrest
    - C. safeguard the rights of citizens against improper arrest
    - D. place the burden of disproving the charges upon the accused

22. A police officer is on patrol in an area on a weekday evening and hears many small explosions of firecrackers coming from various directions. The sale, storage, or use of firecrackers is forbidden.
    Under these circumstances, the BEST course of action for the police officer to take is to
    - A. attempt to find out where the firecrackers are sold
    - B. arrest the first boy seen lighting firecracker since he has violated the law
    - C. make no note in his memo book until he actually sees firecrackers being exploded
    - D. investigate all reports of injuries to see if any were caused by firecrackers

23. As a police officer, you are taking a person under arrest to the station house. While so doing, an influential friend of the prisoner stops you and asks you to release the prisoner.
Of the following, the MOST desirable course of action for you to take is to
    A. ask the friend if he will be personally responsible for the conduct of the prisoner and, if so, let the prisoner go with his friend
    B. explain the reason for the arrest so that the friend can realize it is warranted
    C. arrest the friend of the prisoner for interfering with the performance of a police officer's duty
    D. inform the friend that this is a police matter and proceed with your duty

24. During a riot, it is the practice of the police to take the leaders into custody as soon as possible.
Of the following, the MOST valid reason for this practice is that it will
    A. arrest suspects in order of their importance
    B. remove the leaders from the scene so that the rioting may cease sooner
    C. punish the leaders more than other rioters which is fair since they started the riot
    D. obtain valuable information from the leaders

25. While you are on patrol duty, a woman excitedly complains to you that her purse has been snatched by three boys wearing black leather jackets and dungarees. Later you observe three boys in such clothing. As you approach them, one boy runs away.
Of the following, the BEST course of action for you to take is to
    A. shoot at the fleeing boy since flight indicates he is probably guilty of snatching the purse
    B. fire a warning shot to try to halt the fleeing boy; and if this fails, chase after him
    C. question the two boys who remained
    D. run after the fleeing boy and attempt to overtake him

26. While on patrol of his post, a police officer receives a report that a car has suddenly backed onto a sidewalk and seriously injured an elderly man. Upon arriving at the scene, he finds that a large crowd has gathered. The driver of the car is slumped over the wheel in a state of shock. An ambulance has been summoned for the injured man.
Of the following, the BEST action for the police officer to take next is to
    A. order the crowd to disperse
    B. ask someone to assist him in moving the injured elderly man into a nearby store
    C. ask the driver about the accident
    D. move the car off the sidewalk into the roadway

27. A police officer on duty observes that a window of one of the stores is defaced with indecent and anti-religious remarks written on it. A group of teenage youths is standing nearby.

Of the following, the BEST course of action for the police officer to take is to
- A. explain to the youths the need for tolerance and understanding among the various groups in the community
- B. arrest the leader of the group for defacing property
- C. question the youths to determine if they did it or if they saw anyone do it
- D. ask a fellow officer to assist in bringing all the youths to the station house

28. Many authorities in the field of juvenile delinquency accept youth gangs as a natural development in the community.
If this is correct, the one of the following which is MOST desirable is to attempt to
- A. encourage younger members of gangs to break away
- B. set up an interesting lecture course on the evils of gang warfare
- C. channel gang activity into worthwhile areas
- D. secure legislation making gang activity illegal

28._____

29. An officer conducting an investigation usually avoids expressing his personal opinions on politics or morals when he is interviewing anyone in connection with the investigation.
The BEST reason for this policy is that
- A. discussions of politics frequently lead to argument
- B. the officer's opinions may influence the information offered by the person being interviewed
- C. the interviews will take less time since the officer will be more likely to stick to the facts
- D. public employees should have no opinions on politics or morals

29._____

30. The MOST important factor for you to consider in using information which you have received from a certain person as a basis for further investigation is the
- A. availability of the person for further questioning
- B. expense involved in finding the person
- C. arrest record of the person
- D. value of the information as related to the case in question

30._____

31. An important feature of the modern concept of patrol is to have available an officer whose general location is known to the residents of the area.
The one of the following which is likely to be an IMPORTANT reason for this feature of patrol is to
- A. be able to summon an officer quickly in case of emergency
- B. rotate assignments so that each officer will become familiar with the police problems of the post
- C. prevent undesirable incidents from developing and occurring
- D. insure that all areas in and about the precinct are adequately protected

31._____

32. A police officer has arrested a man for attempted robbery.
    Before taking him to the nearest police station, the FIRST precaution for the police officer to take is to
    A. check the man's identification
    B. return any stolen articles found in the man's possession
    C. determine if the man has a criminal record
    D. see that the man is unarmed

33. A police officer, off duty and going home from work at night, observes three suspicious men loitering near a supermarket that is closed. He stops for a while to watch, unseen by them. Two of the men enter the store and open the wall safe.
    Of the following, the BEST course of action for the police officer to take is to
    A. draw his gun, enter the store, and fire at the two men
    B. ignore the incident since he is off duty
    C. wait until the two men come out, draw his gun, and prepare to arrest all three
    D. ask the man who remained outside if any of them is an employee of the store

34. A police officer is investigating a complaint that a man is brandishing a gun in the rear of a restaurant at a time when customers are present.
    Of the following, the BEST reason for the police officer to exercise caution as he enters is that
    A. the man may open fire without warning and injure others
    B. a police officer should not expose himself to risk which endangers him
    C. the man may injure himself
    D. there may be a second exit from the room

35. Police officers have been ordered to be on the alert for a man who has recently committed a series of robberies. The victims have described the man as being white, of medium height and weight, wearing a black leather jacket and a cap, and having the lower part of his face covered. While on patrol, you observe a man of medium height, wearing a black leather jacket.
    Of the following, the one which is the BEST reason for questioning this man is that he
    A. has his hands in his pockets
    B. is fat
    C. has a scar on the lower part of his cheek
    D. has just driven up in a new car

36. The officer who investigates accidents is always required to make a complete and accurate rate report.
    Of the following, the BEST reason for this procedure is to
    A. protect the operating agency against possible false claims
    B. provide a file of incidents which can be used as basic material for an accident prevention campaign

C. provide the management with concrete evidence of violations of the rules by employees
D. indicate what repairs need to be made

37. It is suggested that an officer keep all persons away from the area of an accident until an investigation has been completed.
    This suggested procedure is
    A. *good*; witnesses will be more likely to agree on a single story
    B. *bad*; such action blocks traffic flow and causes congestion
    C. *good*; objects of possible use as evidence will be protected from damage or loss
    D. *bad*; the flow of normal pedestrian traffic provides an opportunity for an investigator to determine the cause of the accident

37.____

38. An officer receives instructions from his supervisor which he does not fully understand.
    For the officer to ask for a further explanation would be
    A. *good*, chiefly because his supervisor will be impressed with his interest in his work
    B. *poor*, chiefly because the time of the supervisor will be needlessly wasted
    C. *good*, chiefly because proper performance depends on full understanding of the work to be done
    D. *poor*, chiefly because officers should be able to think for themselves

38.____

39. A person is making a complaint to an officer which seems unreasonable and of little importance.
    Of the following, the BEST action for the officer to take is to
    A. criticize the person making the complaint for taking up his valuable time
    B. laugh over the matter to show that the complaint is minor and silly
    C. tell the person that anyone responsible for his grievance will be prosecuted
    D. listen to the person making the complaint and tell him that the matter will be investigated

39.____

40. A member of the department shall not indulge in intoxicating liquor while in uniform. A member of the department not required to wear a uniform and a uniformed member while out of uniform shall not indulge in intoxicants to an extent unfitting him for duty.
    Of the following, the MOST correct interpretation of this rule is that a
    A. member, off duty, not in uniform, may drink intoxicating liquor
    B. member, not on duty, but in uniform, may drink intoxicating liquor
    C. member, on duty, in uniform, may drink intoxicants
    D. uniformed member, in civilian clothes, may not drink intoxicants

40.____

Questions 41-65.

DIRECTIONS: In each of Questions 41 through 65, select the lettered word or phrase which means MOST NEARLY the same as the word in capital letters. Place the letter which corresponds to your choice in the space at the right.

41. INTERROGATE
    A. question   B. arrest   C. search   D. rebuff   41._____

42. PERVERSE
    A. manageable   B. poetic   C. contrary   D. patient   42._____

43. ADVOCATE
    A. champion   B. employ   C. select   D. advise   43._____

44. APPARENT
    A. desirable   B. clear   C. partial   D. possible   44._____

45. INSINUATE
    A. survey   B. strengthen   C. suggest   D. insist   45._____

46. MOMENTOUS
    A. important   B. immediate   C. delayed   D. short   46._____

47. AUXILIARY
    A. exciting   B. assisting   C. upsetting   D. available   47._____

48. ADMONISH
    A. praise   B. increase   C. warn   D. polish   48._____

49. ANTICIPATE
    A. agree   B. expect   C. conceal   D. approve   49._____

50. APPREHEND
    A. confuse   B. sentence   C. release   D. seize   50._____

51. CLEMENCY
    A. silence   B. freedom   C. mercy   D. severity   51._____

52. THWART
    A. enrage   B. strike   C. choke   D. block   52._____

53. RELINQUISH
    A. stretch   B. give up   C. weaken   D. flee from   53._____

54. CURTAIL
    A. stop   B. reduce   C. repair   D. insult   54._____

55. INACCESSIBLE
    A. obstinate   B. unreachable
    C. unreasonable   D. puzzling   55._____

56. PERTINENT
    A. related   B. saucy   C. durable   D. impatient   56._____

57. INTIMIDATE
    A. encourage   B. hunt   C. beat   D. frighten

58. INTEGRITY
    A. honesty   B. wisdom
    C. understanding D. persistence

59. UTILIZE
    A. use   B. manufacture
    C. help   D. include

60. SUPPLEMENT
    A. regulate   B. demand   C. add   D. answer

61. INDISPENSABLE
    A. essential   B. neglected   C. truthful   D. unnecessary

62. ATTAIN
    A. introduce   B. spoil   C. achieve   D. study

63. PRECEDE
    A. break away   B. go ahead   C. begin   D. come before

64. HAZARD
    A. penalty   B. adventure   C. handicap   D. danger

65. DETRIMENTAL
    A. uncertain   B. harmful   C. fierce   D. horrible

Questions 66-70.

DIRECTIONS: Questions 66 through 70 are to be answered on the basis of the information given in the table below. The numbers which have been omitted can be calculated from the other numbers which are given.

NUMBER OF VEHICLE ACCIDENTS IN GREAT CITY FOR THE PERIOD 2015 TO 2020

COUNTY	2015	2016	2017	2018	2019	2020	TOTAL
A	8,141	8,680	8,554	8,213	8,822	8,753	?
B	3,301	3,836	3,623	4,108	4,172	3,735	22,775
C	6,480	7,562	7,275	7,872	8,554	8,341	46,084
D	3,366	3,801	3,715	3,740	4,473	4,390	23,485
E	259	272	9	252	255	457	1,741
TOTAL	21,547	24,151	23,413	24,185	26,276	25,676	145,248

12 (#1)

66. For the total period covered by the table, the average number of vehicle accidents per year in County A exceeded the average number per year in County D by approximately
    A. 4,550   B. 5,450   C. 8,520   D. 27,000

67. In comparing the years 2019 and 2020, the one of the following statements which is MOST accurate is that the
    A. number of accidents in County E and County B combined increased
    B. number of accidents decreased in each of the five counties
    C. number of accidents in County D and County E combined increased
    D. decrease in the number of accidents in County C amounted to more than one-half of the decrease in the total number of accidents for the entire city

68. The percentage increase in 2020 over 2015 in vehicle accidents was LARGEST in County
    A. A   B. B   C. C   D. E

69. If the counties are ranked for each year according to the number of accidents (largest number to rank first), a county which will NOT have the same rank each year is County
    A. A   B. D   C. C   D. E

70. The LARGEST increase in the number of vehicle accidents from any one year to the next was in County
    A. C   B. B   C. A   D. D

71. During the first nine months of 2020, an officer spent an average of $270 a month. In October and November, he spent an average of $315 a month. In December, he spent $385.
    His average monthly spending during the year was MOST NEARLY
    A. $254   B. $287   C. $323   D. $3,000

72. In 2018 there were 8,270 arrests in a certain city. In 2019 the number of arrests increased by 12½%. In 2020 the number of arrests decreased 5% from the 2019 figures.
    The number of arrests in 2020 was MOST NEARLY
    A. 8,840   B. 9,770   C. 6,870   D. 7,600

73. Assume that parking space is to be provided for 25% of the tenants in a new housing development. The project will have five 6-story buildings, having seven tenants on each floor, and eight 11-story buildings, having eight tenants on each floor.
    The number of parking spaces needed is MOST NEARLY
    A. 215   B. 230   C. 700   D. 895

74. A stolen vehicle traveling at 60 miles per hour passes by a police car, which is standing still with the engine running. The police car immediately starts out in pursuit, and one minute later, having covered a distance of half a mile, it reaches a speed of 90 miles per hour and continues at this speed.

In how many minutes after the stolen vehicle passes the police car will the police car overtake it? _____ minute(s)
 A. 1   B. 1½   C. 2   D. 3

75. A police officer found his 42-hour work week was divided as follows: 1/6 of his time in investigating incidents on his patrol post, 1/2 of his time patrolling his post, and 1/8 of his time in special traffic duty. The rest of his time was devoted to assignments at precinct headquarters.
The percentage of his work week which was spent at precinct headquarters is MOST NEARLY
 A. 10%   B. 15%   C. 20%   D. 25%

76. In 2020, the Department of Sanitation towed away 8,430 cars which were abandoned or illegally parked on city streets.
If the value of the abandoned cars was $1,038,200 and that of the illegally parked cars was $6,234,800, then the average value of one of the towed away cars was MOST NEARLY
 A. $400   B. $720   C. $860   D. $1,100

77. Two percent of all school children are problem children. Some 80% of these problem children become delinquents, and about 80% of the delinquent children become criminals.
If the school population is 1,000,000 children, the number of this group who will eventually become criminals, according to this analysis, is
 A. 12,800   B. 1,280   C. 640   D. 128

78. A patrol car began a trip with 12 gallons of gasoline in the tank and ended with 7½ gallons. The car traveled 17.3 miles for each gallon of gasoline. During the trip, gasoline was bought for $23.20 at a cost of $2.90 per gallon.
The total number of miles traveled during this trip was MOST NEARLY
 A. 9   B. 196   C. 216   D. 229

Questions 79-81.

DIRECTIONS: Questions 79 through 81 are to be answered SOLELY on the basis of the following paragraph.

  Foot patrol has some advantages over all other methods of patrol. Maximum opportunity is provided for observation within range of the senses and for close contact with people and things that enable the police officer to provide a maximum service as an information source and counselor to the public and as the eyes and ears of the police department. A foot police officer loses no time in alighting from a vehicle, and the performance of police tasks is not hampered by responsibility for his vehicle while afoot. Foot patrol, however, does not have many of the advantages of a patrol car. Lack of both mobility and immediate communication with headquarters lessens the officer's value in an emergency. The area that he can cover effectively is limited and, therefore, this method of patrol is costly.

79. According to this paragraph, the foot police officer is the eyes and ears of the police department because he is
    A. in direct contact with the station house
    B. not responsible for a patrol vehicle
    C. able to observe closely conditions on his patrol post
    D. a readily available information source to the public

80. The MOST accurate of the following statements concerning the various methods of patrol, according to this paragraph, is that
    A. foot patrol should sometimes be combined with motor patrol
    B. foot patrol is better than motor patrol
    C. helicopter patrol has the same advantages as motor patrol
    D. motor patrol is more readily able to communicate with superior officers in an emergency

81. According to this paragraph, it is CORRECT to state that foot patrol is
    A. economical since increased mobility makes more rapid action possible
    B. expensive since the area that can be patrolled is relatively small
    C. economical since vehicle costs need not be considered
    D. expensive since giving information to the public is time-consuming

Questions 82-84.

DIRECTIONS: Questions 82 through 84 are to be answered SOLELY on the basis of the following paragraph.

All applicants for an original license to operate a catering establishment shall be fingerprinted. This shall include the officers, employees, and stockholders of the company and the members of a partnership. In case of a change, by addition or substitution, occurring during the existence of a license, the person added or substituted shall be fingerprinted. However, in the case of a hotel containing more than 200 rooms, only the officer or manager filing the application is required to be fingerprinted. The police commissioner may also at his discretion exempt the employees and stockholders of any company. The fingerprints shall be taken on one copy of Form C.E. 20 and on two copies of C.E. 21. One copy of Form C.E. 21 shall accompany the application. Fingerprints are not required with a renewal application.

82. According to this paragraph, an employee added to the payroll of a licensed catering establishment which is not in a hotel must
    A. always be fingerprinted
    B. be fingerprinted unless he has been previously fingerprinted for another license
    C. be fingerprinted unless exempted by the police commissioner
    D. be fingerprinted only if he is the manager or an officer of the company

83. According to this paragraph, it would be MOST accurate to state that
    A. Form C.E. 20 must accompany a renewal application
    B. Form C.E. 21 must accompany all applications
    C. Form C.E. 21 must accompany an original application
    D. both Forms C.E. 20 and C.E. 21 must accompany all applications

84. A hotel of 270 rooms has applied for a license to operate a catering establishment on the premises.
According to the instructions for fingerprinting given in his paragraph, the _____ shall be fingerprinted.
   A. officers, employees, and stockholders
   B. officers and the manager
   C. employees
   D. officer filing the application

84._____

Questions 85-86.

DIRECTIONS: Questions 85 through 87 are to be answered SOLELY on the basis of the following paragraph.

It is difficult to instill in young people inner controls on aggressive behavior in a world marked by aggression. The slum child's environment, full of hostility, stimulates him to delinquency; he does that which he sees about him. The time to act against delinquency is before it is committed. It is clear that juvenile delinquency, especially when it is committed in groups of gangs, leads almost inevitably to an adult criminal life unless it is checked at once. The first signs of vandalism and disregard for the comfort, health, and property of the community should be considered as storm warnings which cannot be ignored. The delinquent's first crime has the underlying element of testing the law and its ability to hit back.

85. A suitable title for this entire paragraph based on the material it contains is
   A. The Need for Early Prevention of Juvenile Delinquency
   B. Juvenile Delinquency as a Cause of Slums
   C. How Aggressive Behavior Prevents Juvenile Delinquency
   D. The Role of Gangs in Crime

85._____

86. According to this paragraph, an initial act of juvenile crime usually involves a(n)
   A. group or gang activity
   B. theft of valuable property
   C. test of the strength of legal authority
   D. act of physical violence

86._____

87. According to this paragraph, acts of juvenile delinquency are MOST likely to a criminal career when they are
   A. acts of vandalism
   B. carried out by groups or gangs
   C. committed in a slum environment
   D. such as to impair the health of the neighborhood

87._____

Questions 88-90.

DIRECTIONS: Questions 88 through 90 are to be answered SOLELY on the basis of the following paragraph.

The police laboratory performs a valuable service in crime investigation by assisting in the reconstruction of criminal action and by aiding in the identification of persons and things. When studied by a technician, physical things found at crime scenes often reveal facts useful in identifying the criminal and in determining what has occurred. The nature of substances to be examined and the character of the examinations are to be made so widely that the services of a large variety of skilled scientific persons are needed in crime investigations. To employ such a complete staff and to provide them with equipment and standards needed for all possible analyses and comparisons is beyond the means and the needs of any but the largest police departments. The search of crime scenes for physical evidence also calls for the services of specialists supplied with essential equipment and assigned to each tour of duty so as to provide service at any hour.

88. If a police department employs a large staff of technicians of various types in its laboratory, it will affect crime investigation to the extent that
    A. most crimes will be speedily solved
    B. identification of criminals will be aided
    C. search of crime scenes for physical evidence will become of less importance
    D. investigation by police officers will not usually be required

88.____

89. According to his paragraph, the MOST complete study of objects found at the scenes of crimes is
    A. always done in all large police departments
    B. based on assigning one technician to each tour of duty
    C. probably done only in large police departments
    D. probably done in police departments of communities with low crime rates

89.____

90. According to this paragraph, a large variety of skilled technicians is useful in criminal investigations because
    A. crimes cannot be solved without their assistance as a part of the police team
    B. large police departments need large staffs
    C. many different kinds of tests on various substances can be made
    D. the police cannot predict what methods may be tried by wily criminals

90.____

Questions 91-92.

DIRECTIONS: Questions 91 and 92 are to be answered SOLELY on the basis of the following paragraph.

The emotionally unstable person is always potentially a dangerous criminal, who causes untold misery to other persons and is a source of considerable trouble and annoyance to law enforcement officials. Like his fellow criminals, he will be a menace to society as long as he is permitted to be at large. Police activities against him serve to sharpen his wits and imprisonment gives him the opportunity to learn from others how to commit more serious crimes when he is released. This criminal's mental structure makes it impossible for him to profit by his experience with the police officials, by punishment of any kind or by sympathetic understanding and treatment by well-intentioned persons, professional and otherwise.

91. According to the above paragraph, the MOST accurate of the following statements concerning the relationship between emotional instability and crime is that
    A. emotional instability is proof of criminal activities
    B. the emotionally unstable person can become a criminal
    C. all dangerous criminals are emotionally unstable
    D. sympathetic understanding will prevent the emotionally unstable person from becoming a criminal

92. According to the above paragraph, the effect of police activities on the emotionally unstable criminal is that
    A. police activities aid this type of criminal to reform
    B. imprisonment tends to deter this type of criminal from committing future crimes
    C. contact with the police serves to assist sympathetic understanding and medical treatment
    D. police methods against this type of criminal develop him for further unlawful acts

Questions 93-95.

DIRECTIONS: Questions 93 through 95 are to be answered SOLELY on the basis of the following paragraph.

Proposals to license gambling operations are based on the belief that the human desire to gamble cannot be suppressed and, therefore, it should be licensed and legalized with the people sharing in the profits, instead of allowing the underworld to benefit. If these proposals are sincere, then it is clear that only one is worthwhile at all. Legalized gambling should be completely controlled and operated by the state with all the profits used for its citizens. A state agency should be set up to operate and control the gambling business. It should be as completely removed from politics as possible. In view of the inherent nature of the gambling business with its close relationship to lawlessness and crime, only a man of the highest integrity should be eligible to become head of this agency. However, state gambling would encourage mass gambling with its attending social and economic evils in the same manner as other forms of legal gambling; but there is no justification whatever for the business of gambling to be legalized and then permitted to operate for private profit or for the benefit of any political organization.

93. The central thought of this paragraph may be correctly expressed as the
    A. need to legalize gambling in the state
    B. state operation of gambling for the benefit of the people
    C. need to license private gambling establishments
    D. evils of gambling

94. According to this paragraph, a problem of legalized gambling which will still occur if the state operates the gambling business is
    A. the diversion of profits from gambling to private use
    B. that the amount of gambling will tend to diminish

C. the evil effects of any form of mass gambling
D. the use of gambling revenues for illegal purposes

95. According to this paragraph, to legalize the business of gambling would be
    A. *justified*, because gambling would be operated only by a man of the highest integrity
    B. *justified*, because this would eliminate politics
    C. *unjustified* under any conditions because the human desire to gamble cannot be suppressed
    D. *unjustified* if operated for private or political profit

95.____

Questions 96-97.

DIRECTIONS: Questions 96 and 97 are to be answered SOLELY on the basis of the following paragraph.

For many years, slums had been recognized as breeding disease, juvenile delinquency, and crime which not only threatened the health and welfare of the people who lived there, but also weakened the structure of society as a whole. As far back as 1834, a sanitary inspection report in New York City pointed out the connection between insanitary, overcrowded housing, and the spread of epidemics. Down through the years, evidence of slum-produced evils accumulated as the slums themselves continued to spread. This spread of slums was nationwide. Its symptoms and its ill effects were peculiar to no locality, but were characteristic of the country as a whole and imperiled the national welfare.

96. According to this paragraph, people who live in slum dwellings
    A. cause slums to become worse
    B. are threatened by disease and crime
    C. create bad housing
    D. are the chief source of crime in the country

96.____

97. According to this paragraph, the effects of juvenile delinquency and crime in slum areas were
    A. to destroy the structure of society
    B. noticeable in all parts of the country
    C. a chief cause of the spread of slums
    D. to spread unsanitary conditions in New York City

97.____

Questions 98-100.

DIRECTIONS: Questions 98 through 100 are to be answered SOLELY on the basis of the following paragraph.

Whenever, in the course of the performance of their duties in an emergency, members of the force operate the emergency power switch at any location on the transit system and thereby remove power from portions of the track, or they are on the scene where this has been done, they will bear in mind that, although power is removed, further dangers exist; namely, that a train may coast into the area even though the power is off, or that the rails may be energized by a train which may be in a position to transfer electricity from a live portion of the third rail through its shoe beams. Employees must look in each direction before stepping upon, crossing or standing close to tracks, being particularly careful not to come into contact with the third rail.

98. According to this paragraph, whenever an emergency occurs which has resulted in operating the emergency switch, it is MOST accurate to state that
    A. power is shut off and employees may perform their duties in complete safety
    B. there may still be power in a portion of the third rail
    C. the switch will not operate if a portion of the track has been broken
    D. trains are not permitted to stop in the area of the emergency

98.____

99. An important precaution which this paragraph urges employees to follow after operating the emergency power switch is to
    A. look carefully in both directions before stepping near the rails
    B. inspect the nearest train which has stopped to see if the power is on
    C. examine the third rail to see if the power is on
    D. check the emergency power switch to make sure it has operated properly

99.____

100. A trackman reports to you, the police officer, that a dead body is lying on the road bed. You operate the emergency power switch. A train which has been approaching comes to a stop near the scene.
    In order to act in accordance with the instructions in the above paragraph, you should
    A. climb down to the road bed and remove the body
    B. direct the train motorman to back up to the point where his train will not be in position to transfer electricity through its shoe beams
    C. carefully cross over the road bed to the body, avoiding the third rail and watching for train movements
    D. have the train motorman check to see if power is on before crossing to the tracks

100.____

KEY (CORRECT ANSWERS)

1. C	21. C	41. A	61. A	81. B
2. C	22. A	42. C	62. C	82. C
3. D	23. D	43. A	63. D	83. C
4. B	24. B	44. B	64. D	84. D
5. D	25. C	45. C	65. B	85. A
6. B	26. A	46. A	66. A	86. C
7. C	27. C	47. B	67. C	87. B
8. B	28. C	48. C	68. D	88. B
9. A	29. B	49. B	69. B	89. C
10. B	30. D	50. D	70. A	90. C
11. D	31. A	51. C	71. B	91. B
12. C	32. D	52. D	72. A	92. D
13. C	33. C	53. B	73. B	93. B
14. B	34. A	54. B	74. C	94. C
15. D	35. C	55. B	75. C	95. D
16. B	36. A	56. A	76. C	96. B
17. C	37. C	57. D	77. A	97. B
18. B	38. C	58. A	78. C	98. B
19. D	39. D	59. A	79. C	99. A
20. B	40. A	60. C	80. D	100. C

EXAMINATION SECTION

TEST 1

DIRECTIONS: Each question or incomplete statement is followed by several suggested answers or completions. Select the one that BEST answers the question or completes the statement. *PRINT THE LETTER OF THE CORRECT ANSWER IN THE SPACE AT THE RIGHT.*

1. A sergeant tells an officer to perform a certain duty.
   If the officer does not completely understand the order, she should
   A. carry out the order to the best of her ability and then request further information if necessary
   B. carry out the order to the best of her ability so that she does not give the appearance of being unable to follow orders
   C. inform the sergeant that she does not understand the order
   D. request clarification from a more experienced officer

   1.____

2. While on patrol, you are informed by the manager of a supermarket that an object which appears to be a homemade bomb has been discovered in his market.
   Your FIRST action should be to
   A. go to the market and make sure that everyone leaves it immediately
   B. go to the market, examine the bomb, and then decide what action is to be taken
   C. question the manager in detail in an effort to determine whether this is really a bomb
   D. telephone the Bomb Squad for instructions as to how the bomb should be rendered harmless

   2.____

3. An officer on post would be MOST likely to make a regular hourly signal-box call to his precinct, rather than an immediate call, when he
   A. discovers a traffic signal light which is not functioning properly
   B. discovers what appears to be an abandoned car on his post
   C. notices a street name sign which has been damaged
   D. overhears a conversation relation to a possible disturbance between two groups of teenagers

   3.____

4. An officer is on post, and a citizen sees him *ringing in* on a street police call box to the station house. The citizen asks him what the purpose of the box is.
   Of the following, the BEST course of action for the officer to follow in this situation is to
   A. speak to the desk officer over the call box phone and get his permission to answer the question
   B. suggest that he write to the Community Relations Office of the Police Department for complete information
   C. tactfully suggest to the man it is a police matter and hence confidential
   D. tell the man what the call box is and what it is used for

   4.____

5. The MOST reasonable advice that an officer can give to a merchant who asks what he should do if he receive a telephone call from a person he doesn't recognize regarding an alleged emergency at his store after ordinary business hours is that the merchant should go to the store and, if police officers are not at the scene, he should
   A. continue past the store and call the police for assistance
   B. continue past the store and return and enter it if there doesn't appear to be an emergency
   C. enter the store and ascertain whether the alleged emergency exists
   D. enter the store only if there is no one apparently loitering in the vicinity

6. An officer is asked by a citizen the location of a candy store which the officer knows is under observation for suspected bookmaking activity.
   In such a situation, the officer should
   A. give the proper directions to the citizen
   B. give the proper directions to the citizen, but tell him the store is under observation
   C. state that he does not know the location of the store
   D. tell the citizen that he may be arrested if the store is raided

7. *Whenever a crime has been committed, the criminal has disturbed the surroundings in one way or another by his presence.*
   The LEAST valid deduction for the police to make from this statement is that
   A. clues are thus present at all crime scenes
   B. even the slightest search at crime scenes will turn up conclusive evidence
   C. the greater the number of criminals involved in a crime, the greater the number of clues likely to be available
   D. the completely clueless crime is rarely encountered in police work

8. It is suggested that a suspect should not be permitted to walk in or about the scene of a crime where fingerprints may be present until a thorough search has been made for such evidence.
   This suggested procedure is
   A. *good*; the suspect would, if permitted to walk about the scene, smear all fingerprints that might be found by police investigators
   B. *bad*; the return of a suspect to the scene of a crime provides an opportunity to obtain additional fingerprints from the suspect
   C. *good*; if the suspect handled any objects at the scene, the value of any original fingerprints, as evidence, might be seriously impaired
   D. *bad*; the return of a suspect to the scene of a crime provides an opportunity to identify objects that had been handled during the commission of the crime

9. Of the following, the one which is the purpose of the police fingerprinting procedure is the
   A. identification of deceased persons
   B. identification of the guilty
   C. protection of the innocent
   D. recognition of first offenders

10. An officer is the first one to arrive at the scene of a murder. A suspect offers to make a statement to him concerning the crime. The officer refuses to accept the statement.
    The officer's action was
    A. *good*; interrogation of suspects should be performed by experienced detectives
    B. *poor*; the suspect may later change his mind and refuse to make any statement
    C. *good*; the officer will be too busy maintaining order at the scene to be able to accept the statement
    D. *poor*; a statement made by the suspect would quickly solve the crime

10.____

11. The scene of a crime is the area within the immediate vicinity of the specific location of the crime in which evidence might be found.
    This definition serves as an acceptable working guide for the discovery of evidence by the police because
    A. evidence found outside the crime scene can be just as valuable as evidence found nearly
    B. it assigns the finding of evidence to those responsible for its discovery
    C. it is likely that the most important evidence will be found within the area of the crime scene
    D. evidence found within the area of the crime scene is more readily accepted

11.____

12. It is important that the police give proper attention to the investigation of apparently minor, as well as major, complaints made by citizens.
    Of the following, the one which is the MOST valid reason for doing so is that
    A. minor complaints are frequently of great importance to the complainant
    B. minor complaints are more readily disposed of
    C. minor complaints may be an indication of a serious police problem
    D. police efficiency is determined by their attitude towards citizen complaints

12.____

13. Hearsay evidence may be defined as testimony by one person that another person told him about a criminal act which that other person had witnessed.
    Hearsay evidence is usually NOT admissible in a criminal trial MAINLY because
    A. hearsay evidence is consistently biased and deliberately distorted
    B. hearsay evidence is usually not relevant to the issues of the case
    C. such evidence is usually distorted by both the original witness and the person to whom he stated his observations
    D. the witness to the criminal act is not being cross-examined under oath

13.____

14. Arrests should not be given too much weight in the appraisal of a police officer's performance since a large number of arrests does not necessarily indicate that an officer is doing a good police job.
    This statement is
    A. *true*; factors other than the total of arrests must also be considered in judging police effectiveness
    B. *false*; the basic job of the police is to suppress crime and the surest measure of this is the number of arrests made

14.____

C. *true*; arrest figures are not indicative in any way of an officer's efficiency
D. *false*; although some officers are in a better position to make arrests than others, the law of averages should operate to even this out

15. Arson is a particularly troublesome crime for the police.
Of the following statements, the one which is the MOST important reason why this is so is that
    A. arsonists usually seek the protection of darkness for their crimes
    B. arsons occur so frequently that the police lack a definite approach
    C. important evidence is frequently destroyed by the fire itself
    D. witnesses find it difficult to distinguish arsonists from other criminals

16. Undoubtedly, the police have an important contribution to make to the welfare of youth.
Of the following, the PRINCIPAL reason for this is that
    A. effectiveness is a result of experience and the police have had the longest experience in youth work
    B. no other agency can make use of the criminal aspects of the law as effectively as the police
    C. the police are in a strategic position to observe children actually or potentially delinquent and the condition contributing thereto
    D. welfare agencies lack an understanding of the problems of youth

17. Adolescents, whether delinquent or not, are especially sensitive to the attitudes attitudes of their own small group and are more responsive to the judgments of their companions than to those of their own family.
According to this statement, it would be MOST accurate to conclude that
    A. adolescents are concerned more with their gang's opinion of them than with their own families' reaction to their behavior
    B. adolescents are more personal sensitive to criticism of their conduct than adults
    C. adolescent misbehavior can best be approached through the family
    D. adolescent misbehavior is often caused by the lack of parental interest

18. It is safe to say that the significant patterns of behavior conveyed by movies, press or radio must reach individuals whose behavior resistance is low, in order to be influential.
It follows from the above statement that it would be MOST desirable to
    A. consider the public press a negative factor in the developmental pattern of individuals
    B. encourage youth to imitate significant patterns of behavior which they observe
    C. exclude all children from attending movies which portray patterns of behavior of an anti-social nature
    D. prevent exposure of potentially delinquent children to unfavorable influences

5 (#1)

19. The suggestion has been made that the police department issue identification cards to be used by juveniles over 21 who wish to drink alcoholic beverages in bars.
   The one of the following which is NOT a valid criticism of this proposal is that it might
   A. appear to bestow positive social approval on the consumption of alcoholic beverages by youths
   B. induce more youngsters to congregate in bars
   C. lead to a *black market* in counterfeit identification cards
   D. shield youths from exposure to unwholesome situations

19.____

20. An apparently senile man informs a patrolman that he is returning from a visit to his daughter and that he is unable to find his way back home because he has forgotten his address.
   Of the following courses of action, the FIRST one that should be taken by the patrolman is to
   A. question the man in an effort to establish his identity
   B. request the police missing persons section to describe to you any person recently reported as missing
   C. suggest that the man return to his daughter for travel directions to his home
   D. telephone a description of the man to the precinct station house

20.____

21. Of the following facts about a criminal, the one which would be of MOST value in apprehending and identifying the criminal would be that he
   A. drives a black Cadillac 2019 sedan with chrome license plate holders
   B. invariably uses a .38 caliber Colt blue-steel revolver with walnut stock and regulation front sight
   C talks with a French accent and frequently stutters
   D. usually wears 3-button single-breasted Ivy League suits and white oxford cloth button-down shirts

21.____

22. A pawnshop dealer has submitted to the police an accurate and complete description of a wristwatch which he recently purchased from a customer.
   The one of the following factors that would be MOST important in determining whether this wristwatch was stolen is the
   A. degree of investigative perseverance demonstrated by the police
   B. exactness of police records describing stolen property
   C. honesty and neighborhood reputation of the pawnbroker
   D. time interval between the purchase of the wristwatch by the pawnbroker and his report to the police

22.____

23. An officer noticed a man fumbling at the controls of an automobile, starting with a lurch, grinding the gear, and then driving on the wrong side of the street. The officer signaled the car to stop, warned the driver about his driving and permitted him to depart.

23.____

This procedure was
- A. *right*; it is good public relations for the police to caution rather than punish inadvertent violations of law
- B. *wrong*; the officer should have arrested the driver for driving while in an intoxicated condition
- C. *right*; the bad driving probably was due to nervousness caused by the presence of the officer
- D. *wrong*; the officer should have investigated the possibility that this was a stolen car

24. An officer at the scene of a serious vehicular accident requests two witnesses to the accident not to speak to each other until he has received from each of them a statement concerning the accident.
The MOST likely reason for this request by the officer is that if the witnesses were allowed to speak to each other at this time, they might
- A. become involved in a violent quarrel over what actually occurred
- B. change their opinion so that identical statements to the police would result
- C. discuss the possibility of a bribe offer to either of them by one of the operators involved in the accident
- D. have their original views of the accident somewhat altered by hearing each other's view of the accident

24.____

25. Officer Z is directing traffic when he observes a car approaching him which appears to meet the description of a car stolen several days previously. Officer Z signals the driver of this car to stop. The car does not stop or slacken its speed and proceeds past Officer Z. In an effort to stop the car, Officer Z fires several shots at the car.
The action of Officer Z was
- A. *improper*; Officer Z should know that pistol marksmanship is not always accurate, even at relatively close ranges
- B. *proper*; it is legally justifiable to fire at an escaping felon
- C. *improper*; it is possible that the driver misunderstood the officer's signal to stop
- D. *proper*; Officer Z was on foot duty and there was no other immediately available means of halting the car

25.____

26. Assume that a recent study showed a 2% increase in highway fatalities in the first six months of 2019 over the last six months of 2018.
Of the following factors, generally the LEAST important one to include in a report evaluating this study is the
- A. age and sex distribution of drivers
- B. total number of automobiles in use
- C. total number of miles automobiles were driven
- D. total population

26.____

7 (#1)

27. Tests have shown that sound waves set up by a siren have a greater intensity ahead than at either side or at the rear of a police car.
On the basis of this statement, it would be MOST reasonable for the operator of a police car, when responding to the scene of an emergency and using the siren, to expect that a motorist approaching an intersection from
   A. a side street may not stop his vehicle as soon as a more distant motorist directly ahead of the police car
   B. directly ahead may not stop his vehicle as soon as a more distant motorist approaching from the rear of the police car
   C. directly ahead may not stop his vehicle as soon as a more distant motorist approaching from the side of the police car
   D. the rear of the police car may stop his vehicle before the less distant motorist approaching from the street

27.____

28. An alarm broadcast for criminals escaping by car directs police officers to observe occupants of all cars, even occupants in cars not meeting the description of the fleeing car.
The MOST likely reason for this is that
   A. cars of the same make are not distinctive enough to be of any recognition value
   B. the car's appearance may have been greatly altered after the crime was committed
   C. the criminals may have disguised themselves after the commission of the crime
   D. the escaping criminal may change to a different car after leaving the scene

28.____

29. Five minutes after receiving an alarm for a blue 2010 Buick four-door sedan which had been used as a get-away car by bank robbers, a radio patrol team spots and stops a car which seems to fit the description.
The one of the following which is MOST likely to indicate the need for further careful investigation is that the
   A. car has a cracked rear side window
   B. driver does not have a registration certificate for this car
   C. rear license plate is rusted
   D. occupants of the car consist of three poorly dressed men

29.____

30. A foot patrol officer who is several blocks away observes a woman being dragged into a car, which drives off very rapidly.
Of the following, his FIRST action should be to
   A. call headquarters from the nearest call box or public telephone
   B. commandeer a bus and pursue the other car
   C. shoot in the direction of the scene as a warning
   D. step into a hallway and await the approach of the car

30.____

31. A citizen requests police assistance in locating his adult son who has not been home for a period of twenty-four hours. Questioning of the citizen reveals no reason for the son's absence.

31.____

The MOST appropriate of the following actions that the police should take is to
   A. advise the citizen to contact all nearly hospitals and then contact the police again if this is not successful
   B. conduct a thorough investigation in an attempt to locate the missing son
   C. politely inform the citizen that no police action will be taken since the son is an adult
   D. suggest that the citizen wait several days; and if his son has not then returned home, they will accept the complaint

32. An officer is guarding the entrance of an apartment in which a homicide occurred. While awaiting the arrival of the detectives assigned to the case, he is approached by a newspaper reporter who asks to be admitted. The officer refuses to admit him.
    The officer's action was
    A. *wrong*; the police should cooperate with the press
    B. *right*; the reporter might unintentionally destroy evidence if admitted
    C. *wrong*; experienced police reporters can be trusted to act intelligently in this situation
    D. *right*; this reporter should not be given an advantage over other newspaper men

33. A police officer investigating a reported store hold-up, which occurred shortly before his arrival, enters the store. The salesclerk who witnessed the hold-up starts telling the officer, in a confused and excited manner, what had happened.
    The BEST course for the officer to follow initially is to
    A. ask the clerk to write out an account of what had happened
    B. let the clerk tell her story without interruption
    C. try to confine the clerk to answering relevant questions
    D. wait until the clerk calms down before taking her statement

34. A phone call is received at police headquarters indicating that a burglary is now taking place in a large loft building. Several radio motor patrol teams are dispatched to the scene.
    In order to prevent the escape of the burglars, the two patrolmen arriving first at the building, knowing that there is at least one entrance on each of the four side of the building, should FIRST
    A. station themselves at diagonally opposite corners, outside of the building
    B. enter the building and proceed to search for the criminals
    C. station themselves at the most likely exit from the building
    D. enter the building and remain on the ground floor, attempting to keep all stairways under observation

Questions 36-45.

DIRECTIONS: In each of Questions 36 through 45, select the lettered word which means MOST NEARLY the same as the capitalized word. Place the letter which corresponds to your choice in the space at the right.

35. AVARICE
   A. flight   B. greed   C. pride   D. thrift   35.____

36. PREDATORY
   A. offensive   B. plundering   C. previous   D. timeless   36.____

37. VINDICATE
   A. clear   B. conquer   C. correct   D. illustrate   37.____

38. INVETERATE
   A. backward   B. erect   C. habitual   D. lucky   38.____

39. DISCERN
   A. describe   B. fabricate   C. recognize   D. seek   39.____

40. COMPLACENT
   A. indulgent   B. listless   C. overjoyed   D. satisfied   40.____

41. ILLICIT
   A. insecure   B. unclear   C. unlawful   D. unlimited   41.____

42. PROCRASTINATE
   A. declare   B. multiply   C. postpone   D. steal   42.____

43. IMPASSIVE
   A. calm   B. frustrated   C. thoughtful   D. unhappy   43.____

44. AMICABLE
   A. cheerful   B. flexible   C. friendly   D. poised   44.____

45. FEASIBLE
   A. breakable   B. easy   C. likeable   D. practicable   45.____

KEY (CORRECT ANSWERS)

1. C	11. C	21. C	31. B	41. C
2. A	12. C	22. B	32. B	42. C
3. C	13. D	23. D	33. C	43. A
4. D	14. A	24. D	34. A	44. C
5. A	15. C	25. C	35. B	45. D
6. A	16. C	26. D	36. B	
7. B	17. A	27. A	37. A	
8. C	18. D	28. B	38. C	
9. B	19. D	29. B	39. C	
10. B	20. A	30. A	40. D	

TEST 2

DIRECTIONS: Each question or incomplete statement is followed by several suggested answers or completions. Select the one that BEST answers the question or completes the statement. *PRINT THE LETTER OF THE CORRECT ANSWER IN THE SPACE AT THE RIGHT.*

Questions 1-11.

DIRECTIONS: In each of Questions 1 through 11, select the lettered word which means MOST NEARLY the same as the capitalized word. Place the letter which corresponds to your choice in the space at the right.

1. INNOCUOUS
   A. harmless   B. insecure   C. insincere   D. unfavorable

2. OSTENSIBLE
   A. apparent   B. hesitant   C. reluctant   D. showy

3. INDOMITABLE
   A. excessive
   C. unreasonable
   B. unconquerable
   D. unthinkable

4. CRAVEN
   A. cowardly   B. hidden   C. miserly   D. needed

5. ALLAY
   A. discuss   B. quiet   C. refine   D. remove

6. ALLUDE
   A. denounce   B. refer   C. state   D. support

7. NEGLIGENCE
   A. carelessness   B. denial   C. objection   D. refusal

8. AMEND
   A. correct   B. destroy   C. end   D. list

9. RELEVANT
   A. conclusive   B. careful   C. obvious   D. related

10. VERIFY
    A. challenge   B. change   C. confirm   D. reveal

11. INSIGNIFICANT
    A. incorrect   B. limited   C. unimportant   D. undesirable

2 (#2)

Questions 12-16.

DIRECTIONS: Questions 12 through 16 are to be answered on the basis of the graphs shown below.

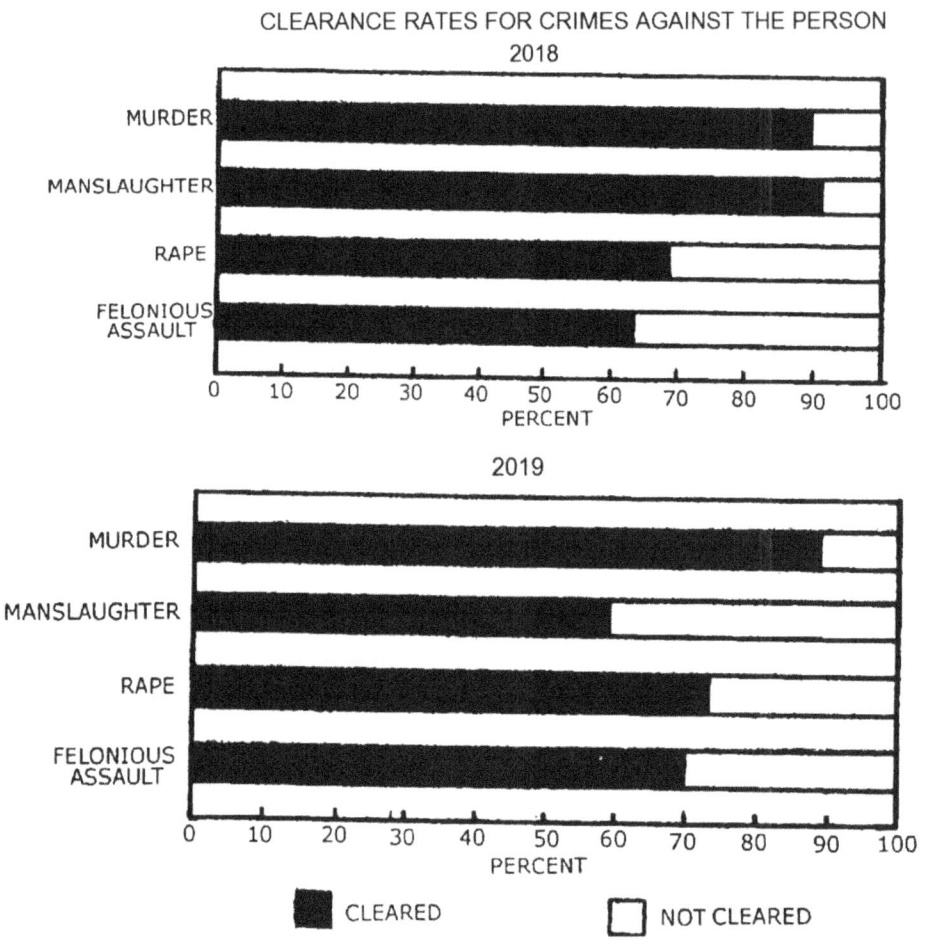

NOTE: The clearance rate is defined as the percentage of reported cases which were closed by the police through arrests or other means.

12. According to the above graphs, the AVERAGE clearance rate for all four crimes for 2019
    A. was greater than in 2018
    B. was less than in 2018
    C. was the same as in 2018
    D. cannot properly be compared to the 2018 figures

12.____

13. According to the above graphs, the crimes which did NOT show an increasing clearance rate from 2018 to 2019 were
    A. manslaughter and murder
    B. rape and felonious assault
    C. manslaughter and felonious assault
    D. rape and murder

13.____

14. According to the above graphs, the average clearance rate for the two-year period 2018-2019 was SMALLEST for the crime of
A. murder
B. manslaughter
C. rape
D. felonious assault

15. If, in 2019, 63 cases of reported felonious assault remained *not cleared*, then the total number of felonious assault cases reported that year was MOST NEARLY
A. 90
B. 150
C. 210
D. 900

16. In comparing the graphs for 2018 and 2019, it would be MOST accurate to state that
A. it is not possible to compare the total number of crimes cleared in 2018 with the total number cleared in 2019
B. the total number of crimes reported in 2018 is greater than the number in 2019
C. there were fewer manslaughter cases cleared during 2018 than in 2019
D. there were more rape cases cleared during 2019 than manslaughter cases cleared in the same year

17. A radio motor patrol car finds it necessary to travel at 90 miles per hour for a period of 1 minute and 40 seconds.
The number of miles which the car travels during this period is
A. $1^5/_6$
B. 2
C. 2½
D. 3¾

18. A radio motor patrol car has to travel a distance of 15 miles in an emergency. If it does the first two-thirds of the distance at 40 m.p.h. and the last third at 60 m.p.h., the total number of minutes required for the entire run is MOST NEARLY
A. 15
B. 20
C. 22½
D. 25

19. A patrol car had 11½ gallons of gasoline at the beginning of a trip of 196 miles and 5½ gallons at the end of the trip. During the trip, gasoline was bought for $21.70 at a cost of $3.10 per gallon.
The average number of miles driven per gallon of gasoline is MOST NEARLY
A. 14
B. 14.5
C. 15
D. 15.5

20. There are 15 police officers assigned to a certain operation. One-third earn $42,000 per year, three earn $44,100 per year, one earns $49,350 per year, and the rest earn $55,810 per year.
The average annual salary of these officers is MOST NEARLY
A. $47,500
B. $48,000
C. $48,500
D. $49,000

21. In 2022, the cost of patrol car maintenance and repair was $2,500 more than in 2021, representing an increase of 10%.
The cost of patrol car maintenance and repair in 2022 was MOST NEARLY
A. $2,750
B. $22,500
C. $25,000
D. $27,500

22. A police precinct has an assigned strength of 180 officers. Of this number, 25% are not available for duty due to illness, vacation, and other reasons. Of those who are available for duty, 1/3 are assigned outside of the precinct for special emergency duty.
The ACTUAL available strength of the precinct, in terms of officers immediately available for precinct duty, is
A. 45   B. 60   C. 90   D. 135

23. Five police officers are taking target practice. The number of rounds fired by each and the percentage of perfect shots is as follows:

Officer	Rounds Fired	Perfect Shots
R	80	30%
S	70	40%
T	75	60%
U	92	25%
V	96	66 2/3%

The average number of perfect shots fired by them is MOST NEARLY
A. 30   B. 36   C. 42   D. 80

24. A dozen 5-gallon cans of paint weigh 494 pounds. Each can, when empty weighs 3 pounds.
The weight of one gallon of paint is MOST NEARLY _____ lbs.
A. 5   B. 6½   C. 7½   D. 8

Questions 25-26.

DIRECTIONS: Questions 25 and 26 are to be answered SOLELY on the basis of the following paragraph.

The medical examiner may contribute valuable data to the investigator of fires which cause fatalities. By careful examination of the bodies of any victims, he not only establishes cause of death, but may also furnish, in many instances, answers to questions relating to the identity of the victim and the source and origin of the fire. The medical examiner is of greatest value to law enforcement agencies because he is able to determine the exact cause of death through an examination of tissue of apparent arson victims. Thorough study of a burned body of even of parts of a burned body will frequently yield information which illuminates the problems confronting the arson investigator and the police.

25. According to the above paragraph, the MOST important task of the medical examiner in the investigation of arson is to obtain information concerning the
A. identity of arsonists
B. cause of death
C. identity of victims
C. source and origin of fires

26. The CENTRAL thought of the above paragraph is that the medical examiner aids in the solution of crimes of arson when
    A. a person is burnt to death
    B. identity of the arsonist is unknown
    C. the cause of the fire is known
    D. trained investigators are not available

Questions 27-30.

DIRECTIONS: Questions 27 through 30 are to be answered SOLELY on the basis of the following paragraph.

A foundling is an abandoned child whose identity is unknown. Desk officers shall direct the delivery, by a policewoman if available, of foundlings actually or apparently under two years of age to the American Foundling Hospital, or if actually or apparently two years of age or over, to the Children's Center. In all other cases of dependent or neglected children, other than foundlings, requiring shelter, desk officers shall provide for obtaining such shelter as follows: between 9 A.M. and 5 P.M., Monday through Friday, by telephone direct to the Bureau of Child Welfare, in order to ascertain the shelter to which the child shall be sent; at all other times, direct the delivery of a child actually or apparently under two years of age to the American Foundling Hospital, of if the child is actually or apparently two years of age or over to the Children's Center.

27. According to the above paragraph, it would be MOST correct to state that
    A. a foundling as well as a neglected child may be delivered to the American Foundling Hospital
    B. a foundling but not a neglected child may be delivered to the Children's Center
    C. a neglected child requiring shelter, regardless of age, may be delivered to the Bureau of Child Welfare
    D. the Bureau of Child Welfare may determine the shelter to which a foundling may be delivered

28. According to the above paragraph, the desk officer shall provide for obtaining shelter for a neglected child, apparently under two years of age, by
    A. directing its delivery to Children's Center if occurrence is on a Monday between 9 A.M. and 5 P.M.
    B. telephoning the Bureau of Child Welfare if occurrence is on a Sunday
    C. directing its delivery to the American Foundling Hospital if occurrence is on a Wednesday at 4 P.M.
    D. telephoning the Bureau of Child Welfare if occurrence is a 10 A.M. on a Friday

29. According to the above paragraph, the desk officer should direct delivery to the American Foundling Hospital of any child who is
    A. actually under two years of age and requires shelter
    B. apparently under two years of age and is neglected or dependent
    C. actually two years of age and is a foundling
    D. apparently under two years of age and has been abandoned

30. A 12-year-old neglected child requiring shelter is brought to a police station on Thursday at 2 P.M.
Such a child should be sent to
   A. a shelter selected by the Bureau of Child Welfare
   B. a shelter selected by the desk office
   C. the Children's Center
   D. the American Foundling Hospital when a brother or sister, under 2 years of age, also requires shelter

Questions 31-33.

DIRECTIONS: Questions 31 through 33 are to be answered SOLELY on the basis of the following paragraph.

In addition to making the preliminary investigation of crimes, police officers should serve as eyes, ears, and legs for the detective division. The patrol division may be used for surveillance, to serve warrants, and bring in suspects and witnesses, and to perform a number of routine tasks for the detectives which will increase the time available for tasks that require their special skills and facilities. It is to the advantage of individual detective, as well as of the detective division, to have officers working in this manner; more cases are cleared by arrest and a greater proportion of stolen property is recovered when, in addition to the detective regularly assigned, a number of officers also work on the case. Detectives may stimulate the interest and participation of officers by keeping them currently informed of the presence, identity, or description, hangouts, associates, vehicles and method of operation of each criminal known to be in the community.

31. According to the above paragraph, an officer should
   A. assist the detective in certain of his routine functions
   B. be considered for assignment as a detective on the basis of his patrol performance
   C. leave the scene once a detective arrives
   D. perform as much of the detective's duties as time permits

32. According to the above paragraph, officers should aid detectives by
   A. accepting assignments from detectives which give promise of recovering stolen property
   B. making arrests of witnesses for the detective's interrogation
   C. performing all special investigative work for detectives
   D. producing for questioning individuals who may aid the detective in his investigation

33. According to the above paragraph, detectives can keep officers interested by
   A. ascertaining that officers are doing investigative work properly
   B. having officers directly under his supervision during an investigation
   C. informing officers of the value of their efforts in crime prevention
   D. supplying the officers with information regarding known criminals in the community

Questions 34-35.

DIRECTIONS: Questions 34 and 35 are to be answered SOLELY on the basis of the following paragraph.

State motor vehicle registration departments should and do play a vital role in the prevention and detection of automobile thefts. The combatting of theft is, in fact, one of the primary purposes of the registration of motor vehicles. In 2018, there were approximately 61,309,000 motor vehicles registered in the United States. That same year, some 200,000 of them were stolen. All but 6 percent have been or will be recovered. This is a very high recovery ratio compared to the percentage of recovery of other stolen personal property. The reason for this is that automobiles are carefully identified by the manufacturers and carefully registered by many of the states

34. The CENTRAL thought of the above paragraph is that there is a close relationship between the 34.____
    A. number of automobiles registered in the United States and the number stolen
    B. prevention of automobile thefts and the effectiveness of police departments in the United States
    C. recovery of stolen automobiles and automobile registration
    D. recovery of stolen automobiles and of other stolen property

35. According to the above paragraph, the high recovery ratio for stolen automobiles is due to 35.____
    A. state registration and manufacturer identification of motor vehicles
    B. successful prevention of automobile thefts by state motor vehicle departments
    C. the fact that only 6% of stolen vehicles are not properly registered
    D. the high number of motor vehicles registered in the United States

Questions 36-39.

DIRECTIONS: Questions 36 through 39 are to be answered SOLELY on the basis of the following paragraph.

It is not always understood that the term *physical evidence* embraces any and all objects, living or inanimate. A knife, gun, signature, or burglar tool is immediately recognized as physical evidence. Less often is it considered that dust, microscopic fragments of all types, even an odor, may equally be physical evidence and often the most important of all. It is well established that the most useful types of physical evidence are generally microscopic in dimensions, that is, not noticeable by the eye and, therefore, most likely to be overlooked by the criminal and by the investigator. For this reason, microscopic evidence persists for months or years after all other evidence has been removed and found inconclusive. Naturally, there are limitations to the time of collecting microscopic evidence as it may be lost or decayed. The exercise of judgment as to the possibility or profit of delayed action in collecting the evidence is a field in which the expert investigator should judge.

36. The one of the following which the above paragraph does NOT consider to be physical evidence is a
    A. criminal thought
    B. minute speck of dust
    C. raw onion smell
    D. typewritten note

    36._____

37. According to the above paragraph, the rechecking of the scene of a crime
    A. is useless when performed years after the occurrence of the crime
    B. is advisable chiefly in crimes involving physical violence
    C. may turn up microscopic evidence of value
    D. should be delayed if the microscopic evidence is not subject to decay or loss

    37._____

38. According to the above paragraph, the criminal investigator should
    A. give most of his attention to weapons used in the commission of the crime
    B. ignore microscopic evidence until a request is received from the laboratory
    C. immediately search for microscopic evidence and ignore the more visible objects
    D. realize that microscopic evidence can be easily overlooked

    38._____

39. According to the above paragraph,
    A. a delay in collecting evidence must definitely diminish its value to the investigator
    B. microscopic evidence exists for longer periods of time than other physical evidence
    C. microscopic evidence is generally the most useful type of physical evidence
    D. physical evidence is likely to be overlooked by the criminal and by the investigator

    39._____

Questions 40-42.

DIRECTIONS: Questions 40 through 42 are to be answered SOLELY on the basis of the following paragraph.

Sometimes, but not always, firing a gun leaves a residue of nitrate particles on the hands. This fact is utilized in the paraffin test which consists of applying melted paraffin and gauze to the fingers, hands, and wrists of a suspect until a cast of approximately 1/8 of an inch is built up. The heat of the paraffin causes the pores of the skin to open and release any particles embedded in them. The paraffin cast is then removed and tested chemically for nitrate particles. In addition to gunpowder, fertilizers, tobacco ashes, matches, and soot are also common sources of nitrates on the hands.

40. Assume that the paraffin test has been given to a person suspected of firing a gun and that nitrate particles have been found.
    It would be CORRECT to conclude that the suspect
    A. is guilty
    B. is innocent
    C. may be guilty or innocent
    D. is probably guilty

    40._____

41. In testing for the presence of gunpowder particles on human hands, the characteristic of paraffin which makes it MOST serviceable is that it
    A. causes the nitrate residue left by a fired gun to adhere to the gauze
    B. is waterproof
    C. melts at a high temperature
    D. helps to distinguish between gunpowder nitrates and other types

41.____

42. According to the above paragraph, in the paraffin test, the nitrate particles are removed from the pores because the paraffin
    A. enlarges the pores
    B. contracts the pores
    C. reacts chemically with nitrates
    D. dissolves the particles

42.____

Questions 43-45.

DIRECTIONS: Questions 43 through 45 are to be answered SOLELY on the basis of the following paragraph.

Pickpockets operate most effectively when there are prospective victims in either heavily congested areas or in lonely places. In heavily populated areas, the large number of people about them covers the activities of these thieves. In lonely spots, they have the advantage of working unobserved. The main factor in the pickpocket's success is the selection of the *right* victim. A pickpocket's victim must, at the time of the crime, be inattentive, distracted, or unconscious. If any of these conditions exist, and if the pickpocket is skilled in his operations, the stage is set for a successful larceny. With the coming of winter, the crowds move southward and so do most of the pickpockets. However, some pickpockets will remain in certain areas all year around. They will concentrate on theater districts, bus and railroad terminals, hotels, or large shopping centers. A complete knowledge of the methods of this type of criminal and the ability to recognize them come only from long years of experience in performing patient surveillance and trailing of them. This knowledge is essential for the effective control and apprehension of this type of thief.

43. According to this paragraph, the pickpocket is LEAST likely to operate in a
    A. baseball park with a full capacity attendance
    B. subway station in an outlying area late at night
    C. moderately crowded dance hall
    D. over-crowded department store

43.____

44. According to the above paragraph, the one of the following factors which is NOT necessary for the successful operation of the pickpocket is that
    A. he be proficient in the operations required to pickpockets
    B. the *right* potential victims be those who have been subject of such a theft previously
    C. his operations be hidden from the view of others
    D. the potential victim be unaware of the actions of the pickpocket

44.____

45. According to the above paragraph, it would be MOST correct to conclude that police officers who are successful in apprehending pickpockets
    A. are generally those who have had lengthy experience in recognizing all types of criminals
    B. must, by intuition, be able to recognize potential *right* victims
    C. must follow the pickpocket in their southward movement
    D. must have acquired specific knowledge and skills in this field

45.____

KEY (CORRECT ANSWERS)

1.	A	11.	C	21.	D	31.	A	41.	A
2.	A	12.	B	22.	C	32.	D	42.	A
3.	B	13.	A	23.	B	33.	D	43.	C
4.	A	14.	D	24.	C	34.	C	44.	B
5.	B	15.	C	25.	B	35.	A	45.	D
6.	B	16.	A	26.	A	36.	A		
7.	A	17.	C	27.	A	37.	C		
8.	A	18.	B	28.	D	38.	D		
9.	D	19.	C	29.	D	39.	C		
10.	C	20.	C	30.	A	40.	C		

EXAMINATION SECTION

TEST 1

DIRECTIONS: Each question or incomplete statement is followed by several suggested answers or completions. Select the one that BEST answers the question or completes the statement. *PRINT THE LETTER OF THE CORRECT ANSWER IN THE SPACE AT THE RIGHT.*

1. The basic purpose of patrol is to create a public impression of police presence everywhere so that potential offenders will think there is no opportunity for successful misconduct.
   In the assignment of police personnel, the type of police activity that MOST NEARLY realizes this purpose is
   A. traffic summons duty
   B. traffic duty
   C. patrol of all licensed premises
   D. patrol by the detective force
   E. radio motor patrol

2. A patrolman, who is asked by a civilian about a legal matter, directs him to the appropriate court.
   Of the following information given by the patrolman, the item which is LEAST likely to be useful to the civilian is
   A. hours during which the court is in session
   B. location of the court
   C. name of the Magistrate sitting in this court
   D. location of the complaint clerk within the court building
   E. transportation directions necessary to get to the court

3. An officer discovers two teenaged gangs, numbering about 50 boys, engaged in a free-for-all fight.
   The BEST immediate course for the officer to adopt is to
   A. call the station house for reinforcements
   B. fire over the heads of the boys and order them to disperse
   C. arrest the ringleaders
   D. call upon adult bystanders to assist him in restoring order
   E. attempt to stop the fight by using his club

4. A radio motor patrol team arrives on the scene a few minutes after a pedestrian has been killed on a busy street by a hit-and-run driver.
   After obtaining a description of the car, the FIRST action the officer should take is to
   A. radio a description of the fleeing car to precinct headquarters
   B. try to overtake the fleeing car
   C. obtain complete statements from everyone at the scene
   D. call for an ambulance
   E. inspect the site of the accident for clues

5. A police officer is approached by an obviously upset woman who reports that her husband is missing.
   The FIRST thing the officer should do is to
   A. check with the hospitals and the police station
   B. tell the woman to wait a few hours and call the police station if her husband has not returned by then
   C. obtain a description of the missing man so that an alarm can be broadcast
   D. ask the woman why she thinks her husband is missing
   E. make certain that the woman lives in his precinct

6. A violin is reported as missing from the home of Mrs. Brown.
   It would be LEAST important to the police, before making a routine check of pawnshops, to know that this violin
   A. is of a certain unusual shade of red
   B. has dimensions which are different from those of most violins
   C. has a well-known manufacturer's label stamped inside the violin
   D. has a hidden number given to the police by the owner
   E. has one tuning key with a chip mark on it in the shape of a triangle

7. In making his rounds, an officer should following the same route and schedule each time.
   The suggested procedure is
   A. *good*; a fixed routine enables the officer to proceed methodically and systematically
   B. *poor*; criminals can avoid observation by studying the officer's routine
   C. *good*; without a fixed routine, an officer may overlook some of his many duties
   D. *poor*; a fixed routine reduces an officer's alertness and initiative
   E. *good*; residents in the area covered will have more confidence in police efficiency

8. Police officers should call for ambulances to transport injured people to the hospital rather than use patrol cars for this purpose.
   Of the following, the MOST valid reason for this policy is that
   A. there is less danger of aggravating injuries
   B. patrol cars cannot be spared from police duty
   C. patrol cars are usually not equipped for giving emergency first aid
   D. medical assistance reaches the injured person sooner
   E. responsibility for treating injured people lies with the Department of Hospitals

9. A businessman requests advice concerning good practice in the use of a safe in his business office.
   The one of the following points which should be stressed MOST in the use of safes is that
   A. a safe should not be placed where it can be seen from the street
   B. the combination should be written down and carefully hidden in the office

C. a safe located in a dark place is more tempting to a burglar than one which is located in a well-lighted place
D. factors of size and weight alone determine the protection offered by a safe
E. the names of the manufacturer and the owner should be painted on the front of the safe

10. During a quarrel on a crowded city street, one man stabs another and flees. An officer arriving at the scene a short time later finds the victim unconscious, calls for an ambulance, and orders the crowd to leave.
His action was
    A. *bad*; there may have witnesses to the assault among the crowd
    B. *good*; it is proper first aid procedure to give an injured person room and air
    C. *bad*; the assailant is probably among the crowd
    D. *good*; a crowd may destroy needed evidence
    E. *bad*; it is poor public relations for the police to order people about needlessly

10.____

11. An officer walking his post at 3 A.M. notices heavy smoke coming out of a top floor window of a large apartment house.
Of the following, the action he should take FIRST is to
    A. make certain that there really is a fire
    B. enter the building and warn all the occupants of the apartment house
    C. attempt to extinguish the fire before it gets out of control
    D. call the Fire Department
    E. call precinct headquarters for Fire Department help

11.____

12. Two rival youth gangs have been involved in several minor classes. The youth officer working in their area believes that a serious clash will occur if steps are not taken to prevent it.
Of the following, the LEAST desirable action for the officer to take in his effort to head of trouble is to
    A. arrest the leaders of both groups as a warning
    B. warn the parents of the dangerous situation
    C. obtain the cooperation of religious and civic leaders in the community
    D. alert all social agencies working in that neighborhood
    E. report the situation to his superior

12.____

13. Police officers are instructed to pay particular attention to anyone apparently making repairs on an auto parked on a street.
The MOST important reason for this rule is that
    A. the auto may be parked illegally
    B. the person making the repairs may be obstructing traffic
    C. working on autos is prohibited on certain streets
    D. many people injure themselves while working on autos
    E. the person making the repairs may be stealing the auto

13.____

14. After making an arrest of a criminal, the officer is LEAST likely to request some kind of transportation if the
 A. prisoner is apparently a violent mental patient
 B. distance to be traveled is considerable
 C. prisoner is injured
 D. prisoner is in an alcoholic stupor
 E. prisoner talks of escaping

14.____

15. The Police Department, in an effort to prevent losses due to worthless checks, suggests to merchants that they place near the cash register a card stating that the merchant reserves the right to require positive identification and fingerprint from all persons who cash checks.
This procedure is
 A. *poor*; the merchant's regular customers may be offended by compulsory fingerprinting
 B. *poor*; the taking of fingerprints would not deter the professional criminal
 C. *good*; the police criminal files may be enlarged by the addition of all fingerprints taken
 D. *poor*; this system could not work unless the fingerprinting was made mandatory
 E. *good*; the card might serve to discourage persons from attempting to cash worthless checks

15.____

16. A factory manager asks an officer to escort his payroll clerk to and from the local bank when payroll money is withdrawn. The officer knows that it is against departmental policy to provide payroll escort service.
The officer should
 A. refuse and explain why he cannot do what is requested
 B. refer the manager to his precinct commander
 C. tell the manager that police officers have more important tasks
 D. advise the manager that he will provide this service if other duties do not interfere
 E. suggest that paychecks be issued to employees

16.____

17. A motorist who has been stopped by a motorcycle police officer for speeding acts rudely. He hints about his personal connections with high officials in the city government and demands the officer's name and shield number.
The officer should
 A. arrest the motorist for threatening an officer in the performance of his duty
 B. give his name and shield number without comment
 C. ignore the question since his name and shield number will be on the summons he is about to issue
 D. give his name and shield number but add to the charges against the motorist
 E. ask the motorist why he wants the information and give it only if the answer is satisfactory

17.____

18. Tire skidmarks provide valuable information to policemen investigating automobile accidents.
    The MOST important information obtained from this source is the
    A. condition of the road at the time of the accident
    B. effectiveness of the automobile's brakes
    C. condition of the tires
    D. point at which the driver first saw the danger
    E. speed of the automobile at the time of the accident

18.____

19. An officer observes several youths in the act of looting a peanut-vending machine. The youths flee in several directions as he approaches, ignoring his order to halt. The officer then shoots at them, and they halt and are captured
    The officer's action was
    A. *right*; it was the most effective way of capturing the criminals
    B. *wrong*; extreme measures should not be taken in apprehending petty offenders
    C. *right*; provided that there was no danger of shooting innocent bystanders
    D. *wrong*; this is usually ineffective when more than one offender is involved
    E. *right*; it is particularly important to teach juvenile delinquents respect for the law

19.____

20. Before permitting automobiles involved in an accident to depart, an officer should take certain measures.
    Of the following, it is LEAST important that the officer make certain that
    A. both drivers are properly licensed
    B. the automobiles are in safe operating condition
    C. the drivers have exchanged names and license numbers
    D. the drivers are physically fit to drive
    E. he obtains the names and addresses of drivers and witnesses

20.____

21. A detective, following a tip that a notorious bank robber is to meet a woman in a certain restaurant, is seated in a booth from which he can observe people entering and leaving. While waiting, he notices a flashily dressed woman get up from a table and slip by the cashier without paying her check. The detective ignored the incident and continued watching for the wanted man.
    This course of action was
    A. *correct*; the woman probably forgot to pay her bill
    B. *incorrect*; he should have arrested the woman since a *bird in the hand is worth two in the bush*
    C. *correct*; it is not the duty of the police department to protect businessmen from loss due to their own negligence
    D. *incorrect*; he should have followed the woman since she may lead to the bank robber
    E. *correct*; the detective should not risk losing the bank robber by checking on this incident

21.____

22. All officers are required to maintain a record of their daily police activity in a memorandum book.
The LEAST likely reason for this requirement is to
    A. make it unnecessary for the officer to remember police incidents
    B. give supervisors information concerning the officer's daily work
    C. serve as a possible basis to refute unjustified complaints against the officer
    D. make a record of information that may have a bearing on a court action
    E. record any action which may later require an explanation

23. Police officers have a duty to take into custody any person who is actually or apparently mentally ill.
Of the following cases, the one LEAST likely to fall under this provision of the law is the
    A. quarrelsome person who makes unjustifiable accusations
    B. elderly man who appears confused and unable to dress or feed himself
    C. young man who sits on the sidewalk curb staring into space and, when questioned, gives meaningless answers
    D. man who shouts obscenities at strangers in the streets
    E. woman who accuses waiters of attempting to poison her

24. An officer should not take notes while first questioning a suspect.
Of the following, the MOST important reason for this procedure is that
    A. information obtained at this time will probably not be truthful
    B. unessential facts can be eliminated if statements are written late
    C. the physical reactions of the suspect during interrogation can be better observed
    D. the exact wording is of no importance
    E. the statement will be better organized if written later

25. An officer should know the occupations and habits of the people on his beat. In heavily populated districts, however, it is too much to ask that the officer know all the people on his beat.
If this statement is correct, the one of the following which would be the MOST practical course for an officer to follow is to
    A. concentrate on becoming acquainted with the oldest residents of the beat
    B. limit his attention to people who work as well as live in the district
    C. limit his attention to people with criminal records
    D. concentrate on becoming acquainted with key people such as janitors, bartenders, and local merchants
    E. concentrate on becoming acquainted with the newest residents of the beat

26. An officer off-duty but in uniform recognizes a stolen car parked outside of a tavern. He notices that the radiator of the car is warm, indicating recent use.
Of the following, the MOST practical course for the officer to follow is to
    A. enter the tavern and ask aloud for the driver of the car
    B. stand in a nearby doorway and watch the car

C. search for the officer on the beat and report the facts to him
D. telephone the station house as soon as he arrives home
E. enter the tavern and privately ask the bartender if he knows who owns the car

27. When a person is arrested, he is always asked whether he uses narcotics, regardless of the charge against him.
Of the following, the MOST important reason for asking this question is that
   A. drug addicts can be induced to confess by withholding narcotics from them
   B. the theft of narcotics is becoming a serious police problem
   C. criminals are usually drug addicts
   D. many drug addicts commit crimes in order to obtain money for the purchase of narcotics
   E. it may be possible to convict the suspect of violation of the narcotics law

27.____

28. Of the following types of crimes, increased police vigilance would probably be LEAST successful in preventing
   A. murder
   B. burglary
   C. prostitution
   D. automobile thefts
   E. robbery

28.____

29. The Police Department has been hiring civilian women to direct traffic at school crossings.
The MOST important reason for this policy is
   A. to stimulate civic interest in police problems
   B. to dramatize the traffic safety problem
   C. that women are more careful of the safety of children
   D. that young school children have more confidence in women who are mothers of their playmates
   E. to free policemen for regular patrol duty

29.____

30. Of the following, the fact that makes it MOST difficult to identify stolen cars is that
   A. thieves frequently damage stolen cars
   B. many cars are similar in appearance
   C. thieves frequently disguise stolen cars
   D. owners frequently don't report stolen cars which are covered by insurance
   E. owners frequently delay reporting the theft

30.____

31. When testifying in a criminal case, it is MOST important that a policeman endeavor to
   A. avoid technical terms which may be unfamiliar to the jury
   B. lean over backwards in order to be fair to the defendant
   C. assist the prosecutor even if some exaggeration is necessary
   D. avoid contradicting other prosecution witnesses
   E. confine his answers to the questions asked

31.____

32. When investigating a burglary, a policeman should obtain as complete descriptions as possible of articles of value which were stolen, but should list, without describing, stolen articles which are relatively valueless.
    This suggested procedure is
    A. *poor*; what is valueless to one person may be of great value to another
    B. *good*; it enables the police to concentrate on recovering the most valuable articles
    C. *poor*; articles of little value frequently provide the only evidence connecting the suspect to the crime
    D. *good*; the listing of the inexpensive items is probably incomplete
    E. *poor*; the police should make the same effort to recover all stolen property, regardless of value

33. At 10 A.M. on a regular school day, an officer notices a boy about 11 years old wandering in the street. When asked the reason he is not in school, he replies that he attends school in the neighborhood, but that he felt sick that morning. The officer then took the boy to the principal of the school.
    This method of handling the situation was
    A. *bad*; the officer should have obtained verification of the boy's illness
    B. *good*; the school authorities are best equipped to deal with the problem
    C. *bad*; the officer should have obtained the boy's name and address and reported the incident to the attendance officer
    D. *good*; seeing the truant boy escorted by an officer will deter other children from truancy
    E. *bad*; the principal of a school should not be saddled with a truancy problem

34. During an investigation of a robbery, an officer caught one of the witnesses contradicting himself on one point. Upon questioning, the witness readily admitted the contradiction.
    The officer should conclude that
    A. the witness was truthful but emotionally disturbed by the experience
    B. all of the statements of the witness should be disregarded as untrustworthy
    C. the statements of the witness should be investigated carefully
    D. the witness was trying to protect the guilty person
    E. contradictions of this sort are inevitable

35. A woman was found dead by her estranged husband in the kitchen of a ground floor apartment. The husband stated that, although the apartment was full of gas and tightly closed, all the burners of the kitchen range were shut. The husband had gone to the apartment to get some clothes. When an officer arrived, the apartment was still heavy with gas fumes.
    Of the following, the MOST likely explanation for these circumstances is that
    A. gas seeped into the apartment under the door from a defective gas furnace in the basement
    B. the husband has given false information to mislead the police

C. the woman changed her mind about committing suicide and shut off the jets just before she collapsed
D. a leak in the kitchen range had developed
E. the woman had died from some other cause than asphyxiation

36. An officer on post hears a cry for help from a woman in a car with two men. He approaches the car and is told by the woman that the men are kidnapping her. The men claim to be the woman's husband and doctor and state that they are taking her to a private mental hospital.
Of the following, the BEST course for the officer is to
    A. take all of them to the station house for further questioning
    B. permit the woman to depart and arrest the men
    C. call for an ambulance to take the woman to the nearest city mental hospital
    D. accompany the car to the private mental hospital
    E. permit the car to depart on the basis of the explanation

36.____

37. Social security cards are not acceptable proof of identification for police purposes.
Of the following, the MOST important reason for this rule is that the social security card
    A. is easily obtained
    B. states on its face *for social security purposes—not for identification*
    C. is frequently lost
    D. does not contain the address of the person
    E. does not contain a photograph, description, or fingerprints of the person

37.____

38. Many well-meaning people have proposed that officers in uniform not be permitted to arrest juveniles.
This proposal is
    A. *good*; the police are not equipped to handle juvenile offenders
    B. *bad*; juvenile offenders would lose respect for all law enforcement agencies
    C. *good*; offending juveniles should be segregated from hardened criminals
    D. *bad*; frequently it is the uniformed officer who first comes upon the youthful offender
    E. *good*; contact with the police would prevent any rehabilitative measures from being taken

38.____

39. An off-duty police officer was seated in a restaurant when two men entered, drew guns, and robbed the cashier. The officer made no effort to prevent the robbery or apprehend the criminals. Later he justified his conduct by stating that an officer when off-duty is a private citizen with the same duties and rights of all private citizens.
The officer's conduct was
    A. *wrong*; an officer must act to prevent crimes and apprehend criminals at all times
    B. *right*; he was out of uniform at the time of the robbery
    C. *wrong*; he had his gun with him at the time of the robbery

39.____

D. *right*; it would have been foolhardy for him to intervene when outnumbered by armed robbers
E. *wrong*; he should have obtained the necessary information and descriptions after the robbers left

40. Drivers with many convictions for traffic law violations sometimes try to conceal this record by cutting off the lower part of the operator's license and attaching to it clean section from a blank application form.
An officer who stops a driver and notices that his operator's license is torn and held together by transparent tape should FIRST
    A. verify the driver's explanation of the torn license
    B. examine both parts of the license to see if they match
    C. request additional proof of identity
    D. check the records of the Bureau of Motor Vehicles for unanswered summonses

Question 41-60.

DIRECTIONS: In answering Questions 41 through 60 select the lettered word or phrase which means MOST NEARLY the same as the word in capitals.

41. IMPLY
    A. agree to   B. hint at   C. laugh at
    D. mimic   E. reduce

42. APPRAISAL
    A. allowance   B. composition   C. prohibition
    D. quantity   E. valuation

43. DISBURSE
    A. approve   B. expend   C. prevent
    D. relay   E. restrict

44. POSTERITY
    A. back payment   B. current procedure   C. final effort
    D. future generations E. rare specimen

45. PUNCTUAL
    A. clear   B. honest   C. polite
    D. prompt   E. prudent

46. PRECARIOUS
    A. abundant   B. alarmed   C. cautious
    D. insecure   E. placid

47. FOSTER
    A. delegate   B. demote   C. encourage
    D. plead   E. surround

48. PINNACLE
    A. center   B. crisis   C. outcome
    D. peak   E. personificaton

49. COMPONENT
    A. flattery   B. opposite   C. part
    D. revision   E. trend

50. SOLICIT
    A. ask   B. prohibit   C. promise
    D. revoke   E. surprise

51. LIAISON
    A. asset   B. coordination   C. difference
    D. policy   E. procedure

52. ALLEGE
    A. assert   B. break   C. irritate
    D. reduce   E. wait

53. INFILTRATION
    A. consumption   B. disposal   C. enforcement
    D. penetration   E. seizure

54. SALVAGE
    A. announce   B. combine   C. prolong
    D. save   E. try

55. MOTIVE
    A. attack   B. favor   C. incentive
    D. patience   E. tribute

56. PROVOKE
    A. adjust   B. incite   C. leave
    D. obtain   E. practice

57. SURGE
    A. branch   B. contract   C. revenge
    D. rush   E. want

58. MAGNIFY
    A. attract   B. demand   C. generate
    D. increase   E. puzzle

59. PREPONDERANCE
    A. decision   B. judgment   C. outweighing
    D. submission   E. warning

60. ABATE
    A. assist
    B. coerce
    C. diminish
    D. indulge
    E. trade

Question 61-65.

DIRECTIONS: Questions 61 through 65 are to be answered on the basis of the table which appears below.

VALUE OF PROPERTY STOLEN – 2019 AND 2020
LARCENY

Category	2019		2020	
	Number of Offenses	Value of Stolen Property	Number of Offenses	Value of Stolen Property
Pocket-picking	20	$1,950	10	$950
Purse-snatching	175	5,750	20	12,500
Shoplifting	155	7,950	225	17,350
Automobile thefts	1,040	127,050	860	108,000
Thefts of auto accessories	1,135	34,950	970	24,400
Bicycle thefts	355	8,250	240	6,350
All other thefts	1,375	187,150	1,300	153,150

61. Of the total number of larcenies reported for 2019, automobile thefts accounted for MOST NEARLY
    A. 5%   B. 15%   C. 25%   D. 50%   E. 75%

62. The LARGEST percentage decrease in the value of the stolen property from 2019 to 2020 was in the category of
    A. pocket-picking
    B. automobile thefts
    C. thefts of auto accessories
    D. bicycle thefts
    E. all other thefts

63. In 2020, the average amount of each theft was LOWEST for the category of
    A. pocket-picking
    B. purse-snatching
    C. shoplifting
    D. thefts of auto accessories

64. The category which had the LARGEST numerical reduction in the number of offenses from 2019 to 2020 was
    A. pocket-picking
    B. automobile thefts
    C. thefts of auto accessories
    D. bicycle thefts
    E. all other thefts

65. When the categories are ranked for each year, according to the number of offenses committed in each category (largest number to rank first), the number of categories which will have the same rank in 2019 as in 2020 is
    A. 3   B. 4   C. 5   D. 6   E. 7

13 (#1)

66. A parade is marching up an avenue for 60 city blocks. A sample count of the number of people watching the parade on one side of the street in the block is taken, first, in a block near the end of the parade, and then in a block at the middle; the former count is 4,000 and the latter is 6,000.
If the average for the entire parade is assumed to be the average of the two samples, then the estimated number of persons watching the entire parade is MOST NEARLY
   A. 240,000   B. 300,000   C. 480,000   D. 600,000   E. 720,000

66._____

67. Suppose that the revenue from parking meters in a city was 5% greater in 2019 than in 2018, and 2% less in 2020 than in 2019.
If the revenue in 2018 was $1,500,000, then the revenue in 2020 was
   A. $1,541,500   B. $1,542,000   C. $1,542,500
   D. $1,543,000   E. $1,543,500

67._____

68. A radio motor patrol car completes a ten mile trip in twenty minutes.
If it does one-half the distance at a speed of twenty miles an hour, its speed, in miles per hour, for the remainder of the distance must be
   A. 30   B. 40   C. 50   D. 60   E. 70

68._____

69. A public beach has two parking areas. Their capacities are in the ratio of two to one and, on a certain day, are filled to 60% and 40% of capacity, respectfully.
The entire parking facilities of the beach on that day are MOST NEARLY _____ filled.
   A. 38%   B. 43%   C. 48%   D. 53%   E. 58%

69._____

70. While on foot patrol, an officer walks north for eleven blocks, turns around and walks south for six blocks, turns around and walks north for two blocks, then makes a right turn and walks one block.
In relation to his starting point, he is now _____ blocks away and facing _____.
   A. twenty; east   B. eight; east   C. seven; west
   D. nine; north   E. seven; north

70._____

Question 71-73.

DIRECTIONS: Questions 71 through 73 are to be answered on the basis of the following paragraph.

   When police officers search for a stolen car, they first check for the color of the car, then for make, model, year, body damage, and finally license number. The first five can be detected from almost any angle, while the recognition of the license number is often not immediately apparent. The serial number and motor number, though less likely to be changed than the easily substituted license number, cannot be observed in initial detection of the stolen car.

71. According to the above paragraph, the one of the following features which is LEAST readily observed in checking for a stolen car in moving traffic is
   A. license number   B. serial number   C. model
   D. make   E. color

71._____

72. The feature of a car that cannot be determined from most angles of observation is the
    A. make B. model C. year
    D. license number E. color

73. Of the following, the feature of a stolen car that is MOST likely to be altered by a car thief shortly after the car is stolen is the
    A. license number B. motor number C. color
    D. model E. minor body damage

Question 74-75.

DIRECTIONS: Questions 74 and 75 are to be answered on the basis of the following paragraph.

The racketeer is primarily concerned with business affairs, legitimate or otherwise, and preferably those which are close to the margin of legitimacy. He gets his best opportunities from business organizations which meet the need of large sections of the public for goods or services which are defined as illegitimate by the same public, such as prostitution, gambling, illicit drugs or liquor. In contrast to the thief, the racketeer and the establishments he controls deliver goods and services for money received.

74. From the above paragraph, it can be deduced that suppression of racketeers is difficult because
    A. victims of racketeers are not guilty of violating the law
    B. racketeers are generally engaged in fully legitimate enterprises
    C. many people want services which are not obtainable through legitimate sources
    D. the racketeers are well organized
    E. laws prohibiting gambling and prostitution are unenforceable

75. According to the above paragraph, racketeering, unlike theft, involves
    A. objects of value B. payment for goods received
    C. organized gangs D. public approval
    E. unlawful activities

Question 76-78.

DIRECTIONS: Questions 76 through 78 are to be answered on the basis of the following paragraph.

A number of crimes, such as robbery, assault, rape, certain forms of theft and burglary, are highly visible crimes in that it is apparent to all concerned that they are criminal acts prior to or at the time they are committed. In contrast to these, check forgeries, especially those committed by first offenders, have low visibility. There is little in the criminal act or in the interaction between the check passer and the person cashing the check to identify it as a crime. Closely related to this special quality of the forgery crime is the fact that, while it is formally defined and treated as a felonious or infamous crime, it is informally held by the legally untrained public to be a relatively harmless form of crime.

76. According to the above paragraph, crimes of high visibility
    A. are immediately recognized as crimes by the victims
    B. take place in public view
    C. always involve violence or the threat of violence
    D. usually are committed after dark
    E. can be observed from a distance

77. According to the above paragraph,
    A. the public regards check forgery as a minor crime
    B. the law regards check forgery as a minor crime
    C. the law distinguishes between check forgery and other forgery
    D. it is easier to spot inexperienced check forgers than other criminals
    E. it is more difficult to identify check forgers than other criminals

78. As used in the above paragraph, an *infamous* crime is
    A. a crime attracting great attention from the public
    B. more serious than a felony
    C. less serious than a felony
    D. more or less serious than a felony, depending upon the surrounding circumstances
    E. the same as a felony

Question 79-81.

DIRECTIONS: Questions 79 through 81 are to be answered on the basis of the following paragraph.

Criminal science is largely the science of identification. Progress in this field has been marked and sometimes very spectacular because new techniques, instruments, and facts flow continuously from the scientist. But the crime laboratories are undermanned, trade secrets still prevail, and inaccurate conclusions are often the result. However, modern gadgets cannot substitute for the skilled intelligent investigator; he must be their master.

79. According to the above paragraph, criminal science
    A. excludes the field of investigation
    B. is primarily interested in establishing identity
    C. is based on the equipment used in crime laboratories
    D. uses techniques different from those used in other sciences
    E. is essentially secret in nature

80. Advances in criminal science have been, according to the above paragraph,
    A. extremely limited   B. slow but steady
    C. unusually reliable   D. outstanding
    E. infrequently worthwhile

81. A problem that has not been overcome completely in crime work is, according to the above paragraph,
    A. unskilled investigators
    B. the expense of new equipment and techniques
    C. an insufficient number of personnel in crime laboratories
    D. inaccurate equipment used in laboratories
    E. conclusions of the public about the value of this field

81.____

Question 82-84.

DIRECTIONS: Questions 82 through 84 are to be answered on the basis of the following paragraph.

The New York City Police Department will accept for investigation no report of a person missing from his residence if such residence is located outside of New York City. The person reporting same will be advised to report such fact to the police department of the locality where the missing person lives, which will, if necessary, communicate officially with the New York City Police Department. However, a report will be accepted of a person who is missing from a temporary residence in New York City, but the person making the report will be instructed to make a report also to the police department of the locality where the missing person lives.

82. According to the above paragraph, a report to the New York City Police Department of a missing person whose permanent residence is outside of New York City will
    A. always be investigated provided that a report is also made to his local police authorities
    B. never be investigated unless requested officially by his local police authorities
    C. be investigated in cases of temporary New York City residence, but a report should always be made to his local police authorities
    D. be investigated if the person making the report is a New York City resident
    E. always be investigated and a report will be made to the local police authorities by the New York City Police Department

82.____

83. Of the following, the MOST likely reason for the procedure described in the above paragraph is that
    A. non-residents are not entitled to free police service from New York City
    B. local police authorities would resent interference in their jurisdiction
    C. local police authorities sometimes try to unload their problems on the New York City Police
    D. local police authorities may be better able to conduct an investigation
    E. few persons are erroneously reported as missing

83.____

84. Mr. Smith, who lives in Jersey City, and Mr. Jones, who lives in Newark, arrange to meet in New York City, but Mr. Jones does not keep the appointment. Mr. Smith telephones Mr. Jones several times the next day and gets no answer. Mr. Smith believes that something has happened to Mr. Jones.

84.____

According to the above paragraph, Mr. Smith should apply to the police authorities of
- A. Jersey City
- B. Newark
- C. Newark and New York City
- D. Jersey City and New York City
- E. Newark, Jersey City, and New York City

Question 85-87.

DIRECTIONS: Questions 85 through 87 are to be answered on the basis of the following paragraph.

Some early psychologists believed that the basic characteristic of the criminal type was inferiority of intelligence, if not outright feeblemindedness. They were misled by the fact that they had measurements for all kinds of criminals but, until World War I gave them a draft army sample, they had no information on a comparable group of non-criminal adults. As soon as acceptable measurements could be taken of criminals and a comparable group of non-criminals, concern with feeblemindedness or with low intelligence as a type took on less and less significance in research in criminology.

85. According to the above paragraph, some early psychologists were in error because they did not
    - A. distinguish among the various types of criminals
    - B. devise a suitable method of measuring intelligence
    - C. measure the intelligence of non-criminals as a basis for comparison
    - D. distinguish between feeblemindedness and inferiority of intelligence
    - E. clearly define the term *intelligence*

86. The above paragraph implies that studies of the intelligence of criminals and non-criminals
    - A. are useless because it is impossible to obtain comparable groups
    - B. are not meaningful because only the less intelligent criminals are detected
    - C. indicate that criminals are more intelligent than non-criminals
    - D. indicate that criminals are less intelligent than non-criminals
    - E. do not indicate that there are any differences between the two groups

87. According to the above paragraph, studies of World War I draft gave psychologists vital information concerning
    - A. adaptability to army life of criminals and non-criminals
    - B. criminal tendencies among draftees
    - C. the intelligence scores of large numbers of men
    - D. differences between intelligence scores of draftees and volunteers
    - E. the behavior of men under abnormal conditions

18 (#1)

Question 88-90.

DIRECTIONS: Questions 88 through 90 are to be answered on the basis of the following paragraph.

The use of a roadblock is simply an adaptation to police practices of the military concept of encirclement. Successful operation of a roadblock plan depends almost entirely on the amount of advance study and planning given to such operations. A thorough and detailed examination of the roads and terrain under the jurisdiction of a given police agency should be made with the locations of the roadblocks pinpointed in advance The first principle to be borne in mind in the location of each roadblock is the time element. Its location must be at a point beyond which the fugitive could not have possibly traveled in the time elapsed from the commission of the crime to the arrival of the officers at the roadblock.

88. According to the above paragraph, 88.____
    A. military operations have made extensive use of roadblocks
    B. the military concept of encirclement is an adaptation of police use of roadblocks
    C. the technique of encirclement has been widely used by military forces
    D. a roadblock is generally more effective than encirclement
    E. police use of roadblocks is based on the idea of military encirclement

89. According to the above paragraph, 89.____
    A. the factor of time is the sole consideration in the location of a roadblock
    B. the maximum speed possible in the method of escape is of major importance in roadblock location
    C. the time of arrival of officers at the site of a proposed roadblock is of little importance
    D. if the method of escape is not known, it should be assumed that the escape is by automobile
    E. a roadblock should be sited as close to the scene of the crime as the terrain will permit

90. According to the above paragraph, 90.____
    A. advance study and planning are of minor importance in the success of roadblock operations
    B. a thorough and detailed examination of all roads within a radius of fifty miles should precede the determination of a roadblock location
    C. consideration of terrain features is important in planning the location of roadblocks
    D. the pinpointing of roadblocks should be performed before any advance study is made
    E. a roadblock operation can seldom be successfully undertaken by a single police agency

KEY (CORRECT ANSWERS)

1. E	21. E	41. B	61. C	81. C
2. C	22. A	42. E	62. A	82. C
3. A	23. A	43. B	63. D	83. D
4. A	24. C	44. D	64. B	84. B
5. D	25. D	45. D	65. C	85. C
6. C	26. B	46. D	66. D	86. E
7. B	27. D	47. C	67. E	87. C
8. A	28. A	48. D	68. D	88. E
9. C	29. E	49. C	69. D	89. B
10. A	30. C	50. A	70. B	90. C
11. D	31. E	51. B	71. B	
12. A	32. C	52. A	72. D	
13. E	33. B	53. D	73. A	
14. E	34. C	54. D	74. C	
15. E	35. B	55. C	75. B	
16. A	36. A	56. B	76. A	
17. B	37. E	57. D	77. A	
18. E	38. D	58. D	78. E	
19. B	39. A	59. C	79. B	
20. C	40. B	60. C	80. D	

EXAMINATION SECTION

TEST 1

DIRECTIONS: Each question or incomplete statement is followed by several suggested answers or completions. Select the one that BEST answers the question or completes the statement. *PRINT THE LETTER OF THE CORRECT ANSWER IN THE SPACE AT THE RIGHT.*

1. Many officers working in the field of juvenile delinquency accept youth gangs as a natural development in community life.
   If this assumption is correct, the one of the following which would be the MOST practical course of action with respect to youth gangs is to
   A. utilize the activity of the gang, diverting it from the criminal to the constructive
   B. change the structure of community life so that gangs will no longer be a natural development
   C. ignore youth gangs and concentrate on youthful offenders
   D. encourage younger members of gangs to break away from the gang leaders
   E. set up an interesting lecture and demonstration course pointing out the evils of gang warfare

2. An officer who is called to the scene of an automobile accident questions two witnesses concerning the accident. The officer knows that the two witnesses are outstanding and upright members of the community. The two witnesses give contradictory testimony.
   He should conclude that the MOST likely reason for the contradiction is that
   A. honest, upright people do not always make the best witnesses
   B. at least one of the witnesses has been upset by the questioning
   C. people do not always observe accurately
   D. at least one of the witnesses is lying
   E. contradictions in cases of this sort are inevitable

3. An officer, making his rounds, notices that one storekeeper has not cleared the snow from the sidewalk in front of his store. After reminding the storekeeper that he is breaking the law if the sidewalk is not cleared, the officer also points out that a dangerous situation may arise if ice forms.
   This method of handling the situation by the officer is USUALLY
   A. *bad*; the storekeeper broke the law and should be punished
   B. *good*; the storekeeper will clear the sidewalk and no one will be hurt
   C. *bad*; the patrolman should have forced the storekeeper to clear the sidewalk of snow immediately
   D. *good*; threatening severe punishment is the most desirable method to achieve compliance with the law
   E. *bad*; the patrolman should not have mentioned the law but asked the storekeeper to clear the walk as a personal favor to him

4. About 9:00 P.M., an officer observes two men loitering near a neighborhood movie theatre. He has not seen either of these two men in the neighborhood before. The agent for the theatre generally deposits the night receipts in the local bank's night deposit vault between 9:00 P.M. an 9:15 P.M.
Of the following, the MOST appropriate action for the officer to take is to
   A. approach the two men and tell them that no loitering is allowed near the theatre
   B. demand that they tell him their place of residence and the reason for their presence near the theatre
   C. pay no further attention since they are obviously waiting for some friend or relative who is in the theatre
   D. enter the theatre by the side entrance and warn the manager to be prepared for a possible attempt at robbery
   E. station himself so that he can observe their further actions until the theatre's money has been deposited

4._____

5. An officer stationed along the route of a parade has been ordered by his superior to allow no cars to cross the route while the parade is in progress. An ambulance driver on an emergency run attempts to drive his ambulance across the route while the parade is passing.
Under these circumstances, the officer should
   A. ask the driver to wait while the officer contacts his superior and obtains a decision
   B. stop the parade long enough to permit the ambulance to cross the street
   C. direct the ambulance driver to the shortest detour available which will add at least ten minutes to run
   D. hold up the ambulance in accordance with the superior's order
   E. advise the driver to telephone the hospital and notify his superior that he is being delayed by the parade

5._____

6. A woman has her husband arrested for severely beating his five-year-old son. A crowd of angry neighbors has gathered around the husband.
In making the arrest, the arresting officer should
   A. treat the husband like any other person accused of breaking the law
   B. deal with the husband sympathetically since the man may be mentally ill
   C. handle him harshly since his crime is a despicable one
   D. treat him roughly only if he shows no remorse for his actions
   E. let him be *roughed up* a bit by neighbors so long as he is not injured severely

6._____

7. An officer notices two students engaged in a fistfight in front of a high school. Three or four students have gathered around the fighting youngsters.
Of the following actions, the one the officer should take FIRST is to
   A. summon assistance before attending to the fight
   B. forcibly disperse the onlooking students and then attend to the belligerents
   C. try to separate the two belligerents without hurting either
   D. fire a shot into the air to warn the onlookers and the belligerents to disperse
   E. use his nightstick on the two belligerents to stop the fight

7._____

8. An officer who responded at 2 A.M. to a radio call that a burglary had been committed in an apartment heard the sound of clashing tools coming from the adjoining apartment.
   For the officer to investigate the noise would be
   A. *undesirable*; he may not search without a warrant
   B. *desirable*; the thief may be found
   C. *undesirable*; unusual noises in apartments are common
   D. *desirable*; the victim would tend to be impressed by the concern shown
   E. *undesirable*; the thief may be armed

8.____

9. An off-duty officer in civilian clothes is riding in the rear of a bus. He notices two teenage boys tampering with the rear emergency door.
   The MOST appropriate action for him to take is to
   A. watch the boys closely but take no action unless they actually open the emergency door
   B. report the boys' actions to the bus operator and let the bus operator take whatever action he deems best
   C. signal the bus operator to stop, show the boys his badge, and then order them off the bus
   D. show the boys his badge, order them to stop their actions, and take down their names and addresses
   E. tell the boys to discontinue their tampering, pointing out the dangers to life that their actions may create

9.____

10. At 3:00 A.M., while on his tour of duty, an officer notices a traffic light at an intersection is not operating. There is little traffic at this intersection.
    Under these circumstances, the MOST appropriate action for the officer to take is to
    A. report this matter to his superior at the end of his tour of duty
    B. station himself at the intersection to direct traffic until the appearance of daylight reduces the hazard of a collision
    C. report this matter immediately to his precinct
    D. post a sign at the intersection stating that the traffic light is not operating
    E. ignore the situation since nothing can be done at this time and the patrolman on the day shift can make the necessary report

10.____

Questions 11-15.

DIRECTIONS: Questions 11 through 15 are to be answered on the basis of the following Police Department rule.

A description of persons or property wanted by the Police Department, which is to be given to the police force through the medium of a general alarm, if not distinctive, is of no value.

11. Mrs. R. Jones reported the theft of a valuable brooch from her apartment. The brooch was of gold and consisted of a very large emerald surrounded by 50 small diamonds.
    The one of the following additional pieces of information which would be MOST helpful to you in identifying the brooch is that

11.____

A. the value of the brooch is $50,000
B. there are 48 small diamonds and 2 slightly larger diamonds
C. the emerald is carved in the form of a woman's head
D. the brooch is made of gold with a slightly green cast
E. the brooch is circular with the emerald in the center and the diamond around it

12. Assume that you have stopped a 2017 Dodge four-door sedan which you suspect is a car which had been reported as stolen the day before.
The one of the following items of information which would be of GREATEST value in determining whether this is the stolen car is that the
    A. stolen car's license number was QA 2356; this car's license number is U21375
    B. stolen car's engine number was AB 6231; this car's engine number is CS2315
    C. windshield of the stolen car was not cracked; this car's windshield is cracked
    D. stolen car had no dents; this car has numerous dents
    E. stolen car had white-walled tires; this car does not have white-walled tires

13. Assume that you are questioning a woman who, you suspect, is wanted by the Department.
Of the characteristics listed below, the one which would be of GREATEST value in determining whether this is the wanted person is:
    A. Age: about 30; Height: 5'8"; Weight: 160 lbs.
    B. Eyes: blue; Hair: blonde; Complexion: fair
    C. that she frequently drinks to excess
    D. Scars: two thin, half-moon scars just on right cheek bone and below eye
    E. that when last seen she was wearing a dark, grey wool dress and was accompanied by the prizefighter John Day

14. You are watching a great number of people leave the sports arena after a boxing match.
Of the characteristics listed below, the one which would be of GREATEST value to you in spotting a man wanted by the Department is
    A. Height: 5'3"; Weight: 200 lbs.
    B. Eyes: brown; Hair: black wavy; Complexion: sallow
    C. that he frequents bars and grills and customarily associates with females
    D. Scars: thin ½" scar on left upper lip; Tattoos: on right forearm – *Pinto*
    E. Mustache: when last seen August 2020, he wore a small black mustache

15. Assume that on a hot summer day you are stationed on the grass of the south bank of a busy parkway looking at eastbound traffic for a light blue 2015 Ford two-door sedan.
If traffic is very heavy, the one of the following additional pieces of information which would be MOST helpful to you in identifying the car is that
    A. all chrome is missing from the left side of the car
    B. there is a bullethole in the left front window

12.____

13.____

14.____

15.____

C. motor number is 22674 AH
D. the front bumper is missing
E. the paint on the right side of the car is somewhat faded

16. While you are on patrol, you notice that the lone occupant of a car parked at the top of a long, steep hill is a boy about 7 years old. The boy is playing with the steering wheel and other controls.
The FIRST action for you to take is to
    A. make sure that the car is safely parked
    B. test the car's emergency brake to make sure it will hold
    C. drive the car to the bottom of the hill and park it there
    D. test the car's controls to make sure that the boy has not changed anything
    E. order the boy to leave the car for his own safety

17. The proprietor of a tavern summons an officer and turns over to him a loaded revolver that was found in one of the tavern's booths.
Of the following, the LEAST appropriate action for the officer to take is to
    A. close off the booth from use by other patrons
    B. determine exactly when the revolver was found
    C. obtain the names or descriptions of the persons who occupied the both before the revolver was found
    D. question the proprietor very closely concerning the matter
    E. unload the gun and place it in an inside pocket

18. The traditional method of training an officer—equipping him and putting him on the street with an experienced man—is no longer adequate.
The one of the following which is the MOST probable reason for this change in viewpoint is that
    A. officers are no longer simply guardians of the peace but each one is a specialist
    B. the kind of recruit that the Police Department gets has changed
    C. the former belief that *the best way to learn is to do* is no longer accepted
    D. there has been a great change in police problems and methods
    E. more money has been made available for training purposes

19. An officer overhears a businessman complain that his sales of tires had fallen off sharply because a new competitor has suddenly appeared in his territory and is underselling him at unbelievably low prices. The officer recalls that a large shipment of tires had been reported stolen a short time ago.
It is ADVISABLE for the officer to
    A. forget the matter as it is probably a coincidence
    B. tell the businessman to report the new competitor to the Better Business Bureau for unfair practices
    C. check to see if there is any connection between the two sets of circumstances
    D. inform the businessman about the robbery and ask him if he thinks that there is a connection
    E. arrest the owner of the new store as he is obviously involved in the robbery

20. While patrolling his post in a section of the county late Saturday night, an officer notices a well-dressed man break a car window with a rock, open a front door, and enter. He is followed into the car by a woman companion.
Of the following, the MOST essential action for the officer to take is to
   A. point his gun at the man, enter the car, and order the man to drive to the station house to explain his action
   B. approach the car and ask the man why it was necessary to break the car window
   C. take down the license number of the car and note the description of both the man and the woman in the event that the car is later reported as stolen
   D. *bawl the man out* for endangering himself by breaking the window
   E. request proof of ownership of the car from the man

20.____

21. Juveniles who rob do not usually use the money they obtain in this manner for essentials but rather to indulge in spending to impress others.
This observation indicates that clues leading to the apprehension of juvenile delinquents may be found by noting
   A. family requirements and needs
   B. the recreation habits of young people
   C. which young people have a tendency to commit robbery
   D. the relationships which exist in criminal gangs between criminals who commit crimes to satisfy essential needs and those who do not
   E. what objects are taken in robberies

21.____

22. A storekeeper complains to an officer that his store window has been broken by a gang of neighborhood hoodlums. The officer tells the storekeeper to notify headquarters.
This action is
   A. *desirable*; the storekeeper will be able to tell the proper official his story firsthand
   B. *undesirable*; the problem is so minor that there is no need to bother headquarters
   C. *desirable*; the storekeeper will be more confidant if his case is handled by a sergeant or lieutenant
   D. *undesirable*; buckpassing of this type makes for inefficiency and poor public relations
   E. *desirable*; investigation of the case would take the officer away from his post for too long a period

22.____

23. In order to reduce the amount of contradictory testimony, the witnesses to a crime should be allowed to discuss, as a group what had happened before they are questioned.
The procedure suggested is
   A. *bad*; a witness is less likely to commit himself if other witnesses to the event are present
   B. *good*; the need to sift stories will be considerably reduced

23.____

C. *bad*; a witness is less likely to blurt out the truth if other witnesses are present to give him moral backing
D. *good*; witnesses will be more apt to recall exactly what happened
E. *bad*; the views of the strongest personalities may be obtained rather than the truth

24. An officer positively recognizes a man on a busy street as one wanted for passing worthless checks.
Of the following, the MOST appropriate action for the officer to take is to
   A. approach and then arrest the man
   B. follow the man until a place is reached where there are few people; then take out his gun and arrest the man
   C. immediately take out his gun, stop the man, and search him
   D. follow the man until he stops long enough for the patrolman to summon aid from his precinct
   E. follow the man as he may lead the way to associates

24.____

25. It is generally agreed that criminal tendencies are present in every person. A basic difference, however, between the normal person and the criminal is that the
   A. normal person, sometimes, commits trivial crimes but the criminal commits crimes of a major nature
   B. criminal is unable to understand the possible results of antisocial acts he commits
   C. normal person is able to control his antisocial tendencies and direct his activity in socially approved channels
   D. criminal believes that he is not different from the person who does not commit crimes
   E. normal person believes that he is not different from the person who commits crimes

25.____

26. It has been claimed that a person who commits a crime sometimes has an unconscious wish to be punished, which is caused by strong unconscious feelings of guilt.
The one of the following actions by a criminal which may be partly due to an unconscious desire for punishment is
   A. claiming that he doesn't know anything about the crime when he is questioned by the police
   B. running away from the state where he committed the crime
   C. revisiting the place where he committed the crime
   D. his care not to leave any clues at the scene of the crime
   E. accusing someone else when he is captured by the police

26.____

27. Experience has shown that many crimes have been planned in prison.
From this finding, it is REASONABLE to assume that
   A. the principal motive for the commission of first crimes is the wish to take revenge on society
   B. some criminals may be influenced to continue their careers of crime because they associate with other criminals

27.____

C. the real motives for the commission of most crimes originate in punishment for criminal acts
D. fear or imprisonment will make a criminal who has been in jail plan his second crime more carefully
E. the criminal mind is sharpened by maturity

28. Any change in insurance coverage immediately prior to a fire should be considered. Strange as it may seem, most such changes made by convicted arsonists are made to a smaller amount.
The MOST probable reason for such changes is that the arsonist
    A. usually is not a rational person
    B. decided to set the fire after the change was made
    C. did not have enough money to pay for the full amount
    D. reduced the insurance to the amount he expected to be lost in the fire
    E. was trying to divert suspicion

28._____

29. Suppose that you are an officer whose tour of duty extends from 12 Midnight to 8:00 A.M. While on the first round of your tour, you notice that the nightlight in the front of a small candy store is out. In the past, the proprietor has always left the light on. The door to the store is locked.
Of the following, the MOST appropriate action for you to take FIRST is to
    A. use your flashlight to light the store interior so that you may inspect it for unusual conditions
    B. continue on your beat since the light probably burned out
    C. break open the door lock so that you may conduct a thorough search of the store
    D. call the storekeeper to notify him that the nightlight is out
    E. call your precinct and report this unusual condition

29._____

30. A criminal becomes either a thief, an assailant, or a sexual offender, never an all-around criminal.
Of the following, an IMPORTANT reason for these basic differences in criminal behavior is probably that
    A. to be an all-around criminal requires more intelligence than the average criminal has
    B. crime syndicates have gained control over certain branches of crime and have made it difficult for a beginner to break in
    C. criminal acts are an expression of the criminal's whole personality
    D. all-around crime is not as profitable as specialization in crime
    E. most crimes are committed on the spur of the moment and without previous thought

30._____

31. A young man who was arrested for smashing a store window and stealing a portable radio was asked why he did it. He answered, *Well, I wanted a radio and I just took it.*
If this answer is characteristic of the behavior of the young criminal, it is MOST reasonable to believe that

31._____

A. the young criminal has a well-organized personality
B. he sizes up each new situation in terms of his past experiences
C. his decision to commit a crime is made after careful consideration of its possible effect on his future
D. his temptation to commit a crime is an isolated situation, having, in his mind, little relation to his life as a whole
E. he hesitates to commit a crime unless he thinks he can get away with it

32. When the bodies of two women were found stabbed in an inner room of an apartment, it was first believed that it was a case of mutual homicide.
Of the following clues found at the scene, the one which indicates that it was more likely a case of murder by a third party is the fact that
    A. the door to the apartment was found locked
    B. there were bloodstains on the outer door of the apartment
    C. there was a switchblade knife in each body
    D. no money could be found in the room where the bodies were
    E. both women were fully clothed

32.____

33. A radio crime program dramatizing a different police case every week showed the capture or death of the criminal and ended with the slogan *Crime Does Not Pay*. It was found that a gang of teenage boys listened to this program every week in order to see what mistake was made by the criminal, and then duplicated the crime, trying to avoid the same mistake.
This case illustrates that
    A. all criminal minds work the same way
    B. attempts to keep young people out of crime by frightening them into obeying the law are not always successful
    C. it is not possible to commit the perfect crime unless care is taken
    D. radio crime programs should not be permitted as they lead to an increase in the number of unsolved crimes
    E. most criminals learn from their own mistakes

33.____

34. While on patrol at 2 A.M., you notice a man and a woman walking down the street talking together in low tones. They do not see you as you are standing in the shadow. The pair stop in front of a large apartment house. The man takes a bunch of keys from his pocket and tries several before he finds one which will open the door. While he is doing this, the woman taps her foot impatiently.
At this point, as the two are entering the apartment house, you should
    A. notify precinct headquarters of the incident
    B. permit them to enter but follow close behind them to see what they do
    C. ignore the incident and continue on your patrol
    D. force them to show their identification papers
    E. arrest them on suspicion of illegal entry

34.____

35. The one of the following which is the probable reason for restricting parking to alternate sides of some streets on successive days is that, without this restriction, the parked cars make it difficult for the
    A. Police Department to direct traffic
    B. Department of Water Supply, Gas and Electricity to service hydrants

35.____

C. Traffic Department to plan the flow of traffic
D. Sanitation Department to clear the streets
E. Fire Department to put out fires

36. Looking through the window of a jewelry store, an officer sees a man take a watch from the counter and drop it into his pocket while the jeweler is busy talking to someone else. The man looks around the store and then walks out. The officer should
    A. follow the man to see what he does with the watch as thieves of this type usually work in pairs
    B. ignore the incident; if the man were performing an illegal act, the jeweler would have called for help
    C. arrest the man, take him to the station house, and then return to obtain the jeweler's statement
    D. ignore the incident; if the man were a thief, the jeweler would not have left the watches unattended
    E. stop the man and bring him back into the shop so that both he and the jeweler can be questioned

36.____

37. It is quite possible to set up a general procedure which will result in the rehabilitation of all juvenile delinquents.
    This statement is, in general
    A. *correct*; the major causes of all juvenile delinquency are improper home life and a general lack of morals; cure these and there will be no problem of juvenile delinquency
    B. *not correct*; juvenile delinquency results from the generally lower moral climate; therefore, rehabilitation is not possible until the world climate changes
    C. *correct*; if juvenile delinquents are severely punished, rehabilitation will follow
    D. *not correct*; each case of juvenile delinquency is different and for most effective treatment must be hand on an individual basis
    E. *correct*: if the proper general procedure is set up, it always can be applied

37.____

38. An officer observes a young man who is obviously very excited, walking unusually fast, and repeatedly halting to look behind him. Upon stopping the young man, the officer finds that he is carrying a gun and has just held up a liquor store a few blocks away.
    This incidence illustrates that
    A. circumstances that are not suspicious in themselves frequently provide clues for the solution of crimes
    B. an experienced officer can pick the criminal type out of a crowd by alert observation
    C. action is always to be preferred to thought
    D. an officer should investigate suspicious circumstances
    E. an officer who stops to think may sometimes fail to get his man

38.____

39. When making arrests, the officer should treat all suspects in the same manner. This suggested rule is
    A. *undesirable*; the specific problems presented should govern the officer's actions
    B. *desirable*; this is the only democratic solution to the problem
    C. *undesirable*; officers should not be expected to abide by rules as criminals do not
    D. *desirable*; only by setting up fixed and rigid rules can patrolmen know what is expected of them
    E. *undesirable*; persons who are only suspected are not criminals and should not be treated as such

39._____

40. One of the most difficult questions in a crime prevention program is to decide how many men are needed to police a particular area. There have been a number of attempts to invent a simple formula, but none has so far been successful.
    Of the following reasons for this, the MOST probable is that
    A. men, not formulas, patrol beats
    B. many factors are involved whose relative importance has not been determined
    C. there is no information on which to base such a formula
    D. such a formula, even if it were accurate, would be of little use as it would be theoretical
    E. police problems in no two areas in the city are alike in any way

40._____

Questions 41-43.

DIRECTIONS: Questions 41 through 43 are to be answered on the basis of the following paragraph.

Modern police science may be said to have three phases. The first phase embraces the identification of living and dead persons. The second embraces the field work carried out by specially trained detectives at the scene of the crime. The third embraces methods used in the police laboratory to examine and analyze clues and traces discovered in the course of the investigation. While modern police science has had a striking influence on detective work and will surely further enhance its effectiveness, the time-honored methods, that is, knowledge of methods used by criminals, patience, tact, industry, thoroughness and imagination, will always be requisites for successful detective work.

41. According to the above paragraph, we may expect modern police science to
    A. help detective work more and more
    B. become more and more scientific
    C. depend less and less on the time-honored methods
    D. bring together the many different approaches to detective work
    E. play a less important role in detective work

41._____

42. According to the above paragraph, a knowledge of the procedures used by criminals is   42._____
    A. solely an element of the modern police science approach to detective work
    B. related to the identification of persons
    C. not related to detective field work
    D. related to methods used in the police laboratory
    E. an element of the traditional approach to detective work

43. Modern police science and practical detective work, according to the above paragraph,   43._____
    A. when used together can only lead to confusion
    B. are based on distinctly different theories of detective work
    C. have had strikingly different influences on detective work
    D. should both be used for successful detective work
    E. lead usually to similar results

Questions 44-47.

DIRECTIONS: Questions 44 through 47 are to be answered on the basis of the following paragraph.

A member of the force shall render reasonable aid to a sick or injured person. He shall summon an ambulance, if necessary, by telephoning the communications bureau of the borough, who shall notify the precinct concerned. If possible, he shall wait in full view of the arriving ambulance and take necessary action to direct the responding doctor or attendant to the patient without delay. If the ambulance does not arrive in twenty minutes, he shall send in a second call. However, if the sick person is in his or her home, a member of the force, before summoning an ambulance, will ascertain whether such person is willing to be taken to a hospital for treatment.

44. According to the above paragraph, if an officer wants to get an ambulance for a sick person, he should telephone   44._____
    A. the precinct concerned
    B. only if the sick person is in his home
    C. the nearest hospital
    D. only if the sick person is not in his home
    E. the borough communications bureau

45. According to the above paragraph, if an officer telephones for an ambulance and none arrives within twenty minutes, he should   45._____
    A. ask the injured person if he is willing to be taken to a hospital
    B. call the borough communications bureau
    C. call the precinct concerned
    D. attempt to give the injured person such assistance as he may need
    E. call the nearest hospital

46. An officer is called to help a woman who has fallen in her own home and has apparently broken her leg.
    According to the above paragraph, he should
    A. ask her if she wants to go to a hospital
    B. try to set her leg if it is necessary
    C. call for an ambulance at once
    D. attempt to get a doctor as quickly as possible
    E. not attempt to help the woman in any way before competent medical aid arrives

47. A man falls from a window into the backyard of an apartment house. Assume that you are an officer and that you are called to assist this man.
    According to the above paragraph, after you have called for an ambulance and comforted the injured man as much as you can, you should
    A. wait in front of the house for the ambulance
    B. ask the injured man if he wishes to go to the hospital for treatment
    C. remain with the injured man until the ambulance arrives
    D. send a bystander to direct the nearest doctor to the patient
    E. not ask the man to explain how the accident happened

Questions 48-50.

DIRECTIONS: Questions 48 through 50 are to be answered on the basis of the following paragraph.

What is required is a program that will protect our citizens and their property from criminal and anti-social acts, will effectively restrain and reform juvenile delinquents, and will prevent the further development of anti-social behavior. Discipline and punishment of offenders must necessarily play an important part in any such program. Serious offenders cannot be mollycoddled merely because they are under twenty-one. Restraint and punishment necessarily follow serious anti-social acts. But punishment, if it is to be effective, must be a planned part of a more comprehensive program of treating delinquency.

48. The one of the following goals NOT included among those listed above is to
    A. stop young people from defacing public property
    B. keep homes from being broken into
    C. develop an intra-city boys' baseball league
    D. change juvenile delinquents into useful citizens
    E. prevent young people from developing anti-social behavior patterns

49. According to the above paragraph, punishment is
    A. not satisfactory in any program dealing with juvenile delinquents
    B. the most effective means by which young vandals and hooligans can be reformed
    C. not used sufficiently when dealing with serious offenders who are under twenty-one
    D. of value in reducing juvenile delinquency only if it is part of a complete program
    E. most effective when it does not relate to specific anti-social acts

50. With respect to serious offenders who are under twenty-one, the above paragraph suggests that they 50.____
   A. be mollycoddled
   B. be dealt with as part of a comprehensive program to punish mature criminals
   C. should be punished
   D. be prevented, by brute force if necessary, from performing anti-social acts
   E. be treated as delinquent children who require more love than punishment

Questions 51-54.

DIRECTIONS: Questions 51 through 54 are to be answered on the basis of the following paragraph.

In all cases of homicide, members of the police department who investigate will make every effort to obtain statements from dying persons. Such statements are of the greatest importance to the District Attorney. In many cases, there may be a failure to solve the crime if they are not taken. The principal element to be considered in taking the declaration of a dying person is his mental attitude. In order to be admissible in evidence, the person must have no hope of recovery. The patient will be fully interrogated on that point before a statement is taken.

51. In cases of homicide, according to the above paragraph, members of the police force will 51.____
   A. try to change the mental attitude of the dying person
   B. attempt to obtain a statement from the dying person
   C. not give the information they obtain directly to the District Attorney
   D. be careful not to injure the dying person unnecessarily
   E. prevent unauthorized persons from taking dying declarations

52. The mental attitude of the person making the dying statement is of great importance because it can determine, according to the above paragraph, whether the 52.____
   A. victim should be interrogated in the presence of witnesses
   B. victim will be willing to make a statement of any kind
   C. victim has been forced to make the statement
   D. statement will tell the District Attorney who committed the crime
   E. statement can be used as evidence

53. District Attorneys find that statements of a dying person are important, according to the above paragraph, because 53.____
   A. it may be that the victim will recover and then refuse to testify
   B. they are important elements in determining the mental attitude of the victim
   C. they present a point of view
   D. it may be impossible to punish the criminal without such a statement
   E. dead men tell no tales

54. A well-known gangster is found dying from a bullet wound. The officer first on the scene, in the presence of witnesses, tells the man that he is going to die and asks, *Who shot you?* The gangster says, *Jones shot me, but he hasn't killed me. I'll live to get him.* He then falls back dead.
According to the above paragraph, this statement is
   A. *admissible* in evidence; the man was obviously speaking the truth
   B. *not admissible* in evidence; the man obviously did not believe that he was dying
   C. *admissible* in evidence; there were witnesses to the statement
   D. *not admissible* in evidence; the victim did not sign any statement and the evidence is merely hearsay
   E. *admissible* in evidence; there was no time to interrogate the victim

54.____

Questions 55-57.

DIRECTIONS: Questions 55 through 57 are to be answered on the basis of the following paragraph.

The factors contributing to crime and delinquency are varied and complex. The home and its immediate environment have been found to be crucial in determining the behavior patterns of the individual, and criminality can frequently be traced to faulty family relationships and a bad neighborhood. But in the search for a clearer understanding of the underlying causes of delinquent and criminal behavior, the total environment must be taken into consideration.

55. According to the above paragraph, family relationships
   A. tend to become faulty in bad neighborhoods
   B. are important in determining the actions of honest people as well as criminals
   C. are the only important element in the understanding of causes of delinquency
   D. are determined by the total environment
   E. of criminals are understandable only in terms of the behavior patterns of the individuals concerned

55.____

56. According to the above paragraph, the causes of crime and delinquency are
   A. not simple   B. not meaningless
   C. meaningless   D. simple
   E. always understandable

56.____

57. According to the above paragraph, faulty family relationships frequently are
   A. responsible for varied and complex results
   B. caused by differences
   C. caused when one or both parents have a criminal behavior pattern
   D. independent of the total environment
   E. the cause of criminal acts

57.____

Questions 58-60.

DIRECTIONS: Questions 58 through 60 are to be answered on the basis of the following paragraph.

A change in the specific problems which confront the police and in the methods for dealing with them has taken place in the last few decades. The automobile is a two-way symbol of this change in policing. It menaces every city with a complicated traffic problem and has speeded up the process of committing a crime and making a getaway, but at the same time has increased the effectiveness of police operations. However, the major concern of police departments continues to be the anti-social or criminal actions and behavior of human beings.

58. On the basis of the above paragraph, it can be stated that for the most part in the past few decades the specific problems of a police force
    A. have changed but the general problems have not
    B. as well as the general problems have changed
    C. have remained the same but the general problems have changed
    D. as well as the general problems have remained the same
    E. have caused changes in the general problems

59. According to the above paragraph, advances in science and industry have, in general, made the police
    A. operations less effective from the overall point of view
    B. operations more effective from the overall point of view
    C. abandon older methods of solving police problems
    D. concern themselves more with the anti-social acts of human beings
    E. concern themselves less with the anti-social acts of human beings

60. The automobile is a two-way symbol, according to the above paragraph, because its use
    A. has speeded up getting to, and away from, the scene of a crime
    B. both helps and hurts police operations
    C. introduces a new anti-social act—traffic violation—and does away with criminals like horse thieves
    D. both increases and decreases speed by introducing traffic problems
    E. helps people get to the city but prevents them from moving once they are there

Questions 61-80.

DIRECTIONS: In each of Questions 61 through 80, select the lettered word or phrase which means MOST NEARLY the same as, or the opposite of, the capitalized word.

61. VINDICTIVE
    A. centrifugal   B. forgiving   C. molten
    D. tedious   E. vivacious

17 (#1)

62. SCOPE
 A. compact   B. detriment   C. facsimile
 D. potable   E. range

63. HINDER
 A. amplify   B. aver   C. method
 D. observe   E. retard

64. IRATE
 A. adhere   B. angry   C. authentic
 D. peremptory   E. vacillate

65. APATHY
 A. accessory   B. availability   C. fervor
 D. pacify   E. stride

66. LUCRATIVE
 A. effective   B. imperfect   C. injurious
 D. timely   E. worthless

67. DIVERSITY
 A. convection   B. slip   C. temerity
 D. uniformity   E. viscosity

68. OVERT
 A. laugh   B. lighter   C. orifice
 D. quay   E. sly

69. SPORADIC
 A. divide   B. encumbrance   C. livid
 D. occasional   E. original

70. RESCIND
 A. annul   B. deride   C. extol
 D. indulge   E. insist

71. AUGMENT
 A. alter   B. decrease   C. obey
 D. perceive   E. supersede

72. AUTONOMOUS
 A. careless   B. conceptual   C. constant
 D. defamatory   E. independent

73. TRANSCRIPT
 A. copy   B. report   C. sentence
 D. termination   E. verdict

74. DISCORDANT
    A. astride   B. comprised   C. effusive
    D. harmonious   E. slick

75. DISTEND
    A. constrict   B. direct   C. redeem

76. EMANATE
    A. bridge   B. coherency   C. conquer
    D. degrade   E. flow

77. EXULTANT
    A. easily upset   B. in bad taste
    C. in high spirits   D. subject to moods
    E. very much over-priced

78. PREVARICATE
    A. hesitate   B. increase   C. lie
    D. procrastinate E. reject

79. COGNIZANT
    A. obvious   B. search   C. stupid
    D. suspicious   E. unaware

80. CREDIBLE
    A. daring   B. helpful   C. surreptitious
    D. unbelievable E. uncontrollable

81. Assume that a parking space for six cars is to be outlined with white paint. The total area to be outlined is 24 feet by 40 feet, and the space for each car, also marked off by white lines, is to be 8 feet by 20 feet.
    The total length of white lines to be painted is MOST NEARLY _____ feet.
    A. 64   B. 128   C. 156   D. 184   E. 232

82. A police car is ordered to report to the scene of a crime 5 miles away.
    If the car travels at an average rate of 40 miles per hour, the length of time it will take to reach its destination is MOST NEARLY _____ minutes.
    A. 3   B. 7   C. 10   D. 13   E. 16

83. A block has metered parking for 19 cars from 7 A.M. to 9 P.M. at a charge of $4 per hour.
    Assuming that each car that is parked remains for a full hour and that on an average for each hour of parking there is a vacancy of five minutes for each meter, the amount of revenue from the meters for a day will be MOST NEARLY
    A. $400   B. $600   C. $800   D. $1000   E. $1200

84. The standard formula for the stopping distance of a car with all four wheels locked is $S = \frac{V \text{ times } V}{30W}$ where S is the stopping distance in feet, V the speed of the car in miles per hour at the moment the brakes are applied, and W is a number which depends on the friction between the tires and the road.
If the speed of a car is 50 miles per hour and W is equal to 5/3, the stopping distance will be MOST NEARLY _____ feet.
   A. 30   B. 40   C. 50   D. 60   E. 70

84._____

85. The radiator of a police car contains 20 quarts of a mixture consisting of 80% water and 20% anti-freeze compound. Assume that you have been ordered to draw off some of the mixture and add pure anti-freeze compound until the mixture is 75% water and 25% anti-freeze compound.
The number of quarts of the mixture which should be removed is MOST NEARLY
   A. 2   B. 3   C. 4   D. 5   E. 6

85._____

Questions 86-90.

DIRECTIONS: Questions 86 through 90 are to be answered on the basis of the following table.

	FATAL HIGHWAY ACCIDENTS					
	Drivers Over 18 Years of Age			Drivers 18 Years of Age & Under		
	Auto	Other Vehicles	Total	Auto	Other Vehicles	Total
January	43	0	43	4	0	4
February	52	0	52	10	0	10
March	36	0	36	8	0	8
April	50	0	50	17	0	17
May	40	2	42	5	0	5
June	26	0	26	8	0	8
July	29	0	29	6	0	6
August	29	1	30	6	0	3
September	36	0	36	4	0	4
October	45	1	46	2	1	3
November	54	1	55	3	0	3
December	66	1	67	0	0	6
TOTALS	506	6	512	76	1	77

86. The average number of fatal auto accidents per month involving drivers older than sixteen was MOST NEARLY
   A. 42   B. 43   C. 44   D. 45   E. 46

86._____

87. The total number of fatal highway accidents was
   A. 506   B. 512   C. 562   D. 582   E. 589

87._____

88. The month during which the LOWEST number of fatal highway accidents occurred was
    A. March   B. June   C. July
    D. August   E. September

89. Of the total number of fatal highway accidents involving drivers older than 18, the percentage of accidents which took place during December is MOST NEARLY
    A. 10   B. 13   C. 16   D. 19   E. 22

90. The GREATEST percentage drop in fatal accidents occurred from
    A. February to March   B. April to May   C. June to July
    D. July to August   E. August to September

KEY (CORRECT ANSWERS)

1.	A	21.	B	41.	A	61.	B	81.	E
2.	C	22.	D	42.	E	62.	E	82.	B
3.	B	23.	E	43.	D	63.	E	83.	D
4.	E	24.	A	44.	E	64.	B	84.	C
5.	B	25.	C	45.	B	65.	C	85.	A
6.	A	26.	C	46.	A	66.	E	86.	A
7.	C	27.	B	47.	A	67.	D	87.	E
8.	B	28.	E	48.	C	68.	E	88.	D
9.	E	29.	A	49.	D	69.	D	89.	B
10.	C	30.	C	50.	C	70.	A	90.	B
11.	C	31.	D	51.	B	71.	B		
12.	B	32.	B	52.	E	72.	E		
13.	D	33.	B	53.	D	73.	A		
14.	A	34.	C	54.	B	74.	D		
15.	D	35.	D	55.	B	75.	A		
16.	A	36.	E	56.	A	76.	E		
17.	E	37.	D	57.	E	77.	C		
18.	D	38.	D	58.	A	78.	C		
19.	C	39.	A	59.	B	79.	E		
20.	E	40.	B	60.	B	80.	D		

EXAMINATION SECTION

DIRECTIONS: Each question consists of a statement. Your are to indicate whether the statement is TRUE (T) or FALSE (F). *PRINT THE LETTER OF THE CORRECT ANSWER IN THE SPACE AT THE RIGHT.*

1. An amendment to the Constitution of the United States provides that no person shall be elected to the office of the President more than twice. 1.____

2. The United States Secret Service is under the jurisdiction of the Department of the Treasury. 2.____

3. The terms of office of U.S. Senators and Representatives are identical. 3.____

4. Determination of the design, type, size and location of all traffic devices, signs and signals in the city is a function of the Traffic Division of the Police Department. 4.____

5. The transportation of criminals is a responsibility of the Department of Correction. 5.____

6. To secure an indictment, 12 members of the Grand Jury must vote in favor thereof. 6.____

7. In case of death from other than natural causes, it is the duty of the Chief Medical Examiner in the city to take charge of the body, examine witnesses and, if necessary, perform an autopsy. 7.____

8. An immigrant can become a naturalized American citizen without giving up his allegiance to the country in which he was born. 8.____

9. A wife can never be a witness against her husband. 9.____

10. All judges of the State Supreme Court are chosen by the Governor with the approval of the State Legislature. 10.____

11. A referendum is the submitting of a measure to the people for approval at an election. 11.____

12. An accused person can be immediately discharged if the jury's verdict is one of acquittal. 12.____

13. A defendant who receives a suspended sentence is deemed innocent of the crime for which he was tried. 13.____

14. The Appellate Division is a part of the Supreme Court of the State. 14.____

15. The power inherent in a government to enact laws to promote the order, safety and health of society is called eminent domain. 15.____

16. After a "pocket veto" the only way to enact a measure into law is to start a new bill in a later session of Congress. 16.____

17. A corporation cannot be charged with the commission of a crime. 17.____

18. The same act may give rise to both civil and criminal liability. 18.____

19. A person can be charged with a crime only if he had the intention of breaking the law when he committed it. 19.____

20. A statute which increases the punishment for an offense after it has been committed is an "ex post facto" law.   20.____

21. To condone an act is to provide a penalty for its commission.   21.____

22. If a person is charged with having performed a particular act wantonly, it means he performed the act in a negligent manner.   22.____

23. The term "corpus delicti" is used in connection with homicide cases to esignate the weapon used to inflict death.   23.____

24. The Bertillion System is a method of fingerprint classification.   24.____

25. A person can claim to have been placed in double jeopardy only if he as been twice convicted and imprisoned for the same crime.   25.____

26. The terms "latent" and "overt" both mean clearly visible.   26.____

27. The verb "harass" means to endanger.   27.____

28. One who uses duress to induce a person to perform an act, tricks that person into doing it willingly but unknowingly.   28.____

29. The term "venue" relates to the place of trial of a civil or criminal action.   29.____

30. The terms "motive" and "intent" are synonymous in crim inal law.   30.____

31. The direct or immediate cause of an injury is called the proximate cause.   31.____

32. Fingerprints are the most reliable means of identifying individuals.   32.____

33. Improper handling of a simple fracture often produces a compound fracture.   33.____

34. In cases of poisoning, the stomach should first be thoroughly washed.   34.____

35. Keeping the body of the patient warm is the most important thing both in treating and preventing shock.   35.____

36. Artificial respiration is a recommended first aid meas ure in all cases of unconsciousness.   36.____

37. In administering first aid for practically all types of injuries, it is important to use measures designed to prevent shock.   37.____

38. The sentence, "Four weeks is a long time to wait," should read, "Four weeks are a long time to wait."   38.____

39. The sentence, "He looked forward to our coming," should read, "He looked forward to us coming."   39.____

40. The sentence, "Intelligence is his principle asset," should read, "Intelligence is his principal asset."   40.____

41. The sentence, "He failed to follow the sergeant's counsel," should read, "He failed to follow the seargent's council."   41.____

42. The sentence, "The course of true love seldom runs smoothly," should read, "The coarse of true love seldom runs smoothly."   42.____

43. The sentence, "I am certain that was he," should read, "I am certain that was him."   43.____

44. The sentence, "He says that you are more clever than me", should read, "He says that you are more clever than I."   44.____

45. The sentence, "Who did you say that was?", should read "Whom did you say that was?".   45.____

46. The sentence, "Whomever you send will be satisfactory," should read, "Whoever you send will be satisfactory."   46.____

47. The past tense of "lay" is "lain."   47.____

48. The plural of "brother-in-law" is "brothers-in-law."   48.____

49. The Pentagon, which houses the offices of the Defense Department, is so called because it is a six-sided building.   49.____

50. William O. Douglas was a Chief Justice of the United States.   50.____

KEY (CORRECT ANSWERS)

1. T	11. T	21. F	31. T	41. F
2. T	12. T	22. F	32. T	42. F
3. T	13. F	23. F	33. T	43. F
4. F	14. T	24. F	34. F	44. T
5. T	15. F	25. F	35. T	45. T
6. T	16. T	26. F	36. F	46. F
7. T	17. F	27. F	37. T	47. F
8. F	18. T	28. F	38. F	48. T
9. F	19. F	29. T	39. F	49. F
10. F	20. T	30. F	40. T	50. F

PERSONALITY/AUTOBIOGRAPHICAL INVENTORY
EXAMINATION SECTION
TEST 1

DIRECTIONS: Each question or incomplete statement is followed by several suggested answers or completions. Select the one that BEST answers the question or completes the statement. *PRINT THE LETTER OF THE CORRECT ANSWER IN THE SPACE AT THE RIGHT.*

1. While a senior in high school, I was absent
    A. never
    B. seldom
    C. frequently
    D. more than 10 days
    E. only when I felt bored

2. While in high school, I failed classes
    A. never
    B. once
    C. twice
    D. more than twice
    E. at least four times

3. During class discussions in my high school classes, I usually
    A. listened without participating
    B. participated as much as possible
    C. listened until I had something to add to the discussion
    D. disagreed with others simply for the sake of argument
    E. laughed at stupid ideas

4. My high school grade point average (on a 4.0 scale) was
    A. 2.0 or lower
    B. 2.1 to 2.5
    C. 2.6 to 3.0
    D. 3.1 to 3.5
    E. 3.6 to 4.0

5. As a high school student, I completed my assignments
    A. as close to the due date as I could manage
    B. whenever the teacher gave me an extension
    C. frequently
    D. on time
    E. when they were interesting

6. While in high school, I participated in
    A. athletic and nonathletic extracurricular activities
    B. athletic extracurricular activities
    C. nonathletic extracurricular activities
    D. no extracurricular activities
    E. mandatory after-school programs

7. In high school, I made the honor roll 7.____
   A. several times
   B. once
   C. more than once
   D. twice
   E. I can't remember if I made the honor role

8. Upon graduation from high school, I received 8.____
   A. academic and nonacademic honors
   B. academic honors
   C. nonacademic honors
   D. no honors
   E. I can't remember if I received honors

9. While attending high school, I worked at a paid job or as a volunteer 9.____
   A. never
   B. every so often
   C. 5 to 10 hours a month
   D. more than 10 hours a month
   E. more than 15 hours a month

10. During my senior year of high school, I skipped school 10.____
    A. whenever I could
    B. once a week
    C. several times a week
    D. not at all
    E. when I got bored

11. I was suspended from high school 11.____
    A. not at all
    B. once or twice
    C. once or twice, for fighting
    D. several times
    E. more times than I can remember

12. During high school, my fellow students and teachers considered me 12.____
    A. above average
    B. below average
    C. average
    D. underachieving
    E. underachieving and prone to fighting

13. The ability to _____ is most important to a Police Officer 13.____
    A. draw his/her gun quickly
    B. see over great distances and difficult terrain
    C. verbally and physically intimidate criminals
    D. communicate effectively in circumstances which can be dangerous
    E. hear over great distances

14. I began planning for college 14.____
    A. when my parents told me to
    B. when I entered high school
    C. during my junior year
    D. during my senior hear
    E. when I signed up for my SAT (or other standardized exam)

15. An effective leader is someone who 15.____
    A. inspires confidence in his/her followers
    B. inspires fear in his/her followers
    C. tells subordinates exactly what they should do
    D. creates an environment in which subordinates feel insecure about their job security and performance
    E. makes as few decisions as possible

16. I prepared myself for college by 16.____
    A. learning how to get extensions on major assignments
    B. working as many hours as possible at my after-school job
    C. spending as much time with my friends as possible
    D. getting good grades and participating in extracurricular activities
    E. watching television shows about college kids

17. I paid for college by 17.____
    A. supplementing my parents contributions with my own earnings
    B. relying on scholarships, loans, and my own earnings
    C. relying on my parents and student loans
    D. relying on my parents to pay my tuition, room and board
    E. relying on sources not listed here

18. While a college student, I spent my summers and holiday breaks 18.____
    A. in summer or remedial classes   B. traveling
    C. working   D. relaxing
    E. spending time with my friends

19. My final college grade point average (on a 4.0 scale) was 19.____
    A. 3.8 to 4.0   B. 3.5 to 3.8   C. 3.0 to 3.5
    D. 2.5 to 3.0   E. 2.0 to 2.5

20. As a college student, I cut classes 20.____
    A. frequently   B. when I didn't like them
    C. sometimes   D. rarely
    E. when I needed the sleep

21. In college, I received academic honors 21.____
    A. not at all
    B. once
    C. twice
    D. several times
    E. I can't remember if I received academic honors

4 (#1)

22. While in college, I declared a major
    A. during my first year
    B. during my sophomore year
    C. during my junior year
    D. during my senior year
    E. several times

    22._____

23. While on patrol as a Police Officer, you spot someone attempting to flee the scene of a crime. Your first reaction is to
    A. draw your weapon
    B. observe the person until he or she completes the fleeing
    C. identify yourself as a Police Officer
    D. fire your weapon over the person's head in order to scare him or her
    E. call immediately for backup

    23._____

24. As a college student, I failed _____ classes.
    A. no
    B. two
    C. three
    D. four
    E. more than four

    24._____

25. Friends describe me as
    A. introverted
    B. hot-tempered
    C. unpredictable
    D. quiet
    E. easygoing

    25._____

KEY (CORRECT ANSWERS)

PLEASE NOTE: The answers listed are the best answers. However, you are to answer the exam honestly. Your personal answer may differ from the *best* answers.

1.	A		11.	A
2.	A		12.	A
3.	C		13.	D
4.	E		14.	B
5.	D		15.	A
6.	A		16.	D
7.	A		17.	B
8.	A		18.	C
9.	E		19.	A
10.	D		20.	D

21. D
22. A
23. C
24. A
25. E

TEST 2

DIRECTIONS: Each question or incomplete statement is followed by several suggested answers or completions. Select the one that BEST answers the question or completes the statement. *PRINT THE LETTER OF THE CORRECT ANSWER IN THE SPACE AT THE RIGHT.*

1. As a Police Officer, you apprehend three men whom you believe are in the country illegally. However, none of the men speaks English, and you don't speak their language.
   Your reaction should be to
   A. draw your weapon so that they understand the seriousness of the situation
   B. take them into custody, where they will have access to a translator
   C. attempt to communicate through hand gestures and shouting
   D. call for a translator to come and meet you at your location
   E. pretend you understand their language and apprehend them

   1.____

2. During my college classes, I preferred to
   A. remain silent during class discussions
   B. do other homework during class discussions
   C. participate frequently in class discussions
   D. argue with others as much as possible
   E. laugh at the stupid opinions of others

   2.____

3. As a Police Officer, you are chasing a small group of people who are running away from the scene of a crime. During your pursuit, one member of the group is left behind. You see that she is injured and in need of medical attention.
   Your reaction is to
   A. fire your weapon at the group members to get them to stop
   B. cease pursuit of the group members and take the woman into custody
   C. continue pursuit of the group members, leaving the woman behind since acting ill is a common trick
   D. radio for backup to stay with the woman while medical help arrives while you continue pursuit of the group members
   E. radio for backup to continue pursuit of the group members while you stay with the woman and wait for medical help to arrive

   3.____

4. As a college student, I was placed on academic probation
   A. not at all   B. once
   C. twice   D. three times
   E. more than three times

   4.____

5. At work, being a team player means to
   A. compromise your ideals and beliefs
   B. compensate for the incompetence of others
   C. count on others to compensate for my inexperience
   D. cooperate with others to get a project finished
   E. rely on others to get the job done

   5.____

6. As a Police Officer, you confront someone you believe has just committed a crime. After identifying yourself, you notice the suspect holding something that looks like a knife.
   Your FIRST reaction should be to
   A. draw your weapon and fire
   B. call immediately for backup
   C. keep your weapon drawn until you get the suspect into a position that is controllable
   D. ask the suspect if he is armed
   E. talk to the suspect without drawing your weapon

6.____

7. My friends from college remember me primarily as a(n)
   A. person who loved to party   B. ambitious student
   C. athlete   D. joker
   E. fighter

7.____

8. My college experience is memorable primarily because of
   A. the friends I made
   B. the sorority/fraternity I was able to join
   C. the social activities I participated in
   D. my academic achievements
   E. the money I spent

8.____

9. A friend who is applying for a job asks you to help him pass the mandatory drug test by substituting a sample of your urine for his.
   You should
   A. help him by supplying the sample
   B. help him by supplying the sample and insisting he seek drug counseling
   C. supply the sample, but tell him that this is the only time you'll help in this way
   D. call the police
   E. refuse

9.____

10. As a college student, I handed in my assignments
    A. when they were due   B. whenever I could get an extension
    C. when they were interesting D. when my friends reminded me to
    E. when I was able

10.____

11. At work you are accused of a minor infraction which you didn't commit.
    Your FIRST reaction is to
    A. call a lawyer
    B. speak to your supervisor about the mistake
    C. call the police
    D. yell at the person who did commit the infraction
    E. accept the consequences regardless of your guilt or innocence

11.____

12. While on patrol, you are surprised by a large group of disorderly teenage gang members. You are greatly outnumbered.
    As a Police Officer, your FIRST reaction is to
    A. draw your weapon and identify yourself
    B. get back into your vehicle and wait for help to arrive
    C. call for backup
    D. pretend you are part of a large group of police in the area
    E. identify yourself and get the group members into a controllable position

12.____

13. As a college student, I began to prepare for final exams
    A. the night before taking them
    B. when the professor handed out the review sheets
    C. several weeks before taking them
    D. when my friends began to prepare for their exams
    E. the morning of the exam

13.____

14. As a Police Officer in the field, you confront a small group of people you believe to be wanted criminals.
    Your MOST important consideration during this exchange should be
    A. apprehension of criminals
    B. safety of county citizens in nearby towns
    C. safety of the criminals
    D. number of criminals you must apprehend in order to receive a commendation'
    E. the amount of respect the criminals show to you and your position

14.____

15. At work, I am known as
    A. popular   B. quiet   C. intense
    D. easygoing   E. dedicated

15.____

16. The MOST important quality in a coworker is
    A. friendliness   B. cleanliness
    C. a good sense of humor   D. dependability
    E. good listening skills

16.____

17. In the past year, I have stayed home from work
    A. frequently   B. only when I felt depressed
    C. rarely   D. only when I felt overwhelmed
    E. only to run important errands

17.____

18. As a Police Officer, the BEST way to collect information from a suspect during an interview is to
    A. physically intimidate the suspect
    B. verbally intimidate the suspect
    C. threaten the suspect's family and/or friend with criminal prosecution
    D. encourage a conversation with the suspect
    E. sit in silence until the suspect begins speaking

18.____

19. For me, the BEST thing about college was the
    A. chance to strengthen my friendships and develop new ones
    B. chance to test my abilities and develop new ones
    C. number of extracurricular activities and clubs
    D. chance to socialize
    E. chance to try several different majors

19.____

20. As an employee, my WEAKEST skill is
    A. controlling my temper
    B. my organizational ability
    C. my ability to effectively understand directions
    D. my ability to effectively manage others
    E. my ability to communicate my thoughts in writing

20.____

21. As a Police Officer, my GREATEST strength would be
    A. my sense of loyalty
    B. my organizational ability
    C. punctuality
    D. dedication
    E. my ability to intimidate others

21.____

22. As a Police Officer, you find a group of suspicious youths gathered around a truck which is on fire.
    Your FIRST reaction is to
    A. call the fire department
    B. arrest them all for destruction of property
    C. draw your weapon and begin questioning them
    D. return to your vehicle and wait for the fire department
    E. instruct the group to remain while you return to your vehicle and request backup

22.____

23. If asked by my company to learn a new job-related skill, my reaction would be to
    A. ask for a raise
    B. ask for overtime pay
    C. question the necessity of the skill
    D. cooperate with some reluctance
    E. cooperate with enthusiasm

23.____

24. When I disagree with others, I tend to
    A. listen quietly despite my disagreement
    B. laugh openly at the person I disagree with
    C. ask the person to explain their views before I respond
    D. leave the conversation before my anger gets the best of me
    E. point out exactly why the person is wrong

24.____

5 (#2)

25. When I find myself in a situation which is confusing or unclear, my reaction is to
    A. pretend I am not confused
    B. remain calm and, if necessary, ask someone else for clarification
    C. grow frustrated and angry
    D. walk away from the situation
    E. immediately insist that someone explain things to me

25.____

KEY (CORRECT ANSWERS)

PLEASE NOTE: The answers listed are the best answers. However, you are to answer the exam honestly. Your personal answer may differ from the *best* answers.

1. B
2. C
3. E
4. A
5. D

6. C
7. B
8. D
9. E
10. A

11. B
12. E
13. C
14. A
15. E

16. D
17. C
18. D
19. B
20. E

21. D
22. A
23. E
24. C
25. B

TEST 3

DIRECTIONS: Each question or incomplete statement is followed by several suggested answers or completions. Select the one that BEST answers the question or completes the statement. *PRINT THE LETTER OF THE CORRECT ANSWER IN THE SPACE AT THE RIGHT.*

1. While on patrol as a Police Officer, you find a dead body lying in the open. Hiding a few feet away, behind some rocks, you find a suspicious person who is holding items which seem to have been taken from the dead body, including a pair of shoes and some jewelry.
   You should
   A. apprehend the suspect and bring him to the station for further questioning
   B. arrest the suspect for murder and robbery
   C. arrest the suspect for murder
   D. subdue the suspect with force and check the area for his accomplices
   E. subdue the suspect with force and call for backup to check the area for his accomplices

1.____

2. If you were placed in a supervisory position, which of the following abilities would you consider to be MOST important to your job performance?
   A. Stubborness
   B. The ability to hear all sides of a story before making a decision
   C. Kindness
   D. The ability to make and stick to a decision
   E. Patience

2.____

3. What is your HIGHEST level of education?
   A. Less than a high school diploma
   B. A high school diploma or equivalency
   C. A graduate of community college
   D. A graduate of a four-year accredited college
   E. A degree from graduate school

3.____

4. When asked to supervise other workers, your approach should be to
   A. ask for management wages since you're doing management work
   B. give the workers direction and supervise every aspect of the process
   C. give the workers direction and then allow them to do the job
   D. and the workers their job specifications
   E. do the work yourself, since you're uncomfortable supervising others

4.____

5. Which of the following BEST describes you?
   A. Need little or no supervision
   B. Resent too much supervision
   C. Require as much supervision as my peers
   D. Require slightly more supervision than my peers
   E. Require close supervision

5.____

6. You accept a job which requires an ability to perform several tasks at once. What is the BEST way to handle such a position?
   A. With strong organizational skills and a close attention to detail
   B. By delegating the work to someone with strong organizational skills
   C. Staying focused on one task at a time, no matter what happens
   D. Working on one task at a time until each task is successfully completed
   E. Asking my supervisor to help me

7. As a Police Officer, you take a suspected perpetrator into custody. After returning to the field, you notice that your gun is missing.
   You should
   A. retrace your steps to see if you dropped it somewhere
   B. report the loss immediately
   C. ask your partner to borrow his or her gun
   D. pretend that nothing's happened
   E. rely on your hands for defense and protection

8. Which of the following BEST describes your behavior when you disagree with someone?
   You
   A. state your own point of view as quickly and loudly as you can
   B. listen quietly and keep your opinions to yourself
   C. listen to the other person's perspective and then carefully point out all the flaws in their logic
   D. list all of the ignorant people who agree with the opposing point of view
   E. listen to the other person's perspective and then explain your own perspective

9. As a new Police Officer, you make several mistakes during your first week of work.
   You react by
   A. learning from your mistakes and moving on
   B. resigning
   C. blaming it on your supervisor
   D. refusing to talk about it
   E. blaming yourself

10. My ability to communicate effectively with others is _____ average.
    A. below   B. about   C. above
    D. far above   E. far below

11. In which of the following areas are you MOST highly skilled?
    A. Written communication
    B. Oral communication
    C. Ability to think quickly in difficult situations
    D. Ability to work with a broad diversity of people and personalities
    E. Organizational skills

12. As a Police Officer, you are assigned to work with a partner whom you dislike. You should
    A. immediately report the problem to your supervisor
    B. ask your partner not to speak to you during working hours
    C. tell your colleagues about your differences
    D. tell your partner why you dislike him/her
    E. work with your partner regardless of your personal feelings

12.____

13. During high school, what was your MOST common after-school activity?
    A. Remaining after school to participate in various clubs and organizations (such as band, sports, etc.)
    B. Remaining after school to make up for missed classes
    C. Remaining after school as punishment (detention, etc.)
    D. Going straight to an after-school job
    E. Spending the afternoon at home or with friends

13.____

14. During high school, in which of the following subjects did you receive the HIGHEST grades?
    A. English, History, Social Studies
    B. Math, Science
    C. Vocational classes
    D. My grades were consistent in all subjects
    E. Classes I liked

14.____

15. When faced with an overwhelming number of duties at work, your reaction is to
    A. do all of the work yourself, no matter what the cost
    B. delegate some responsibilities to capable colleagues
    C. immediately ask your supervisor for help
    D. put off as much work as possible until you can get to it
    E. take some time off to relax and clear your mind

15.____

16. As a Police Officer, your supervisor informs you that a prisoner whom you arrested has accused you of beating him. You know you are innocent. You react by
    A. quitting your job
    B. hiring a lawyer
    C. challenging your supervisor to prove the charges against you
    D. calmly tell your supervisor what really happened and presenting evidence to support your position
    E. insisting that you be allowed to speak alone to the prisoner

16.____

17. Which of the following BEST describes your desk at your current or most recent job?
    A. Messy and disorganized   B. Neat and organized
    C. Messy but organized   D. Neat but disorganized
    E. Messy

17.____

18. The _____ BEST describes your reasons for wanting to become a Police Officer. 18.____
    A. ability to carry and use a weapon
    B. excitement and challenges of the career
    C. excellent salary and benefits package
    D. chance to tell other people what to do
    E. chance to help people find a better life

19. As a Police Officer in the field, you are approached by a man who is frantic 19.____
    but unable to speak English. After several minutes of trying to communicate,
    you realize that the man is asking you to come with him in order to help
    someone who has been hurt.
    You should
    A. ignore him, since it might be a trap
    B. call for backup
    C. immediately offer to help the man
    D. return to your vehicle and wait for the man to leave
    E. radio your position and situation to another officer, then go with the man
       to offer help

20. When asked to take on extra responsibility at work, in order to help out a 20.____
    coworker who is overwhelmed, your response is to
    A. ask for overtime pay
    B. complain to your supervisor that you are being taken advantage of
    C. help the coworker to the best of your ability
    D. ask the coworker to come back some other time
    E. give the coworker some advice on how to get his/her job done

21. At my last job, I was promoted 21.____
    A. not at all   B. once
    C. twice   D. three times
    E. more than three times

22. As a Police Officer, you discover the body of a person whom you suspect 22.____
    to be a gang member. You also suspect that there are several other gang
    members hiding in the nearby vicinity.
    Your FIRST reaction should be to
    A. begin a search of the nearby area for the other gang members
    B. return to your vehicle and call for backup
    C. return to your vehicle with the body of the person you found
    D. check whether the person you found is dead or alive
    E. draw your weapon and identify yourself

23. You are faced with an overwhelming deadline at work. Your reaction is to
    A. procrastinate until the last minute
    B. procrastinate until someone notices you need some help
    C. notify your supervisor that you can't complete the work on your own
    D. work in silence without asking any questions
    E. arrange your schedule so that you can get the work done before the deadline

24. When you feel yourself under deadline pressures at work, your response is to
    A. make sure you keep to a schedule which allows you to complete the work on time
    B. wait until just before the deadline to complete the work
    C. ask someone else to do the work
    D. grow so obsessive about the work that your coworkers feel compelled to help you
    E. ask your supervisor immediately for help

25. Which of the following BEST describes your appearance at your current or most recent position?
    A. Well-groomed, neat, and clean
    B. Unkempt, but dressed neatly
    C. Messy and dirty clothing
    D. Unshaven and untidy
    E. Clean-shaven, but sloppily dressed

6 (#3)

KEY (CORRECT ANSWERS)

PLEASE NOTE: The answers listed are our preferred answers. However, you are to answer the exam honestly. Your personal answer may differ from our answers.

1.	A	11.	C
2.	D	12.	E
3.	E	13.	A
4.	C	14.	D
5.	A	15.	B
6.	A	16.	D
7.	B	17.	B
8.	E	18.	B
9.	A	19.	E
10.	C	20.	C

21.	C
22.	D
23.	E
24.	A
25.	A

TEST 4

DIRECTIONS: Each question or incomplete statement is followed by several suggested answers or completions. Select the one that BEST answers the question or completes the statement. *PRINT THE LETTER OF THE CORRECT ANSWER IN THE SPACE AT THE RIGHT.*

1. Which of the following BEST describes the way you react to making a difficult decision?
    A. Consult with the people you're closest to before making the decision
    B. Make the decision entirely on your own
    C. Consult only with those people whom your decision will affect
    D. Consult with everyone you known, in an effort to make a decision that will please everyone
    E. Forget about the decision until you have to make it

1.____

2. If placed in a supervisory role, which of the following characteristics would you rely on most heavily when dealing with the employees you supervise?
    A. Kindness   B. Cheeriness   C. Honesty
    D. Hostility   E. Aloofness

2.____

3. As a Police Officer, you are pursuing a suspect when he turns and pulls something out of his pocket that looks like a gun.
You should
    A. run away and call for backup
    B. assure the man that you mean him no harm
    C. draw your gun and order the man to stop and drop his weapon
    D. draw your gun and fire a warning shot
    E. draw your gun and fire immediately

3.____

4. In addition to English, in which of the following languages are you also fluent?
    A. Spanish   B. French   C. Italian
    D. German   E. Other

4.____

5. When confronted with gossip at work, your typical reaction is to
    A. participate
    B. listen without participating
    C. notify your supervisor
    D. excuse yourself from the discussion
    E. confront your coworkers about their problem

5.____

6. In the past two years, how many jobs have you held?
    A. None   B. One   C. Two
    D. Three   E. More than three

6.____

7. In your current or most recent job, you favorite part of the job is the part which involves
   A. telling other people what they're doing wrong
   B. supervising others
   C. working without supervision to finish a project
   D. written communication
   E. oral communication

7.____

8. Your supervisor asks you about a colleague who is applying for a position which you also want.
   You react by
   A. commenting honestly on the person's work performance
   B. enhancing the person's negative traits
   C. informing your supervisor about your colleague's personal problems
   D. telling your supervisor that would be better in the position
   E. refusing to comment

8.____

9. As a Police Officer, you confiscate some contraband which was being imported by an illegal alien who is now in your custody. Your partner asks you not to turn the contraband in to your supervisor.
   Your response is to
   A. inform your supervisor of your partner's request immediately
   B. tell your partner you feel uncomfortable with his request
   C. pretend you didn't hear you partner's request
   D. tell your supervisor and all your colleagues about your partner's request
   E. give the contraband to your partner and let him handle it

9.____

10. Which of the following BEST describes your responsibilities in your last job?
    A. Entirely supervisory
    B. Much supervisory responsibility
    C. Equal amounts of supervisory and nonsupervisory responsibility
    D. Some supervisory responsibilities
    E. No supervisory responsibilities

10.____

11. How much written communication did your previous or most recent job require of you?
    A. A great deal of written communication
    B. Some written communication
    C. I don't remember
    D. A small amount of written communication
    E. No written communication

11.____

12. In the past two years, how many times have you been fired from a job?
    A. None   B. Once
    C. Twice   D. Three times
    E. More than three times

12.____

13. How much time have you spent working for volunteer organizations in the past year?
    A. 10 to 20 hours per week
    B. 5 to 10 hours per week
    C. 3 to 5 hours per week
    D. 1 to 3 hours per week
    E. I have spent no time volunteering in the past year

    13.____

14. Your efforts at volunteer work usually revolve around which of the following types of organizations?
    A. Religious
    B. Community-based organizations working to improve the community
    C. Charity organizations working on behalf of the poor
    D. Charity organizations working on behalf of the infirm or handicapped
    E. Other

    14.____

15. Which of the following BEST describes your professional history?
    Promoted at _____ coworkers
    A. a much faster rate than
    B. a slightly faster rate than
    C. the same rate as
    D. a slightly slower rate than
    E. a much slower rate than

    15.____

16. Which of the following qualities do you MOST appreciate in a coworker?
    A. Friendliness
    B. Dependability
    C. Good looks
    D. Silence
    E. Forgiveness

    16.____

17. When you disagree with a supervisor's instructions or opinion about how to complete a project, your reaction is to
    A. inform your supervisor that you refuse to complete the project according to his or her instructions
    B. inform your colleague of you supervisor's incompetence
    C. accept your supervisor's instructions in silence
    D. voice your concerns and then complete the project according to your own instincts
    E. voice your concerns and then complete the project according to your supervisor's instructions

    17.____

18. Which of the following BEST describes your reaction to close supervision and specific direction from your supervisor?
    You
    A. listen carefully to the directions, and then figure out a way to do the job more effectively
    B. complete the job according to the given specifications
    C. show some initiative by doing the job your way
    D. ask someone else to do the job for you
    E. listen carefully to the directions, and then figure out a better way to do the job which will save more money

    18.____

19. How should a Police Officer handle a situation in which he or she is offered a bribe not to issue a traffic ticket?
    A. Pretend the bribe was never offered
    B. Accept the money as evidence and release the person
    C. Draw your weapon and call for backup
    D. Refuse the bribe and then arrest the person
    E. Accept the bribe and then arrest the person

    19.____

20. At work you are faced with a difficult decision.
    You react by
    A. seeking advice from your colleagues
    B. following your own path regardless of the consequences
    C. asking your supervisor what you should do
    D. keeping the difficulties to yourself
    E. working for a solution which will please everyone

    20.____

21. If asked to work with a person whom you dislike, your response would be
    A. to ask your supervisor to allow you to work with someone else
    B. to ask your coworker to transfer to another department or project
    C. talk to your coworker about the proper way to behave at work
    D. pretend the coworker is your best friend for the sake of your job
    E. to set aside your personal differences in order to complete the job

    21.____

22. As a supervisory, which of the following incentives would you use to motivate your employees?
    A. Fear of losing their jobs
    B. Fear of their supervisors
    C. Allowing employees to provide their input on a number of policies
    D. Encouraging employees to file secret reports regarding colleagues' transgressions
    E. All of the above

    22.____

23. A fellow Police Officer, with whom you enjoy a close friendship, has a substance-abuse problem which has gone undetected. You suspect the problem may be affecting his job.
    You would
    A. ask the Police Officer if the problem is affecting his job performance
    B. warn the Police Officer that he must seek counseling or you will report him
    C. wait a few weeks to see whether the officer's problem really is affecting his job
    D. discuss it with your supervisor
    E. wait for the supervisor to discover the problem

    23.____

24. In the past two months, you have missed work
    A. zero times   B. once
    C. twice   D. three times
    E. more than three times

    24.____

25. As a Police Officer, you are pursuing a group of robbers when you discover two small children who have been abandoned near a railroad crossing.
You should
   A. tell the children to stay put while you continue your pursuit
   B. lock the children in your vehicle and continue your pursuit
   C. stay with the children and radio for help in the pursuit of the robbers
   D. use the children to set a trap for the robbers
   E. ignore the children and continue your pursuit

25.____

KEY (CORRECT ANSWERS)

PLEASE NOTE: The answers listed are our preferred answers. However, you are to answer the exam honestly. Your personal answer may differ from our answers.

1.	A		11.	B
2.	C		12.	A
3.	C		13.	C
4.	A		14.	B
5.	D		15.	A
6.	B		16.	B
7.	C		17.	E
8.	A		18.	B
9.	A		19.	D
10.	D		20.	A

21. E
22. C
23. D
24. A
25. C

READING COMPREHENSION
UNDERSTANDING AND INTERPRETING WRITTEN MATERIAL

EXAMINATION SECTION

TEST 1

DIRECTIONS: Each question or incomplete statement is followed by several suggested answers or completions. Select the one that BEST answers the question or completes the statement. *PRINT THE LETTER OF THE CORRECT ANSWER IN THE SPACE AT THE RIGHT.*

Questions 1-3.

DIRECTIONS: Questions 1 through 3 are to be answered SOLELY on the basis of the following passage.

Foot patrol has some advantages over all other methods of patrol. Maximum opportunity is provided for observation within range of the senses and for close contact with people and things that enable the patrolman to provide a maximum service as an information source and counselor to the public and as the eyes and ears of the police department. A foot patrolman loses no time in alighting from a vehicle, and the performance of police tasks is not hampered by responsibility for his vehicle while afoot. Foot patrol, however, does not have many of the advantages of a patrol car. Lack of both mobility and immediate communication with headquarters lessens the officer's value in an emergency. The area that he can cover effectively is limited and, therefore, this method of patrol is costly.

1. According to the above passage, the foot patrolman is the eyes and ears of the police department because he is
    A. in direct contact with the station house
    B. not responsible for a patrol vehicle
    C. able to observe closely conditions on his patrol post
    D. a readily available information source to the public

1._____

2. The MOST accurate of the following statements concerning the various methods of patrol, according to the above passage, is that
    A. foot patrol should sometimes be combined with a motor patrol
    B. foot patrol is better than motor patrol
    C. helicopter patrol has the same advantages as motor patrol
    D. motor patrol is more readily able to communicate with superior officers in an emergency

2._____

3. According to the above passage, it is CORRECT to state that foot patrol is
    A. economical since increased mobility makes more rapid action possible
    B. expensive since the area that can be patrolled is relatively small
    C. economical since vehicle costs need not be considered
    D. expensive since giving information to the public is time consuming

3._____

Questions 4-6.

DIRECTIONS: Questions 4 through 6 are to be answered SOLELY on the basis of the following passage.

All applicants for an original license to operate a catering establishment shall be fingerprinted. This shall include the officers, employees, and stockholders of the company and the members of a partnership. In case of a change, by addition or subtraction, occurring during the existence of a license, the person added or substituted shall be fingerprinted. However, in the case of a hotel containing more than 200 rooms, only the officer or manager filing the application is required to be fingerprinted. The police commissioner may also at his discretion exempt the employees and stockholders of any company. The fingerprints shall be taken on one copy of form C.E. 20 and on two copies of C.E. 21. One copy of form C.E. 21 shall accompany the application. Fingerprints are not required with a renewal application.

4. According to the above passage, an employee added to the payroll of a licensed catering establishment which is not in a hotel must
   A. always be fingerprinted
   B. be fingerprinted unless he has been previously fingerprinted for another license
   C. be fingerprinted unless exempted by the police commissioner
   D. be fingerprinted only if he is the manager or an officer of the company

5. According to the above passage, it would be MOST accurate to state that
   A. form C.E. 20 must accompany a renewal application
   B. form C.E. 21 must accompany all applications
   C. form C.E. 21 must accompany an original application
   D. both forms C.E. 20 and C.E. 21 must accompany all applications

6. A hotel of 270 rooms has applied for a license to operate a catering establishment on the premises.
   According to the instructions for fingerprinting given in the above passage, the _____ shall be fingerprinted.
   A. officers, employees, and stockholders
   B. officers and the manager
   C. employees
   D. officer filing the application

Questions 7-9.

DIRECTIONS: Questions 7 through 9 are to be answered SOLELY on the basis of the following passage.

It is difficult to instill in young people inner controls on aggressive behavior in a world marked by aggression. The slum child's environment, full of hostility, stimulates him to delinquency; he does that which he sees about him. The time to act against delinquency is before it is committed. It is clear that juvenile delinquency, especially when it is committed in groups or gangs, leads almost inevitably to an adult criminal life unless it is checked at once.

The first signs of vandalism and disregard for the comfort, health, and property of the community should be considered as storm warnings which cannot be ignored. The delinquent's first crime has the underlying element of testing the law and its ability to hit back.

7. A SUITABLE title for this entire paragraph based on the material it contains is 7.____
   A. The Need for Early Prevention of Juvenile Delinquency
   B. Juvenile Delinquency as a Cause of Slums
   C. How Aggressive Behavior Prevents Juvenile Delinquency
   D. The Role of Gangs in Crime

8. According to the above passage, an initial act of juvenile crime USUALLY involves a(n) 8.____
   A. group or gang activity
   B. theft of valuable property
   C. test of the strength of legal authority
   D. act of physical violence

9. According to the above passage, acts of juvenile delinquency are MOST likely to lead to a criminal career when they are 9.____
   A. acts of vandalism
   B. carried out by groups or gangs
   C. committed in a slum environment
   D. such as to impair the health of the neighborhood

Questions 10-12.

DIRECTIONS: Questions 10 through 12 are to be answered SOLELY on the basis of the following passage.

The police laboratory performs a valuable service in crime investigation by assisting in the reconstruction of criminal action and by aiding in the identification of persons and things. When studied by a technician, physical things found at crime scenes often reveal facts useful in identifying the criminal and in determining what has occurred. The nature of substances to be examined and the character of the examinations to be made vary so widely that the services of a large variety of skilled scientific persons are needed in crime investigations. To employ such a complete staff and to provide them with equipment and standards needed for all possible analyses and comparisons is beyond the means and the needs of any but the largest police departments. The search of crime scenes for physical evidence also calls for the services of specialists supplied with essential equipment and assigned to each tour of duty so as to provide service at any hour.

10. If a police department employs a large staff of technicians of various types in its laboratory, it will affect crime investigation to the extent that 10.____
    A. most crimes will be speedily solved
    B. identification of criminals will be aided
    C. search of crime scenes for physical evidence will become of less importance
    D. investigation by police officers will not usually be required

11. According to the above passage, the MOST complete study of objects found at the scenes of crimes is   11.____
    A. always done in all large police departments
    B. based on assigning one technician to each tour of duty
    C. probably done only in large police departments
    D. probably done in police departments of communities with low crime rates

12. According to the above passage, a large variety of skilled technicians is useful in criminal investigations because   12.____
    A. crimes cannot be solved without their assistance as a part of the police team
    B. large police departments need large staffs
    C. many different kinds of tests on various substances can be made
    D. the police cannot predict what methods may be tried by wily criminals

Questions 13-14.

DIRECTIONS: Questions 13 and 14 are to be answered SOLELY on the basis of the following passage.

The emotionally unstable person is always potentially a dangerous criminal, who causes untold misery to other persons and is a source of considerable trouble and annoyance to law enforcement officials. Like his fellow criminals, he will be a menace to society as long as he is permitted to be at large. Police activities against him serve to sharpen his wits and imprisonment gives him the opportunity to learn from others how to commit more serious crimes when he is released. This criminal's mental structure makes it impossible for him to profit by his experience with the police officials, by punishment of any kind or by sympathetic understanding and treatment by well-intentioned persons, professional and otherwise.

13. According to the above passage, the MOST accurate of the following statements concerning the relationship between emotional instability and crime is that   13.____
    A. emotional instability is proof of criminal activities
    B. the emotionally unstable person can become a criminal
    C. all dangerous criminals are emotionally unstable
    D. sympathetic understanding will prevent the emotionally unstable person from becoming a criminal

14. According to the above passage, the effect of police activities on the emotionally unstable criminal is that   14.____
    A. police activities aid this type of criminal to reform
    B. imprisonment tends to deter this type of criminal from committing future crimes
    C. contact with the police serves to assist sympathetic understanding and medical treatment
    D. police methods against this type of criminal develop him for further unlawful acts

Questions 15-17.

DIRECTIONS: Questions 14 through 17 are to be answered SOLELY on the basis of the following passage.

Proposals to license gambling operations are based on the belief that the human desire to gamble cannot be suppressed and, therefore, it should be licensed and legalized with the people sharing in the profits, instead of allowing the underworld to benefit. If these proposals are sincere, then it is clear that only one is worthwhile at all. Legalized gambling should be completely controlled and operated by the state with all the profits used for its citizens. A state agency should be set up to operate and control the gambling business. It should be as completely removed from politics as possible. In view of the inherent nature of the gambling business, with its close relationship to lawlessness and crime, only a man of the highest integrity should be eligible to become head of this agency. However, state gambling would encourage mass gambling with its attending social and economic evils in the same manner as other forms of legal gambling; but there is no justification whatever for the business of gambling to be legalized and then permitted to operate for private profit or for the benefit of any political organization.

15. The central thought of this passage may be CORRECTLY expressed as the   15.____
    A. need to legalize gambling in the state
    B. state operation of gambling for the benefit of the people
    C. need to license private gambling establishments
    D. evils of gambling

16. According to the above passage, a problem of legalized gambling which will   16.____
    still occur if the state operates the gambling business is
    A. the diversion of profits from gambling to private use
    B. that the amount of gambling will tend to diminish
    C. the evil effects of any form of mass gambling
    D. the use of gambling revenues for illegal purposes

17. According to the above passage, to legalize the business of gambling would be   17.____
    A. *justified*, because gambling would be operated only by a man of the highest integrity
    B. *justified*, because this would eliminate politics
    C. *unjustified* under any conditions because the human desire to gamble cannot be suppressed
    D. *unjustified* if operated for private or political profit

Questions 18-19.

DIRECTIONS: Questions 18 and 19 are to be answered SOLELY on the basis of the following passage.

For many years, slums had been recognized as breeding disease, juvenile delinquency, and crime which not only threatened the health and welfare of the people who lived there, but also weakened the structure of society as a whole. As far bac as 1834, a sanitary inspection report in New York City pointed out the connection between unsanitary, overcrowded housing and the spread of epidemics. Down through the years, evidence of slum-produced evils accumulated as the slums themselves continued to spread. This spread of slums was nationwide. Its symptoms and its ill effects were peculiar to no locality, but were characteristic of the country as a whole and imperiled the national welfare.

18. According to the above passage, people who live in slum dwellings   18.____
    A. cause slums to become worse
    B. are threatened by disease and crime
    C. create bad housing
    D. are the chief source of crime in the country

19. According to the above passage, the effects of juvenile delinquency and crime   19.____
    in slum areas were
    A. to destroy the structure of society
    B. noticeable in all parts of the country
    C. a chief cause of the spread of slums
    D. to spread unsanitary conditions in New York City

Questions 20-22.

DIRECTIONS: Questions 20 through 22 are to be answered SOLELY on the basis of the following passage.

Whenever, in the course of the performance of their duties in an emergency, members of the force operate the emergency power switch at any location on the transit system and thereby remove power from portions of the track, or they are on the scene where this has been done, they will bear in mind that, although power is removed, further dangers exist; namely, that a train may coast into the area even though the power is off, or that the rails may be energized by a train which may be in a position to transfer electricity from a live portion of the third rail through its shoe beams. Employees must look in each direction before stepping upon, crossing, or standing close to tracks, being particularly careful not to come into contact with the third rail.

20. According to the above passage, whenever an emergency occurs which has   20.____
    resulted in operating the emergency power switch, it is MOST accurate to state that
    A. power is shut off and employees may perform their duties in complete safety
    B. there may still be power in a portion of the third rail
    C. the switch will not operate if a portion of the track has been broken
    D. trains are not permitted to stop in the area of the emergency

21. An IMPORTANT precaution which this passage urges employees to follow after   21.____
    operating the emergency power switch is to
    A. look carefully in both directions before stepping near the rails
    B. inspect the nearest train which has stopped to see if the power is on
    C. examine the third rail to see if the power is on
    D. check the emergency power switch to make sure it has operated properly

22. A trackman reports to you, the patrolman, that a dead body is lying on the road bed. You operate the emergency power switch. A train which has been approaching comes to a stop near the scene.
In order to act in accordance with the instructions in the above passage, you should
   A. climb down to the road bed and remove the body
   B. direct the train motorman to back up to the point where his train will not be in position to transfer electricity through its shoe beams
   C. carefully cross over the road bed to the body, avoiding the third rail and watching for train movements
   D. have the train motorman check to see if power is on before crossing to the tracks

Questions 23-25.

DIRECTIONS: Questions 23 through 25 are to be answered SOLELY on the basis of the following passage.

Pickpockets operate most effectively when there are prospective victims in either heavily congested areas or in lonely places. In heavily populated areas, the large number of people about them covers the activities of these thieves. In lonely spots, they have the advantage of working unobserved. The main factor in the pickpocket's success is the selection of the *right* victim. A pickpocket's victim must, at the time of the crime, be inattentive, distracted, or unconscious. If any of these conditions exist, and if the pickpocket is skilled in his operations, the stage is set for a successful larceny. With the control of winter, the crowds move southward—and so do most of the pickpockets. However, some pickpockets will remain in certain areas all year around. They will concentrate on theater districts, bus and railroad terminals, hotels or large shopping centers. A complete knowledge of the methods of this type of criminal and the ability to recognize them come only from long years of experience in performing patient surveillance and trailing of them. This knowledge is essential for the effective control and apprehension of this type of thief.

23. According to the above passage, the pickpocket is LEAST likely to operate in a
   A. baseball park with a full capacity attendance
   B. subway station in an outlying area late at night
   C. moderately crowded dance hall
   D. overcrowded department store

24. According to the above passage, the one of the following factors which is NOT necessary for the successful operation of the pickpocket is that
   A. he be proficient in the operations required to pick pockets
   B. the *right* potential victims be those who have been the subject of such a theft previously
   C. his operations be hidden from the view of others
   D. the potential victim be unaware of the actions of the pickpocket

25. According to the above passage, it would be MOST correct to conclude that police officers who are successful in apprehending pickpockets
    A. are generally those who have had lengthy experience in recognizing all types of criminals
    B. must, by intuition, be able to recognize potential *right* victims
    C. must follow the pickpockets in their southward movement
    D. must have acquired specific knowledge and skills in this field

25.____

KEY (CORRECT ANSWERS)

1.	C	11.	C
2.	D	12.	C
3.	B	13.	B
4.	C	14.	D
5.	C	15.	B
6.	B	16.	C
7.	A	17.	D
8.	C	18.	D
9.	B	19.	B
10.	B	20.	B

21.	A
22.	C
23.	C
24.	B
25.	D

TEST 2

DIRECTIONS: Each question or incomplete statement is followed by several suggested answers or completions. Select the one that BEST answers the question or completes the statement. *PRINT THE LETTER OF THE CORRECT ANSWER IN THE SPACE AT THE RIGHT.*

Questions 1-2.

DIRECTIONS: Questions 1 and 2 are to be answered SOLELY on the basis of the following passage.

    The medical examiner may contribute valuable data to the investigator of fires which cause fatalities. By careful examination of the bodies of any victims, he not only establishes cause of death, but may also furnish, in many instances, answers to questions relating to the identity of the victim and the source and origin of the fire. The medical examiner is of greatest value to law enforcement agencies because he is able to determine the exact cause of death through an examination of tissue of apparent arson victims. Thorough study of a burned body or even of parts of a burned body will frequently yield information which illuminates the problems confronting the arson investigator and the police.

1. According to the above passage, the MOST important task of the medical examiner in the investigation of arson is to obtain information concerning the
   A. identity of arsonists
   B. cause of death
   C. identity of victims
   D. source and origin of fires

1.____

2. The central thought of the above passage is that the medical examiner aids in the solution of crimes of arson when
   A. a person is burnt to death
   B. identity of the arsonist is unknown
   C. the cause of the fire is known
   D. trained investigators are not available

2.____

Questions 3-6.

DIRECTIONS: Questions 3 through 6 are to be answered SOLELY on the basis of the following passage.

    A foundling is an abandoned child whose identity is unknown. Desk officers shall direct the delivery, by a policewoman if available, of foundlings actually or apparently under two years of age to the American Foundling Hospital, or if actually or apparently two year of age or over to the Children's Center. In all other cases of dependent or neglected children, other than foundlings, requiring shelter, desk officers shall provide for obtaining such shelter as follows: between 9 A.M. and 5 P.M., Monday through Friday, by telephone direct to the Bureau of Child Welfare, in order to ascertain the shelter to which the child shall be sent; at all other time, direct the delivery of a child actually or apparently under two years of age to the American Foundling Hospital, or if the child is actually or apparently two years of age or over to the Children's Center.

3. According to the above passage, it would be MOST correct to state that
   A. a foundling as well as a neglected child may be delivered to the American Foundling Hospital
   B. a foundling but not a neglected child may be delivered to the Children's Center
   C. a neglected child requiring shelter, regardless of age, may be delivered to the Bureau of Child Welfare
   D. the Bureau of Child Welfare may determine the shelter to which a foundling may be delivered

3.____

4. According to the above passage, the desk officer shall provide for obtaining shelter for a neglected child apparently under two years of age by
   A. directing its delivery to Children's Center if occurrence is on a Monday between 9 A.M. and 5 P.M.
   B. telephoning the Bureau of Child Welfare if occurrence is on a Sunday
   C. directing its delivery to the American Foundling Hospital if occurrence is on a Wednesday at 4 P.M.
   D. telephoning the Bureau of Child Welfare if occurrence is at 10 A.M. on a Friday

4.____

5. According to the above passage, the desk officer should direct delivery to the American Foundling Hospital of any child who is
   A. actually under 2 years of age and requires shelter
   B. apparently under 2 years of age and is neglected or dependent
   C. actually 2 years of age and is a foundling
   D. apparently under 2 years of age and has been abandoned

5.____

6. A 12-year-old neglected child requiring shelter is brought to a police station on Thursday at 2 P.M.
   Such a child should be sent to
   A. a shelter selected by the Bureau of Child Welfare
   B. a shelter selected by the desk officer
   C. the Children's Center
   D. the American Foundling Hospital when a brother or sister under 2 years of age also requires shelter

6.____

Questions 7-10.

DIRECTIONS: Questions 7 through 10 are to be answered SOLELY on the basis of the following passage.

In addition to making the preliminary investigation of crimes, patrolmen should serve as eyes, ears, and legs for the detective division. The patrol division may be used for surveillance, to serve warrants and bring in suspects and witnesses, and to perform a number of routine tasks for the detectives which will increase the time available for tasks that require their special skills and facilities. It is to the advantage of individual detectives, as well as of the detective division, to have patrolmen working in this manner; more cases are cleared by arrest and a greater proportion of stolen property is recovered when, in addition to the detective regularly assigned, a number of patrolmen also work on the case. Detectives may stimulate the interest and participation of patrolmen by keeping them currently informed of the presence, identity or description, hangouts, associates, vehicles, and method of operation of each criminal known to be in the community.

7. According to the above passage, a patrolman should
   A. assist the detective in certain of his routine functions
   B. be considered for assignment as a detective on the basis of his patrol performance
   C. leave the scene once a detective arrives
   D. perform as much of the detective's duties as time permits

8. According to the above passage, patrolmen should aid detectives by   8._____
   A. accepting assignments from detectives which give promise of recovering stolen property
   B. making arrests of witnesses for the detective's interrogation
   C. performing all special investigative work for detectives
   D. producing for questioning individuals who may aid the detective in his investigation

9. According to the above passage, detectives can keep patrolmen interested by   9._____
   A. ascertaining that patrolmen are doing investigative work properly
   B. having patrolmen directly under his supervision during an investigation
   C. informing patrolmen of the value of their efforts in crime prevention
   D. supplying the patrolmen with information regarding known criminals in the community

10. Which of the following is NOT a result of cooperation between detectives and patrolmen?   10._____
    A. A greater proportion of stolen property is recovered.
    B. Detectives have more time to make preliminary investigations.
    C. Detectives have more time to finish tasks requiring their special skills.
    D. Patrolmen may become more interested and participate more in solving the case.

Questions 11-12.

DIRECTIONS: Questions 11 and 12 are to be answered SOLELY on the basis of the following passage.

State motor vehicle registration departments should and do play a vital role in the prevention and detection of automobile thefts. The combatting of theft is, in fact, one of the primary purposes of the registration of motor vehicles. In 2020 there were approximately 61,309,000 motor vehicles registered in the United States. That same year some 200,000 of them were stolen. All but 6 percent have been or will be recovered. This is a very high recovery ratio compared to the percentage of recovery of other stolen personal property. The reason for this is that automobiles are carefully identified by the manufacturers and carefully registered by many of the states.

11. The central thought of this passage is that there is a close relationship between the
    A. number of automobiles registered in the United States and the number stolen
    B. prevention of automobile thefts and the effectiveness of police departments in the United States
    C. recovery of stolen automobiles and automobile registration
    D. recovery of stolen automobiles and of other stolen property

11.____

12. According to the above passage, the high recovery ratio for stolen automobiles is due to
    A. state registration and manufacturer identification of motor vehicles
    B. successful prevention of automobile thefts by state motor vehicle departments
    C. the fact that only 6% of stolen vehicles are not properly registered
    D. the high number of motor vehicles registered in the United States

12.____

Questions 13-16.

DIRECTIONS: Questions 13 through 16 are to be answered SOLELY on the basis of the following passage.

It is not always understood that the term *physical evidence* embraces any and all objects, living or inanimate. A knife, gun, signature, or burglar tool is immediately recognized as physical evidence. Less often is it considered that dust, microscopic fragments of all types, even an odor, may equally be physical evidence and often the most important of all. It is well established that the most useful types of physical evidence are generally microscopic in dimensions, that is, not noticeable by the eye and, therefore, most likely to be overlooked by the criminal and by the investigator. For this reason, microscopic evidence persists for months or years after all other evidence has been removed and found inconclusive. Naturally, there are limitations to the time of collecting microscopic evidence as it may be lost or decayed. The exercise of judgment as to the possibility or profit of delayed action in collecting the evidence is a field in which the expert investigator should judge.

13. The one of the following which the above passage does NOT consider to be physical evidence is a
    A. criminal thought   B. minute speck of dust
    C. raw onion smell   D. typewritten note

13.____

14. According to the above passage, the rechecking of the scene of a crime
    A. is useless when performed years after the occurrence of the crime
    B. is advisable chiefly in crimes involving physical evidence
    C. may turn up microscopic evidence of value
    D. should be delayed if the microscopic evidence is not subject to decay or loss

14.____

15. According to the above passage, the criminal investigator should
    A. give most of his attention to weapons used in the commission of the crime
    B. ignore microscopic evidence until a request is received from the laboratory
    C. immediately search for microscopic evidence and ignore the more visible objects
    D. realize that microscopic evidence can be easily overlooked

16. According to the above passage,
    A. a delay in collecting evidence must definitely diminish its value to the investigator
    B. microscopic evidence exists for longer periods of time than other physical evidence
    C. microscopic evidence is generally the most useful type of physical evidence
    D. physical evidence is likely to be overlooked by the criminal and by the investigator

Questions 17-20.

DIRECTIONS: Questions 17 through 20 are to be answered SOLELY on the basis of the following passage.

Sometimes, but not always, firing a gun leaves a residue of nitrate particles on the hands. This fact is utilized in the paraffin test which consists of applying melted paraffin and gauze to the fingers, hands, and wrists of a suspect until a cast of approximately 1/8 of an inch is built up. The heat of the paraffin causes the pores of the skin to open and release any particles embedded in them. The paraffin cast is then removed and tested chemically for nitrate particles. In addition to gunpowder, fertilizers, tobacco ashes, matches, and soot are also common sources of nitrates on the hands.

17. Assume that the paraffin test has been given to a person suspected of firing a gun and that nitrate particles have been found.
    It would be CORRECT to conclude that the suspect
    A. is guilty   B. is innocent
    C. may be guilty or innocent   D. is probably guilty

18. In testing for the presence of gunpowder particles on human hands, the characteristic of paraffin which makes it MOST serviceable is that it
    A. causes the nitrate residue left by a fired gun to adhere to the gauze
    B. is waterproof
    C. melts at a high temperature
    D. helps to distinguish between gunpowder nitrates and other types

19. According to the above passage, in the paraffin test the nitrate particles are removed from the pores because the paraffin
    A. enlarges the pores   B. contracts the pores
    C. reacts chemically with nitrates   D. dissolves the particles

20. The presence of a residue of nitrate particles on the hands is a COMMON result of 20.____
    A. the paraffin test
    B. handling fertilizer
    C. a bullet wound
    D. enlarged pores

KEY (CORRECT ANSWERS)

1.	B	11.	C
2.	A	12.	A
3.	A	13.	A
4.	D	14.	C
5.	D	15.	D
6.	A	16.	C
7.	A	17.	C
8.		18.	A
9.	D	19.	A
10.	B	20.	B

REPORT WRITING

EXAMINATION SECTION

TEST 1

DIRECTIONS: Each question or incomplete statement is followed by several suggested answers or completions. Select the one that BEST answers the question or completes the statement. *PRINT THE LETTER OF THE CORRECT ANSWER IN THE SPACE AT THE RIGHT.*

Questions 1-10.

DIRECTIONS: Questions 1 through 10 are to be answered SOLELY on the basis of the following passage and Stolen Vehicle Report Form, which appears on the following page. The form contains 43 numbered boxes. Read the passage and look at the form before answering the questions.

    Police Officers Walton and Wright, patrolling in their radio patrol car in the industrial area of the 29th Precinct, were dispatched to 523 Johnson Boulevard at 10:30 A.M. on October 30, 2020 by the Police Radio Dispatcher. The Dispatcher had received a telephone call from a Ms. Ann Graham at 10:28 A.M. that her friend's car was being stolen from in front of her house.

    Officers Walton and Wright arrived at 523 Johnson Boulevard at 10:32 A.M. Ms. Graham was waiting outside and informed them that the car had already been stolen. She stated that her friend, Samantha Merlin, had gone on vacation to California three days before and had left her car in Ms. Graham's care. Ms. Graham had parked the car in front of her own house the night before.

    Ms. Graham stated that she looked out of her window at 10:25 A.M. that day and saw a strange man breaking into the car using a wire coat hanger. The car's hood was raised. She ran to her telephone to call the police. When she returned to her window, she saw the man doing something under the hood and, within a minute, he drove the car away. She had been too frightened to try to stop him, and there was no one else on the street.

    Ms. Graham described the car as a black 2002 Buick 2-door sedan, New York license plate number 113-ABT, Vehicle Identification Number 7641239877. She stated that her friend, Ms. Merlin, lives at 1905 Junis Road, her telephone number is 978-4123, she is unmarried, 30 years old, and will return from vacation on November 13. Until then, she can be reached by telephone at 213-804-9112. She is employed at the law firm of Adams and Adams, 360 Park Avenue, as an office manager.

    Ms. Graham described the man who stole the car as white, in his early twenties, about 5'7", 155 lbs., and wearing blue pants, a black jacket, and an earring in his left ear. He had dark brown, short curly hair.

    Ms. Graham gave her telephone number as 275-8722 and stated that she is divorced, employed as a securities analyst at F.G. Sutton and Company, 125 Wall Street, and is 32 years old. Her birth date is June 13, 1976. Her telephone number at work is 217-7273.

2 (#1)

STOLEN VEHICLE REPORT FORM

COMPLAINT INFORMATION	Complaint Number (1)	Precinct (2)	Date Complaint Reported (3)	Time Reported (4)	Place Complaint Taken (5)
VEHICLE DESCRIPTION	Year (6)	Make (7)	Color (8)		License Number (9)
	I.D. Number (10)		Type (11)		Location of Theft (122)
OWNER INFORMATION	Name (13)		Address (14)		Home Telephone (15)
	Age (16)		Marital Status (17)		Occupation (18)
	Business Address (19)			Business Telephone (20)	
WITNESS INFORMATION	Name (21)		Address (22)		Home Telephone (23)
	Age (24)		Marital Status (25)		Occupation (26)
	Business Address (27)			Business Telephone (28)	
	Witness' Description of Incident (29)				
DESCRIPTION OF SUSPECT	Name (If Known) (30)	Age (31)	Race (32)	Sex (33)	Height (34)	Weight (35)	Hair (36)
	Eyes (37)		Clothing (38)		Distinctive Marks (39)
	Other (40)				
OFFICER INFORMATION	Name (41)			Date (42)	
	Shield Number (43)				

1. Which one of the following should be entered in Box 3?
   A. June 13
   B. October 13
   C. October 30
   D. November 13

1.____

2. Which one of the following should be entered in Box 31?
   A. Late teens   B. Early twenties   C. 30   D. 32

3. Which one of the following should be entered in Box 12?
   In front of
   A. 1905 Junis Road   B. 523 Johnson Boulevard
   C. 125 Wall Street   D. 360 Park Avenue

4. Which one of the following should be entered in Box 8?
   A. Blue   B. Brown   C. Black   D. Red

5. Which one of the following should be entered in Box 11?
   A. 2-door sedan   B. 4-door sedan
   C. 4-door station wagon D. 2-door sportscar

6. Which one of the following should be entered in Box 15?
   A. 804-9112   B. 217-7273   C. 275-8722   D. 978-4123

7. Which one of the following should be entered in Box 17?
   A. Married   B. Legally separated
   C. Single   D. Divorced

8. Which one of the following should be entered in Box 21?
   A. Samantha Merlin   B. Samantha Graham
   C. Ann Merlin   D. Ann Graham

9. Which one of the following should be entered in Box 26?
   A. Securities analyst   B. Housewife
   C. Office Manager   D. Secretary

10. Which one of the following should be entered in Box 40?
    A. Scar on left cheek   B. Earring in left ear
    C. Short curly brown hair   D. Blue pants, black jacket

Questions 11-20.

DIRECTIONS: Questions 11 through 20 are to be answered SOLELY on the basis of the following story and Complaint Report Form.

Officers Fred Johnson and Carl Adams, patrolling in their radio car in the Riverfront section of Precinct #8, were dispatched to 124 Selwyn Lane at 3:23 P.M. on April 26 by the dispatcher. The dispatcher had received a telephone call at 3:20 P.M. from a Mrs. Green who said that her house had been burglarized and all of the contents of her house had been stolen.

Officers Johnson and Adams arrived at 124 Selwyn Lane at 3:28 P.M. Mrs. Green and two neighbors were waiting for them on the front steps. The Officers parked their patrol car in front of the house and locked the doors. Mrs. Green explained that she is a schoolteacher and her husband is a lawyer. They usually leave the house around 8:00 A.M. each morning. She is the first to arrive home since school lets out at 3:00 P.M. She tells the Officers that today, when she arrived home, she found the door to her house slightly open. She was frightened and went to her neighbor's house. Both women then returned to 124 Selwyn and, upon entering the house, found that the contents of the house had been removed. At that point, Mrs. Green called the Police Department.

While Officer Johnson took statements from Mrs. Green and Mrs. Walters, her neighbor, Officer Adams questioned other residents of the street. Most of the other residents were standing outside of the Green's house.

Mrs. Schneider, age 56, who lives 5 doors down at 138 Selwyn, told Officer Adams that she arrived home at 2:45 P.M. She then told Adams that she saw a large truck parked near 124 Selwyn and remembers wondering if anyone new was moving into the neighborhood. She remembers the truck was dented, painted bright blue with a white top, and it had New Jersey plates. Also she was able to describe one of the suspects. She saw him get into the truck before it pulled away. The man was white, about 6'2" tall, about 220 lbs., and thinning brown hair. He was wearing a pair of dirty white overalls and brown work boots. He appeared to walk with a limp. There was another man already in the truck, and Mrs. Schneider described him as a very short Black man wearing a white hat. Mrs. Schneider said the truck turned left on Second Street as it pulled away.

Mrs. Jones, Mrs. Dartnell, and Mrs. Leopold, when questioned by Officer Adams, said that they saw nothing. They were all at Mrs. Leopold's house playing cards and didn't come outside until they heard Mrs. Green screaming.

Officer Adams found that Mrs. Schneider's home phone number was 683-2291 and that she lives alone. Officer Johnson found that both Mrs. Green and her neighbor were 48 years of age and that the school's telephone number was 925-6394. Mrs. Walters' home telephone number is 683-7642, and she lives with her husband at 126 Selwyn Lane. Mr. Green's office number is 238-4296. It is located at 555 Fifth Avenue, Suite 816.

Officers Johnson and Adams then completed the complaint form. The complaint number assigned by the dispatcher was 479638G.

5 (#1)

COMPLAINT REPORT					
COMPLAINT INFORMATION	Complaint Number (1)	Precinct (2)	Date of Complaint (3)	Time of Complaint (4)	Place Complaint Taken (5)
INFORMATION ABOUT PERSON MAKING COMPLAINT	Name of Person Making Complaint (6) Last Name First Name Middle			Address of Person Making Complaint (7) Street City State	
	Age (8)	Marriage (9) Married ☐ Not-Married ☐		Occupation (If Any) (10)	
	Spouse's Occupation (If Any) (11)			Spouse's Business Address (12) Street City State	
WITNESS INFORMATION	Name of Witness (If Any) (13) Last Name First Name Middle			Address of Witness (If Any) (14) Street City State	
	Age (15)	Occupation (If Any) (16)			
	Spouse's Occupation (If Any) (17)			Spouse's Business Address (18) Street City State	
DESCRIPTION OF INCIDENT	Description (19)				
DESCRIPTION OF SUSPECTS (if Any)	Suspect #1	Name (20)	Age (21)	Race (22) *white*	Sex (23) *male*	Height (24)	Weight (25)	Hair (26)	Eyes (27)
	Suspect #2	Name (28)	Age (29)	Race (30) *black*	Sex (31) *male*	Height (32)	Weight (33)	Hair (34)	Eyes (35)
	Suspect #3	Name (36)	Age (37)	Race (38)	Sex (39)	Height (40)	Weight (41)	Hair (42)	Eyes (43)
	Special Suspect Description (44) Suspect Number _____			Description (45) *Walked with limp*	
SUSPECT VEHICLE DESCRIPTION (If Any)	Year (46)		Make (47)	Color (48)	License Number 49)
OFFICER INFORMATION	Name (50)			Date (51)	
	Shield No. (52)				

11. Which one of the following should be entered in Box 4?   11.____
    A. 8:00 AM   B. 2:45 PM   C. 3:20 PM   D Not known

12. Which one of the following should be entered in Box 6?   12.____
    A. Mrs. Schneider   B. Mrs. Green
    C. Officer Johnson   D. Not known

13. Which one of the following should be entered in Box 7?   13.____
    A. 138 Selwyn Lane   B. 125 Selwyn Lane
    C. 124 Selwyn Lane   D. Not known

14. Which one of the following should be entered in Box 8? 14.____
    A. 48 B. 52 C. 46 D. Not known

15. Which one of the following should be entered in Box 10? 15.____
    A. Lawyer B. Widow C. Teacher D. Not known

16. Which one of the following should be entered in Box 11? 16.____
    A. Lawyer B. Widow C. Teacher D. Not known

17. Which one of the following should be entered in Box 13? 17.____
    A. Mrs. Green B. Mrs. Schneider
    C. Mrs. Leopold D. Not known

18. Which one of the following should be entered in Box 16? 18.____
    A. Lawyer B. Teacher C. Widow D. Not known

19. Which one of the following should be entered in Box 26? 19.____
    A. Black B. Brown C. Blonde D. Not known

20. Which one of the following should be entered in Box 44? 20.____
    A. 1 B. 2 C. 3 D. Not known

KEY (CORRECT ANSWERS)

1.	C	11.	C
2.	B	12.	B
3.	B	13.	C
4.	C	14.	A
5.	A	15.	C
6.	D	16.	A
7.	C	17.	B
8.	D	18.	D
9.	A	19.	B
10.	B	20.	A

TEST 2

DIRECTIONS: Each question or incomplete statement is followed by several suggested answers or completions. Select the one that BEST answers the question or completes the statement. *PRINT THE LETTER OF THE CORRECT ANSWER IN THE SPACE AT THE RIGHT.*

Questions 1-10.

DIRECTIONS: Questions 1 through 10 are to be answered SOLELY on the basis of the following story and Complaint Report Form.

Officers Hunt and Torry respond to a suspected burglary-in-process call at 285 E. Reed Street. They arrive there at 2:32 P.M. A man wearing gray slacks, white dress shirt, and red tie is standing in front of the store yelling, *Stop, robbers!* He is pointing east. Officer Hunt sees three men running about one hundred and fifty feet away. He immediately starts to chase after them. One suspect is 5'9" and weighs about 140 lbs. He has black hair in an Afro cut and is wearing tan pants with a blue work shirt. He is wearing white tennis shoes with blue stripes. He turns the corner and runs south on Elm Street. Another one is 6'2" and weighs about 200 lbs. He has long dark brown hair and is wearing a green headband, white jacket, and blue jeans. He is carrying a brown paper bag in his left hand. He also turns south on Elm. The third man is 5'9" and weighs about 180 lbs. He has long dark brown hair and is wearing a white cap. He is wearing blue jeans and a light blue jacket with a white stripe around it. He continues running east on Reed.

Officer Torry questions the man in the red tie and finds he is the manager of the Elite Jewelry Store and that he has just been robbed by the men running away. Torry radios in the information and continues his questioning. The manager, Mr. Oscar Freehold, says that he was showing a ruby and diamond necklace to Mrs. Mandt, a customer, when these men entered the store. One of them, the tallest one, pointed a gun at Freehold and grabbed the necklace. He put the necklace in the pocket of his white jacket. The other two men were shorter and the same height. The heaver one of the two opened the cash register and emptied the money into a brown paper bag.

The thinner short man opened a display case and put several sapphire and emerald rings in his pants pocket. He then took a knife from his pocket and held it on Mrs. Mandt. The tall one forced Mr. Freehold to open the safe. The tall one took jewels and money from the safe and put them in another brown paper bag. The three men ran out.

Officer Hunt chased the two suspects who turned south on Elm Street. At the next corner, they turned east on Maple. They ran one block to the corner of Beech, where the one with the Afro cut turned south. The other suspect got into a car and drove east on Maple. It was a dark blue 2018 Ford sedan with New York license number 677-HKL. As he drove east on Maple, he sideswiped a 2016 red Dodge and a 2019 tan Volvo.

Officer Hunt returns to the jewelry store and radios in the additional information. Officer Torry completes the Complaint Report.

COMPLAINT REPORT

COMPLAINT INFORMATION	Complaint Number (1)	Precinct (2)	Date of Complaint (3)	Time of Complaint (4)	Place Complaint Taken (5)		
INFORMATION ABOUT PERSON MAKING COMPLAINT	Name of Person Making Complaint (6) — Last Name, First Name, Middle			Address of Person Making Complaint (7) — Street, City, State			
	Age (8)	Marriage (9) Married ☐ Not-Married ☐		Occupation (If Any) (10)			
	Spouse's Occupation (If Any) (11)			Spouse's Business Address (12) — Street, City, State			
WITNESS INFORMATION	Name of Witness (If Any) (13) — Last Name, First Name, Middle			Address of Witness (If Any) (14) — Street, City, State			
	Age (15)	Occupation (If Any) (16)					
	Spouse's Occupation (If Any) (17)			Spouse's Business Address (18) — Street, City, State			
DESCRIPTION OF INCIDENT	Description (19)						
DESCRIPTION OF SUSPECTS (if Any)	Suspect #1	Name (20)	Age (21)	Race (22)	Sex (23) *male*	Height (24) 5'9"	Weight (25) 140	Hair (26)	Eyes (27)
	Suspect #2	Name (28)	Age (29)	Race (30) *black*	Sex (31) *male*	Height (32) 6'2"	Weight (33) 200	Hair (34)	Eyes (35)
	Suspect #3	Name (36)	Age (37)	Race (38)	Sex (39) *male*	Height (40) 5'9"	Weight (41) 180	Hair (42)	Eyes (43)
	Special Suspect Description (44) Suspect Number _____			Description (45) *Walked with limp*			
SUSPECT VEHICLE DESCRIPTION (If Any)	Year (46)	Make (47)		Color (48)		License Number 49)	
OFFICER INFORMATION	Name (50)			Date (51)			
	Shield No. (52)						

1. Which of the following should be entered in Box 6? 1.____
   A. Officer Hunt B. Mr. Oscar Freehold
   C. Mrs. Mandt D. Not known

2. Which of the following should be entered in Box 10? 2.____
   A. Jewelry store manager B. Police officer
   C. Clerk D. Not known

3. Which of the following should be entered in Box 13? 3.____
   A. Mr. Oscar Freehold B. Mrs. Mandt
   C. Officer Hunt D. Not known

4. Which of the following should be entered in Box 14? 4.____
   A. East Reed Street   B. East Elm Street
   C. South Beech Street   D. Not known

5. Which of the following should be entered in Box 26? 5.____
   A. Blonde   B. Brown   C. Black   D. Not known

6. Which of the following should be entered in Box 34? 6.____
   A. Blonde   B. Brown   C. Black   D. Not known

7. Which of the following should be entered in Box 42? 7.____
   A. Blonde   B. Brown   C. Black   D. Not known

8. Which of the following should be entered in Box 46? 8.____
   A. 2016   B. 2018   C. 2019   D. Not known

9. Which of the following should be entered in Box 48? 9.____
   A. Green   B. Tan   C. Blue   D. Not known

10. Which of the following should be entered in Box 50? 10.____
    A. Officer Hunt   B. Officer Freehold
    C. Officer Torry   D. Not known

Questions 11-20.

DIRECTIONS: Questions 11 through 20 are to be answered SOLELY on the basis of the following story and Arrest Form.

Officer John Smith, on foot patrol near a delicatessen, heard a man's cry for help. When he reached the man, Peter Laxalt Green, Green told him that he had just been robbed by a young white male who could be seen running down the street. The officer ran after the youth and saw him jump into a 2019 two-door white Buick, New York plate number 761-QCV. While the youth was trying to start the car, the officer caught up with him and arrested him in front of 49 Second Avenue, Brooklyn. The arrest took place ten minutes after the robbery occurred. The officer brought his prisoner to the 65th Precinct station house at 57 Second Avenue, Brooklyn. At the station house, thirty minutes after the robbery, it was determined that the prisoner's legal name was John Wright Doman and his nickname was *Beefy*. Mr. Doman lives at 914 East 140th Street, Brooklyn, Apartment 3G, telephone number 737-1392. He was born in Calgary, Canada, on February 3, 2005. He became a U.S. citizen on February 3, 2012. His Social Security number is 056-46-7056. Doman is not married. He is employed at the Bollero Wine Company, 213 Fourth Avenue, Brooklyn. An arrest report was prepared at the Precinct. The number assigned to the report was 17460.

At the station house, Mr. Green described the incident in detail. Mr. Green stated that at 11:55 P.M. on July 18, 2023, a young, heavy-set white male, 5'11" tall, weighing 220 pounds, with brown hair and blue eyes, entered Mr. Green's delicatessen, at 141 Second Avenue, Brooklyn, New York. Green, who lives in the apartment above the delicatessen, asked him if he could help him. The male replied, *Yes, you can*, and then immediately pulled out a knife. Mr.

4 (#2)

Green then noticed that the male had a red tattoo of an ax on his right arm. The male demanded that Mr. Green give him all the money from the cash register or else Mr. Green would get hurt. Mr. Green picked up a bottle that was on the counter and threw it at the male, striking him in the chest. The male fled from the delicatessen and headed south on Second Avenue. Mr. Green then ran out of the delicatessen and yelled for the police.

Mr. Green was born on March 17, 1969. His business phone number is 871-3113; his home phone number is 330-5286.

ARREST REPORT					
ARREST INFORMATION	Arrest Number (1)	Precinct (2)	Date of Arrest (3)	Time of Arrest (4)	Place of Arrest (5)
DESCRIPTION OF INCIDENT	Date & Time (6)			Prisoner's Weapon (Description (7)	
	Prisoner's Auto (color, year, make, model, license plate number, state) (8)				
	Location of Incident (be specific) (9)			Type of Business (10)	
DESCRIPTION OF PRISONER	Last Name First Name Middle (11)			Date of Birth (12)	
	Age (13)	Sex (14)	Race (15)	Eyes (16)	Hair (17)	Weight (18)	Height (19)
	Address City State			Apt. No. (21)	Home Phone Number (22)
	Place of Birth (23)		Citizenship (24) Citizen ☐ Non-citizen ☐		Marital Status (25)
	Social Security Number (26)		Where Employed (Company and Address) (27)		
	Nickname (28)		Scars, Tattoos (Describe fully and give location) (29)		
DESCRIPTION OF COMPLAINANT	Last Name First Name Middle (30)			Date of Birth (31)	
	Address City State (32)			Telephone Numbers Business: (33) Home: (34)	

11. Which of the following should be entered in Box 3? _____, 2018
    A. February 3   B. March 17   C. July 18   D. July 19

11.____

12. Which of the following should be entered in Box 4?
    A. 11:55 P.M.   B. 12:05 A.M.   C. 12:25 A.M.   D. 12:35 A.M.

12.____

5 (#2)

13. Which of the following should be entered in Box 6? 13.____
    A. 7/18/23, 11:55 P.M.   B. 7/18/23, 11:55 A.M.
    C. 7/19/23, 11:55 P.M.   D. 7/19/23, 11:55 A.M.

14. Which of the following should be entered in Box 7? 14.____
    A. Ax   B. Gun   C. Bottle   D. Knife

15. Which of the following should be entered in Box 8? 15.____
    White _____ Buick, _____, New York
    A. 2019; two-door; 761-QCV   B. 2020; four-door; 762-QCV
    C. 2019; two-door; 761-VCQ   D. 2020; four-door; 167-QCV

16. Which of the following should be entered in Box 12? 16.____
    A. 3/17/69   B. 2/3/05   C. 7/18/05   D. 2/3/12

17. Which of the following should be entered in Box 27? 17.____
    Bollero _____, Brooklyn, N.Y.
    A. Beer Company, 213 Fourth Avenue
    B. Wine Company, 213 Fourth Avenue
    C. Beer & Wine Company, 213 Second Avenue
    D. Wine Company, 213 Fourth Street

18. Which of the following should be entered in Box 32? _____, Brooklyn. 18.____
    A. 49 Second Avenue   B. 57 Second Avenue
    C. 141 Second Avenue   D. 914 East 140th Street

19. Which of the following should be entered in Box 33? 19.____
    A. 330-1392   B. 330-5286   C. 737-1392   D. 871-3113

20. Which of the following should be entered in Box 28? 20.____
    A. Doman   B. Axe   C. Beefy   D. Maniac

KEY (CORRECT ANSWERS)

1.	B	11.	D
2.	A	12.	B
3.	B	13.	A
4.	D	14.	D
5.	C	15.	A
6.	B	16.	B
7.	B	17.	B
8.	B	18.	C
9.	C	19.	D
10.	C	20.	C

POLICE SCIENCE NOTES
PATROL

INTRODUCTION

Patrol is commonly referred to as the "backbone" of police activity. It serves as the foundation upon which all other police functions rest. It is the fundamental operation which contributes greatly to the successful curtailment of criminal activities. Police patrol is also a basic factor in providing the public with the type of police service that it has a right to expect.

The word "patrol" comes from the French "Pattrouiller" meaning "to go through puddles." This is an excellent description of the task because good patrolling means going through puddles, through garbage-filled alleys, and up rickety back stairs in all kinds of weather and at all times of day or night.

While patrol is neither glamorous nor exciting at all times, it can be interesting and rewarding for the individual officer. It gives the officer an opportunity to observe a wide variety of people and supplies insight into their problems. By being alert and understanding, he can analyze his beat area and render effective public service.

The continuous patrol of an area, whether on foot or in a vehicle, makes or breaks a law enforcement agency. Nothing contributes more to police efficiency and the belief of the community in its security and protection by its police than the manner in which patrol duty is performed. Patrol is truly the police department's first line of defense against crime.

PURPOSES OF PATROL

The general purposes of patrol might be stated as follows:

1. The protection of life and property.
2. The preservation of the peace.
3. The prevention of crime.
4. The detection and apprehension of criminals.
5. The regulation of conduct (noncriminal).
6. The performance of required services such as giving aid and information.

These are the tangible, definite things for which police patrols are designed, but on the other side, there are certain intangible things that are very important, but cannot be reduced to exact actions. The policeman on the street is more than just an officer on patrol; he is the police department in the eyes of many of the people and indeed, he represents all of government to a large portion of the public. This factor indicates the leadership role which the policeman is called upon to play in time of civil defense emergency or natural disaster. So, it is doubly important that he know and execute his task well. In no area of his work is the policeman required to exercise tact, good judgment, and leadership as often as while he is patrolling.

TYPES OF PATROL

There are three general classifications of police patrol which are pertinent here. They are foot patrol, vehicular patrol, and plainclothes patrol.

Every patrolman is a foot patrolman at one time or another. There are two types of foot patrol, moving and fixed. An officer on moving patrol is assigned to a designated route or beat to cover. This route is generally in an area where there is a concentration of police hazards. An officer on a fixed post has primary assignment at one location, such as traffic direction at a specific intersection. Much of the work to be done falls within this category.

Vehicular patrol includes the performance of many of the same functions that are required of the foot patrolman. The basic difference can be found among these factors:

1. The use of some mode of transportation, i.e., bicycle, motorcycle, horse, boat, aircraft, or most often, automobile.

2. The ability to cover a larger geographic area.

3. The existence of constant radio contact in most instances.

While vehicular patrol may also involve moving or fixed assignments, fixed vehicular patrol is normally only employed when communications contact is imperative.

Plainclothes patrol may be foot or vehicular, moving or fixed. It is normally used only to handle special problems such as the control of criminal activities in areas of high-crime frequency or surveillance of specific persons or locations.

POLICE PATROL TECHNIQUES

Efficiency in patrol can be attained only through considerable experience. There are, however, a number of tested techniques that the auxiliary policeman should know and practice.

While patrolling his assigned area, the patrolman should "be systematically unsystematic." The officer should frequently backtrack and take an unexpected route whether in a vehicle or on foot. He should maneuver so as to observe the people and locations on his beat without in turn being observed. This can be done properly only if the dead ends, construction work and any other factor which might cause delay. The patrolman must also have knowledge of the legitimate activities and crime potentialities of his area.

The location of stores, service stations, other houses of business and their hours, is vital knowledge to the beat officer. Knowledge of these things will enable him to more readily recognize some unusual activity that may possess criminal implications. This knowledge is also useful to the officer because it will enable him to intelligently direct persons asking for information. It is, thus, essential for the officer to know the area which he is patrolling.

Observation is also an important tool for the patrolman. It includes the utilization of all of his senses in ascertaining just what is occurring in his area of responsibility. Observation is a result of intelligent curiosity, and it can and should be developed. The officer should carefully take in all aspects of life around him as he walks his beat. When anything out of the ordinary takes place, he should evaluate it and take the steps that are necessary. The required evaluation is of the utmost importance and it will necessitate years of experience before the officer's faculties are developed to a peak of efficiency. The officer should, however, constantly practice his observational technique because only through such constant exercise can he expect to achieve effectiveness.

Particular care should be taken when observing individuals. Personal description is critical to the patrolman's task. Every officer should learn the procedure employed by his department for identifying suspects or wanted persons.

SOME THINGS TO WATCH FOR WHILE ON PATROL

While patrolling an area, an officer should be careful to observe the following things:

1. Doors and windows in buildings those are not secure. If any are found, the officer should search the premises, secure the premises with any means at hand, and notify the owner through appropriate channels.

2. Conditions conducive to crime such as: improperly secured buildings, partitions between stores, things of value left unattended, and window displays and counter displays of unusual value.

3. Suspicious persons or known criminals. The officer should also observe suspicious behavior such as: loitering around banks, warehouses, shipping rooms, dock terminals, schools, hotels, stores, etc.; door-to-door peddling, begging, delivery services strange to the area; and persons with no apparent destination or purpose.

4. Business places. These should be scrutinized carefully on each tour. The officer should ascertain the following information concerning each of them: location of safes and cash registers; location and type of night lights, and alarm systems; habits of the staff; exits; means of locking doors, windows, gratings, skylights, basements, etc.

5. Vehicles. The patrolling officer will find them important to his work. They will often be the thing most likely observable in connection with criminal activities. Many excellent arrests and much fine police work have resulted from observation of vehicles. Traffic enforcement, of course, requires close observation of vehicles, but the officer on patrol must not confine his interests only to traffic violations.

6. Signs of disorder, excitement or unusual activity such as: large groups of people, hysteria at the scene of a fire or other disaster, drunk or quarrelsome persons, persons running away from or toward some incident or location, or people avoiding the police or watching police activity.

7. Conditions which are hazardous or require actions such as the repair of sidewalks, streets, street lights, and various fire hazards. In some instances, the officer should take remedial action himself. In other cases, he should report the condition through the proper channels.

INFORMATION AND ASSISTANCE

Besides his various activities in the area of crime control, the police officer to called upon by the public for information and assistance. It is important that he handle these request with dispatch and accuracy. This is especially true in time of emergency and disaster. The correct performance of such actions also tends to result in greater public cooperativeness.

AT CRISIS LOCATIONS

Patrol duties in fallout and crisis locations, while involving the same basic principles discussed above, will also be concerned with situations peculiar to crowded and unfamiliar conditions. The following list of such situations is suggestive, not exhaustive.

1. Hazardous conditions, such as insufficient ventilation, fire hazards, etc.

2. Violations of regulations, such as smoking at unauthorized times or places, unnecessary noise while others are trying to sleep, horseplay, scuffling, etc.

3. Evidences of poor morale or emotional disturbances.

4. In general, all situations about which the authorities should be kept informed, such as evidence of boredom, illness, behavior problems of small children, etc.

CONCLUSION

Patrol is the backbone of police service. Without constant vigilance on the part of the basic patrol unit, the patrolman, the police cannot hope to accomplish their objectives under normal or emergency conditions. It is, then, critical that the individual officer extend himself as far as possible in the performance of this indispensable police activity.

POLICE SCIENCE NOTES

BASIC CONCEPTS OF LAW AND ARREST

Man has been puzzling over the appropriateness of community controls throughout his recorded history and undoubtedly before that. What he has been trying to decide are the answers to: "Who is/are going to run the show?" "Under what restrictions must authority operate?" and "What acts by community members shall be required or prohibited?" Basic to an understanding of the complexity of answers to these questions is an awareness of the variety of systems and laws under which various societies have lived and are living. At some time some community has lived under laws directly opposite to those under which we now control ourselves, and their requirements were "right" for that time and place. In fact, we can bring to mind examples of changes which have occurred in our own United States of America during its existence—even within our own lifetime. The requirements placed upon the members of any community by its government consist of laws which filter out by prevailing over others in the market place of ideas and which are manifested by their issuance through formal governmental organizations.

Every police office should be aware of the fact that there is no law which has not been enacted in response to and for the purpose of correcting a problem which has become significant by the degree to which some member of the community have acted in opposition to the common belief. In short, where there is no meaningful opposition to the feelings of the majority there is no law in support of those beliefs. For example, cannibalism is not prohibited in the United States because opposition to it is so pervasive that it is reasonable to say that only the mentally ill have engaged in that gruesome activity.

Individuals and communities require guidelines defining acceptable conduct and reciprocal duties and responsibilities in order to attain feelings of tranquility, a sense of well-being, and a belief that conformance to group requirements will result in the society's respect for and supply of individual needs in response. Basic to any society, primitive or modern, is the necessity for disciplined behavior, and the necessity for community tranquility. Each individual must relinquish his right to act entirely for his own self-interest in return for the agreement of others not to deprive him unduly of his right to personal freedom or to impinge upon his reciprocal rights under the law. Every requirement of law acts to some degree to reduce individual freedom of action, but reasonable restrictions on absolute freedom are essential to community living and to protect individuals against others. As the danger to any community belief increases so will the group response grow in severity to reduce that threat, especially when the common belief is basic and widely accepted without reservation.

Police officers are faced with daily frustration caused by their inability to understand clearly that the freedom-loving citizens of our Nation have learned from past experience (some of which initiated our Nation's birth) that absolute authority demands rigid compliance with even the smallest and relatively unimportant requirement and results in stultifying repression of personal freedom. The ultimately efficient government can only be one in which power is so centralized that it is dictatorial and undemocratic. Therefore, laws have developed which restrict the police to that level of efficiency which is acceptable to the citizens and which permits the greatest possible individual freedom. Again, there is no law where there is no problem. Therefore, there should be little serious doubt that one of the highest duties of a police officer is to know and follow the law because it has been developed in answer to previously existing actions which were conducted in opposition to the beliefs of the people. Officials who are responsible for law enforcement must personify lawfulness as they interact with offenders. A peace officer is endowed with awesome power over life and property, and he must not only restrict his actions to those the law but also restrain himself personally to be considered a thoughtful, objective, police professional.

It is important that every police officer understands the basics of the checks and balances system under which we govern ourselves. Our forefathers so constructed our governmental system that none of the three branches of our government—the legislature, the executive, and the judicial—could become so strong that it would be able to dominate the people completely. The basic objective of this system is to prevent one or a few people from absolute control and overwhelming power. In its operation, the checks and balances system prevents domination by providing stumbling blocks in the paths of requirements which do not meet with the approval of the great majority of the citizens. Without considerable support, legislatures will not pass laws, the executive branch will not actively enforce them, and the courts will overturn them. However, those requirements which are backed by the great majority of the people are enacted by legislatures, enforced with great universality and vigor by the executive branch, and upheld by the courts.

The individual professional police officer understands the checks and balances system and acts within the law because of this knowledge. At the operational level, even though a patrol officer is aware of a problem he does not attempt to "enforce the law" when the legislature has not passed a statute dealing with it. He neither strains to fit the facts of an incident into another statute nor makes an arrest for an unrelated offense in order to harrass the "law breaker." At the executive level, the professional police administrator or agency head allocates the resources of his department according to priorities so that enforcement of important offenses is emphasized. The accompanying spinoff is naturally the de-emphasis of enforcement against those offenses which are determined to be of lesser importance. The term which applies to this assignment of priorities is *selective enforcement*.

Professional Demeanor

The appropriateness of the reasons for and the manner by which members of a community are deprived of their liberty is one of the most difficult problems to be solved by members of a society and its lawmakers. An arrest or detention is a matter of preventing the free movement of a person. In most cases, what is more important to the person subject to this deprivation of liberty is the manner in which an arrest or detention is effected. There is a great difference between simply following the directions of another without the free will to do any other thing one might wish to do and that loss *plus* being searched, handcuffed, placed in obvious incarceration, and even being stripped of all clothing and dignity for the purpose of maximizing security. In fact, most people will understand the necessity of appropriate loss of liberty, but what makes them seriously upset is the public spectacle and loss of face which it can entail when improperly conducted, especially when the arresting officer shows personal antagonism toward the prisoner.

The professional officer balances the importance of each factor involved in an arrest situation. Although safety to himself, his fellow officers and the general public is very important, he is well aware that it is not always the most important factor. In fact, he knows that some persons will submit to an arrest quietly unless demeaning security precautions are utilized or personal antagonism is manifested by the arresting officer. Unfortunately, the unprofessional officer often considers security and safety to be uppermost and controlling in nearly every case and is personally offended by lawbreakers. When these conditions prevail, arrested and detained persons are often subjected to such overwhelming threats to their psychological well-being (or face) that they find it necessary to fight back against those who are creating the threat. in some cases their loss of face or distress is so great that they physically attack any person who obstructs their liberty and are willing to kill to escape rather than to suffer the public humiliation of detention or arrest. Therefore, the professional officer effects his detentions and arrests with circumspection and avoids excessive psychological distress to those being restricted. By making the arrest as easy as possible on the offender, the arresting officer also makes it as easy as possible on himself and his coworkers. The professional exerts his will over those whom he is arresting by the use of reasoning rather than his club. The officer who is involved in fights significantly more often than his coworkers, however soon becomes well known and is avoided as a partner.

Persons usually react in three general ways to a police officer who is enforcing the law or is about to make an arrest. They may submit to his directions or the arrest without resistance. Such persons follow the directions of the officer because they believe that the officer is correct in what he is doing or they simply bow to the inevitable. The professional, skilled police officer will so conduct himself that the great majority of persons will react to his directions in this way.

Other persons may feel gravely threatened by the officer's actions and believe it necessary to attack either verbally or physically, or flee. Whatever their action may be, it is an attempt to reduce the real or imagined threat to their physical or mental well-being. Although the attack will usually be directed at the source of the threat, the officer, it may be against another person—an "innocent" third party. This is still an attempt to reduce their feelings of frustration, however, but the target will be an object or person who cannot "fight back." We have all witnessed examples of distressed persons who kick their cats, shout at their children, or drive their automobiles recklessly when frustrated. In fact, many times officers find themselves to be the "cat" whom it is necessary for the person to "kick" to compensate for a frustrating experience which occurred prior to the officer's arrival on the scene. The professional officer, because of his self-confidence, is never threatened by verbal "cat kicking." He is able to control these excited persons through the use of his calm, professional, competent manner so that they soon begin to accept his directions. This same technique is usually effective with those offenders who are inclined towards physical attack. The experienced professional officer knows with reasonable accuracy those who cannot be dissuaded and with reasonable force acts to protect himself and others from physical attack.

The professional officer asks himself questions such as these: "This person is attacking me verbally, therefore, he (NOT I) is greatly threatened by something. Am I the threat, or is it something else?" "Is this attack going to be all talk, or will it turn into a physical attack?" "What can I do to reduce his feeling of distress?" The unprofessional reacts out of his own fear of the verbal attack, retaliates in kind, and the situation rapidly escalates into physical combat or the bringing of inappropriate charges out of spite. Invariably the result of retaliatory action by an officer who attacks to save his own face, no matter how poorly the offender may have acted to initiate the incident, is the salvation of the offender's conscience. This is because the offender will be able to say to himself that the officer attacked him, therefore, no matter what the offender has done, the officer has become the "bad guy" who is subject to all the blame—the "offensive cat," if you will

The third reaction is that of ignoring or remaining unaffected by the threat. Persons who manifest this type of reaction are those who are secure, unconcerned, and believe that they are truly not endangered by the threat. They are convinced that those who are acting aggressively towards them cannot in fact harm them in any basic way. In everyday language, this type of individual is called a person with "self-confidence." It is this type of confidence that the professional police officer exhibits. It is a quiet confidence, as opposed to the blatant, pushy, aggressive, officious manner of those who are unsure of themselves and who try to make up for it with bluster, which is immediately recognizable as a lack of confidence.

Self-confidence is the kind of attitude which makes it possible to exert one's will upon others while encountering the least resistance from them. The officer who exhibits this confidence brings the belief into the minds of those he is controlling that: "This officer will not ask anything of me which is not only lawful but also reasonable and necessary, and if I refuse to act in response to his requests, I will be not only lawful but also unreasonable and appear foolish to others." On the other hand, if it is the person who is to be arrested who exhibits the self-confidence, that person is the one who has the greatest chance of defeating the officer and taking over control of the situation. The officer who allows himself to be manipulated is in for a very uncomfortable experience. The danger to the officer is rarely that of physical attack, rather he will feel greatly threatened psychologically. He may begin to believe that he is appearing foolish and damaged in his self-image (loss of face; receiving severe blows to his ego, etc.). Unless he retains his self-control, he may well commit a rash or illegal act which can easily result in disciplinary action or a civil suit naming him and his department as defendants. But the experienced professional officer never loses during these encounters because: He never presses or demands more than is absolutely necessary; Even though the law may empower him to do more; He always acts within the law and utilized it to accomplish its basic purpose, not just technical requirements which were designed to accomplish some other objective. His actions assure that his opponent becomes aware that: What the officer requires is within the law; The full extent of the available powers are never utilized without full reason; The officer never acts out of personal vengeance.

Professional Direction

ONLY ROOKIES TRY TO ENFORCE ALL THE LAWS ALL THE TIME, AND ONLY ROOKIES CONFINE THEIR ENFORCEMENT ACTIVITY ALMOST EXCLUSIVELY TO AN ARREST. The experienced professional officer has learned that enforcement of some laws is best accomplished by simply being present and visible. Other laws can be enforced by a warning or an educationally oriented conversion with actual or potential offenders. There are certain laws which do require that offenders be processed through the criminal justice system by either a summons or physical arrest. In most jurisdictions, with rare exceptions, no officer is in fact required to arrest for an offense except when ordered to do so by a magistrate, either by the judge in person or under his written order in the form of a warrant.

Criminal Law

A crime or an offense is an act or omission forbidden by law, prosecuted by the governmental officials of the jurisdiction, and punishable upon conviction. The statutes which define what acts or omissions are crimes or offenses must clearly state the kind of conduct which is prohibited or required and designate the punishment which is to be applied to those adjudged guilty.

Each statute which defines a crime is constructed of elements or criteria which the prosecution must prove before a defendant may be found guilty of the charge. The words used in statutes each have very special and particular meaning under law, and an officer must be careful to be aware of these legal terms because definitions in law sometimes differ from the meanings they convey when used in informal or daily conversation. For example, larceny or theft involves the *taking of the personal property of another*. Each of the underlined words is an element of the offense, and they are not the only elements. The "thief has not taken if he has not gained possession, it is not personal property if it is an attachment to a house, and it is not another's if the thief is a part owner or the property has been abandoned. Furthermore, even f he does commit all those acts, he has not committed theft unless he intended to steal. For example, the acts were committed under his reasonable belief that the property was his. Also, no matter how fervent was his intention to steal, there cannot be a conviction where the item "stolen" was not subject to ownership which is protected by law, for example an illegal lottery ticket.

Detentions

Police officers are empowered to make detentions and arrests under appropriate restrictions. A detention is a temporary restriction of one's liberty during which the detaining person is permitted to make a short investigation for the purpose of determining whether or not the person detained is subject to arrest for an offense. The authority and restrictions upon it which apply to this power of an officer are delineated by either court decisions or statutes, dependent upon the law which prevails within a particular jurisdiction. This type of detention is generally referred to as "stop and frisk." These three little words, however, have become the subject of thousands of pages of court decisions and statutes. This manual must cover the subject with just a few words, and readers should bear in mind that jurisdictions differ in what is permissible. Each officer should become well versed in the law on this subject as it is applied in his jurisdiction.

The stop and detention of a person is generally authorized when an officer has reasonable grounds for suspecting that the individual whom he intends to detain: has committed a crime, is committing a crime, is about to commit a crime.

Note that the facts on which the officer bases his stop and detention are less than those necessary for him to effect an arrest, and it is essential to his authority that the person to be detained must be suspected of criminal activity. An arrest requires that the officer has reasonable grounds for *believing* that the person has committed or is committing a crime, but a detention requires the officer to have reasonable grounds for *suspecting* involvement in criminal activity. Because the officer is possessed of information short of that required to make an arrest, he may not use deadly force to stop or detain the person.

An important factor in the laws dealing with detentions is that of the duration which will be permitted. In jurisdictions where the courts have delineated the law on this subject, case law permits officers to detain persons a reasonable time. The duration permitted is determined by the relative importance of permitting the officer time necessary to ascertain whether or not the person has committed a crime and the loss of freedom suffered by the person detained. Each case is decided on its own facts. Where statutes control, legislatures either permit a reasonable time, similar to court holdings, or specifically limit the duration, varying from ten minutes to two hours. Under both case law and statutes, however, an officer in every jurisdiction is required to release the person immediately after he has determined that the person has not committed a crime. Where the duration is limited to a specified time period, when the time limit has expired, the officer must either arrest the person for a crime or immediately release him, even though with more time to investigate the officer might have been able to develop sufficient information to effect an arrest.

Another critical difference among the various jurisdictions is the right of the officer to transport the person detained during the course of the investigation. In some jurisdictions the officer is not permitted to remove the person from the place at which the detention was initiated. In areas where it is permitted, the transportation must be conducted only when it is reasonably necessary for the purpose of investigating the possible criminal involvement of the person detained, and unless the investigation results in the person's arrest he should be returned to the place from which he was removed. The officer may ask any pertinent question of the person detained, for example his name, an explanation of what he is doing or where he is going, the ownership of any property in his possession, etc., but the officer must constantly remain aware that the person detained is under no obligation to answer any question. The detained individual may remain absolutely silent during the whole period of detention, is under no obligation to produce any identification or other property for the officer's inspection, and the office has no right to take *anything* from the person except a weapon.

Frisks

The frisk is a very limited search which may be conducted by an officer who has detained a person. It may be performed only when the officer: knows that the person has a weapon in his immediate possession; reasonably suspects that the person has a weapon in his immediate possession.

Note that the frisk is for weapons only, and that the officer must be able to state the facts which caused the development of his belief that the person possessed a weapon. The frisk: must be only for the purpose of locating the weapon; must be initially restricted to touching or grasping only the *outer* clothing of the individual; may be continued inside the outer clothing, pockets, etc. only after the officer has felt something which reasonably causes him to believe that a weapon is contained within.

If the officer finds a weapon, he may remove it from the person's possession. If the possession of the weapon on the part of the person constitutes a crime, the officer may arrest for that offense and retain the weapon as evidence. If the person is not arrested, the officer shall return the weapon at the end of the detention.

Arrests

An arrest is the deprivation of one's liberty by another for the purpose of initiating the arrested person's processing through the justice system, usually the criminal justice system. An arrest must be made in compliance with the restrictions which surround such an action. Otherwise, it is considered a false arrest and will cause the loss of the admissibility of any resulting evidence and possible loss of a conviction. The arresting officer may also possibly be subject to a suit for civil damages and be charged with a crime. An "arrest" which is made without the intention for processing the party into or through the justice system would be kidnapping within the statutes of most jurisdictions. Arrests can be made either under the authority of an arrest warrant or without a warrant, and the arresting person can be either a police officer or a person.

An arrest involves the following elements:

1. The arresting party "intends" to take the arrested person into custody. Although in most cases the arresting party's actual intention is to take the person into custody, and the best way to express this is by stating words such as, "You are under arrest for…," courts determine the intention from all the defend himself from false arrest liability by simply claiming that he had no intention to arrest.

2. The arresting party acts under the belief that he has legal authority. If the arresting party is correct in his belief the arrest is valid, but if he actually does not have the authority, it is an illegal arrest. Examples of lack of authority would be arrests made under a void or non-existent warrant, even though the officer had been informed that there was a warrant, and arresting for a misdemeanor not committed in his presence, if this is not permitted in his jurisdiction.

3. The arresting party gains custody and control of the arrested person. An arrest is not complete until the arrested person comes within the custody and control of the arresting party, and this state exists when either the person submits or his resistance is overcome. It is not necessary that the person be touched or that any force be applied if he understands that he is in the power of the arresting person and submits to control; that his liberty is restrained is sufficient. On the other hand, if the officer's words, "You are under arrest for…" are immediately followed by the suspect's running away, there has been no arrest. In fact, unless the flight includes some physical contact or the application of force between the suspect and the arresting party, the flight does not constitute resisting arrest.

An arrest warrant is an order of a court directing police officers to arrest and bring before the court the person named in the warrant. If it is practicable, an officer should obtain a warrant before making an arrest. The basic purpose served by the warrant process is to protect persons from unjustified arrests and prosecutions. The warrant is one of the manifestations of the checks and balances system in that a member of the judicial branch passes upon the legitimacy of actions intended by the executive branch. Given the same circumstances or facts known to an officer, if he arrests after obtaining a warrant, the courts will in all probability sustain the arrest, but if he arrests without one his action will be much more closely scrutinized for probable cause.

Following are common requirements for a valid arrest warrant:

1. Probable Cause: The magistrate issuing the warrant must make an impartial judgment on the basis of the evidence presented that probable cause exists that a crime has been committed by the person to be arrested. Probable cause is more than mere suspicion on the part of the officer requesting the warrant, but he is not required to present proof beyond a reasonable doubt of the person's guilt. Information supplied by informants may be used, even if their identity is not disclosed, but officers must be able to state facts which indicate the probable reliability of such information which they have not acquired through their own observation.

2. Affidavit supported by oath or affirmation. Some person must swear to his belief in the truth of the statements contained in the affidavit.

3. Person Particularly Described: The description must be such that the officer serving the warrant is supplied with information sufficient for him to believe with reasonable certainty that the person whom he is about to arrest is the person described. Ordinarily the warrant includes the name of the person, but sometimes this is not known. In such cases, a physical description, occupation or place of employment, residence address or other information may be utilized to particularly describe the person.

4. Nature of the Offense: Although the language need not describe the offense with the same detail as in an indictment or information, it must be sufficient to inform the person of the subject of the accusation.

5. Officers Designated: The warrant may direct an individual officer or a class of officers to arrest the person. For example, the warrant may be addressed to all police officers in the state.

6. Issued in the Name of the Jurisdiction: Warrants must be issued either in the name of the state under which the issuing magistrate's authority exists or in the name of the United States when issued by a federal official.

7. Signed by the Issuing Official: Only an official authorized by law may sign a warrant, and he must be a neutral and impartial person, a magistrate, or judicial officer.

Requirements to Be Followed in Serving a Warrant:

1. Person serving warrant must be named in it. Either the officer or person serving the warrant must be specifically named in the warrant or he must be within the class of persons designated.

2. Must Be Served Within the Jurisdiction: A warrant issued in one state may not be served in another unless the second state has authorized this service by statute. An officer in the second state may arrest if he has knowledge of the warrant's issuance; however, his knowledge constituting the reasonable grounds for his belief that a felony has been committed by the person.

3. Officer Make Known His Purpose: Unless the information will imperil the arrest or the person flees or resists before the officer can convey his intention, the officer must inform the person of his intention to arrest and the cause of it.

4. Show the Warrant or Inform Person It Exists: Under common law, the officer must possess the warrant and show it to the person if he demands it, but most modern codes have relaxed this requirement under the needs of today's society. However, the officer's belief in the existence of the warrant must be reasonable, and it shall be shown to the person as soon as practicable if he so requests.

Arrests can be made without a warrant by both officers and private persons. The authority of a police officer is more extensive, but not as much so as most people believe.

1. Both an officer and a private person can arrest for a felony committed in their presence and for a felony which has actually been committed but not in their presence.

2. An officer can arrest for a felony which he reasonably believes has been committed by the individual to be arrested, even though the crime has not been committed, but a private person may not. Stated in another way, the officer is protected if he makes a reasonable mistake, but the private person is not.

3. In all jurisdictions an officer can arrest for a misdemeanor which is committed in his presence, but in some jurisdictions a private person may not.

4. In some jurisdictions an officer may arrest for a misdemeanor not committed in his presence when he has reasonable cause to believe that it has been committed by the suspect, but a private person may not do so in any jurisdiction.

The Constitution, statutes, and court decisions refer to the necessity of the "reasonable cause" and "probable cause" which must exist before the authority to arrest arises. This degree of proof, evidence, or information to be possessed by the officer who intends an arrest must be more than good faith suspicion (enough to effect a detention for investigation), but it need not be proof beyond a reasonable doubt of the person's guilt. The reasonable cause is determined as of the time the arrest is effected. Evidence acquired after the arrest may not be utilized to validate a preceding arrest. In fact, if the arrest is not based on probable cause that evidence will be excluded no matter how condemning and conclusive it might have been in proving the defendant's guilt.

The standards by which an officer's reasonable cause to arrest is ascertained is determined individually for each case. That is, the information in his possession and its relationship to the development of probable cause in his mind (as opposed to a reasonable man test) in the light of his personal experience and the circumstances of the case before the court will all be considered by the court in arriving at its holding that there was or was not probable cause to arrest. Actions which do not attract the attention of untrained or inexperienced persons or officers may convince the experienced and trained officer that a particular offense is being committed. This experience may include not only the activity but also the person performing it. An officer who knows of the past criminal record of a suspect may consider that history along with other facts in developing reasonable cause, but the officer may not arrest on only the basis of one's previous criminal record.

The following are sources which can develop reasonable cause to arrest for the officer:

1. Complaints From Victims and Information From Witnesses: Statements and information received which indicate that a crime has been committed and which provide evidence by which the offender can be ascertained by developing reasonable cause to arrest. An officer must bear in mind that if the crime complained of is less than a felony no arrest will be valid unless a warrant is first issued, unless their jurisdiction is one in which officers are permitted to arrest for misdemeanors on reasonable cause. But if the jurisdiction is one in which private persons can arrest for misdemeanors, the victim or a witness can make the arrest and turn the prisoner over to the officer.

2. Information From an Informant: The reliability of the informant is an important factor. An officer should maintain records on the cases in which the particular informant's information has proven to be accurate, and whenever possible the officer should make further investigation to determine that the information is correct prior to making his arrest without a warrant.

3. Observation of the Officer: When the officer witnesses the actual commission of the crime, there is reasonable grounds to arrest without serious question. But when his observations lead him to a reasonable suspicion only, then he must first detain until his investigation leads to reasonable cause to arrest. When all the circumstances lead the officer to the reasonable belief that a felony has been committed, he may arrest under his reasonable belief in any jurisdiction, but for a misdemeanor only if his jurisdiction permits that type of arrest. An officer can always obtain a warrant and effect the arrest later for the misdemeanor.

4. Physical Evidence: Fingerprints, identification dropped at the scene of the crime, footprints leading from the scene of the crime to the place of apprehension, and other physical evidence closely tying the suspect to the crime would be sufficient to give rise to reasonable cause to arrest.

5. Information Received from the Officer's Department or From Another Agency: Information received over the police radio, at briefings, or from wanted circulars or lists may

form the basis for reasonable cause; however, persons initiating these messages must have reasonable cause for doing so.

Citation/Summons Process

The processing of offenders into the justice system is ordinarily begun when he is contacted by the police. At this point the person may be "physically" arrested and taken to jail or other place of detention to await his appearance before the court. Very few defendants want to spend time in jail, and the purpose of such incarceration is only to assure the appearance of the defendant before the magistrate. Originally, under our criminal law, incarceration to await court appearance was the only process utilized no matter what the degree of the offense. Beginning with the widespread use of the automobile and the numerous offenses committed by motorists, spurred by the growth of more liberal feelings toward offenders by both the general community and persons involved in the administration of justice, and because of the great savings in time and money which the method causes, written notification to an offender of the charge to be made and the time and place to appear before a magistrate has now become prevalent. Commonly called "a ticket," the citation or summons process is now not only used universally for traffic code offenses but has expanded to include many other types as well such as theft, assault, battery, a variety of regulatory statutes, and other misdemeanor offenses. Whenever possible or permitted, an officer should use this process.

The "ticket" procedure can proceed in three ways: an arrest followed by release, a detention followed by release, or the delivery of a notice of charges to be filed to the person charged. Although definitions differ somewhat, the citation process is that which involves an arrest by an officer followed by the offender's signing on the citation that he promises to appear in court at the time indicated, at which time he is given a copy of the citation and released from arrest. The defendant's signature and promise is his "bail." Should he fail to appear, he commits an offense which is separate from that of the original charge. The offender may refuse to sign the citation, but if he chooses to exert this right the officer is required to incarcerate him.

In jurisdictions in which the summons process is utilized, the offender is detained (not arrested) for a period necessary for the officer to determine the defendant's identity and write the summons, a copy is given to the person (he is not required to take it, and he is then released from detention. The suspect is not required to sign the summons, he commits no offense if he does not appear, and upon his non-appearance the court simply issues a warrant of arrest for the charge made.

The notice process involves leaving a written notice to be discovered by the person to be charged or otherwise delivering such notice, for example by mail. The vast majority of cases in which this process is used involves parking offenses, but it can also be utilized for many other offenses. Whether the person receives the notice or not, the charge is filed before the court, and if the defendant does not appear as directed in the notice, an arrest warrant will be issued by the court. Each officer must be aware of the law concerning these processes in his area because in many jurisdictions numerous offenses have been required by statutes and departmental regulations to be so handled. Therefore, an officer who incarcerates a person who is entitled under law or departmental regulation to be offered a citation or summons will be subject to prosecution, civil suit, and/or disciplinary action.

POLICE SCIENCE NOTES

FORCE, SEARCH, AND SEIZURE

Use of Force

The right to use force against another varies according to the reasonable and apparent necessity that it be applied. The most important factors considered in the determination of how much force may be used by an officer are the following:

1. Is the force used or contemplated essential, or could the actor reasonably foresee that less force would be sufficient?
2. Does the crime to be prevented or the arrest to be attempted involve a felony or misdemeanor?
3. Does the act or crime to be prevented by force endanger property rights or human life and limb, and to what extent?
4. What are the responsibilities under law between the actor and what or whom he is attempting to protect with force?
5. Do departmental regulations restrict officers to less force than that permitted by statutes and court decisions?

When necessary, a police officer is permitted to use force in the performance of his duty to accomplish the following objectives:

1. To preserve the peace, prevent commission of offenses, or prevent suicide or self-inflicted injury.
2. To make *lawful* arrests and searches, to overcome resistance to such arrests and searches, and to prevent escapes from custody.
3. To defend himself or another against unlawful evidence to his person or property.
4. To interrupt an intrusion on or interference with the lawful possession of property.

Lawful force is an aggressive act committed by a police officer in the performance of his duty when it is necessary to accomplish any of the objectives listed above. Deadly force is that which under the prevailing circumstances is capable of or intended to cause death or great bodily injury. Although lawful, or necessary, force is the minimum amount sufficient to achieve a legitimate objective, this does not mean that an officer is permitted to escalate the force he uses without limit until the police objective is accomplished. For example, it would be illegal and immoral for an office to use deadly force to prevent a person from unlawfully interfering with or even destroying anothers personal property such as an automobile, even if under the circumstances, shooting the person would be the only way the destruction could be stopped.

Deadly force may be used to prevent a felony which threatens the life or safety of a person. However, when the felony does not involve such danger, the tendency of the law among jurisdictions to prohibit such extreme measures is steadily growing. Even in those jurisdictions in which the statutes and court cases continue to permit deadly force to be used to prevent felonies in which life is not endangered police departments are prohibiting it through their policies and regulations.

Once a crime has been committed, the chief law enforcement interest is the apprehension of the offender. Although laws vary, deadly force may generally be used to effect the arrest of a dangerous criminal who is endangering or has threatened human life, but this amount of force may not be used on a thief no matter how much he stole. No jurisdiction punishes theft with the death penalty, so no officer should apply "capital punishment" to a thief.

In no jurisdiction is deadly force permitted to effect an arrest for a misdemeanor. If the subject resists, the officer may escalate the amount of his force until it becomes deadly, it this is necessary to protect himself from death or great bodily injury, and the officer is not required to retreat. However, the use of deadly force is not justified to apprehend a misdemeanant even though he is in flight and there is no other way to capture him.

The right of self-defense is based on the necessity of permitting a person who is attacked to take reasonable steps to prevent harm to himself. This right permits him to use any reasonable force to prevent threatened harm, offensive bodily contact, or confinement. Since it is a defense to a charge or accusation of use of force, the burden is on the actor to show the facts which caused him to use force and that it was reasonable.

The privilege to act to defend oneself arises not only when the danger is real but even when the danger does not in fact exist, providing that the belief in the presence and degree of anger is reasonable. For example, if after a long, high speed, wild and reckless attempt on the part of a motorist to escape an officer the offender stops, leaps from his car and whips his hand inside his jacket, it would be reasonable for the officer to believe that he was about to be fired upon. It would be lawful use of deadly force for the officer to draw and fire his sidearm at the offender even if, in fact, the motorist was unarmed and reaching for only his wallet and driver license. The belief that he is threatened, however, must be that which a reasonable man would have under the circumstances. The person defending himself is not required to restrain himself with outstanding bravery, but on the other hand the reasonable man standard does not permit an abject coward to attack when there is no reasonable ground for his belief that he is in danger.

If force is continued after at attacker is disarmed, defeated, helpless, or the danger has passed, it is unlawful. No matter how gross he provocation had been on the part of the original attacker, there is no right to continue the use of force for revenge or punishment.

No officer should possess or use any weapon or incapacitating device which is neither issued nor approved by his department, including the ammunition in his firearm. Naturally, issued or approved weapons which have been materially altered to increase the force which they may apply should also not be possessed or used.

Under normal circumstances only the methods or weapons listed below should be used to apply force. It is the officer's responsibility to first exhaust every reasonable means of employing lesser force before escalating to a more severe application of force. The following methods are listed in ascending order from the least severe to the most drastic:

1. Physical strength and skill
2. Approved noxious substance, mace, gas, etc.
3. Approved baton, sap, or blackjack
4. Approved sidearm or other firearm loaded with approved ammunition.

Weapons should never be brandished or displayed as a threat unless their use under the circumstances would be reasonable and lawful.

Only those security devices or measures issued or approved by the department should be used to restrain those in custody, and the devices and measures should be used reasonably and only for the purpose of preventing:

1. Escape
2. Destruction of evidence
3. Attack
4. Self-inflicted injury
5. Commission of an offense

An officer who, out of anger or for the purpose of inflicting punishment or pain, cinches handcuffs too tightly, places a person in a straight jacket, strips a prisoner naked, puts an offender into a padded cell, incarcerates an offender with others who may attack him, or continues security measures when they are no longer reasonably necessary is acting unlawfully and reprehensibly. It is the responsibility of the courts to punish, not the police.

The decision of an officer to use handcuffs or not is a difficult one. Opinions on this subject vary among experienced, professional officers. Where departmental regulations have been issued which state the circumstances under which handcuffs shall, may, or must not be utilized they should be followed. However, because of the difficulty involved in covering all the possible situations in a regulation, they have not been written for officers' guidance in many agencies. The officer must then utilize his professional discretion.

The officer who decides whether or not to use handcuffs on the basis of his answer to, "If I were this prisoner, would I realize or could I be lead to understand that handcuffs are reasonable and necessary?" will arrive at the appropriate conclusion. An officer who states that "I handcuff everybody I arrest," does not, it is to be hoped, really do so. It is obviously ridiculous to handcuff "little old ladies" and small children without exception. On the other hand, the officer who fails to restrain dangerous felons, persons in a state of rage, or others who can be reasonably expected to do any of the acts which security measures are designed to prevent certainly should be handcuffed.

An officer who fails to use his cuffs when it is appropriate endangers himself, his coworkers, the prisoner, and others. Persons who are restrained by security devices are helpless, and officers must remain constantly aware of the possibility that such prisoners may be injured or suffer needlessly if precautions are not utilized. Therefore, secured persons must not be left unattended unnecessarily or otherwise subjected to needless danger or discomfort. The variety of possible situations to be avoided are too numerous to mention, but two must be. Prisoners should never be handcuffed to a vehicle which is used to transport them. If the vehicle is involved in an accident, they cannot be removed from it if the officer is incapacitated or otherwise incapable of releasing them. It is appropriate to restrain handcuffed prisoners with safety belts because anyone can release the belts. However, if the person is handcuffed to the vehicle, only an officer can provide the key to the cuffs. Prisoners who indicate that they need to relieve themselves must be permitted to do so as soon as possible. The officer who refuses to permit his prisoner to use toilet facilities or to aid the nauseated person who must vomit is inflicting cruel and unusual punishment upon him.

Search and Seizure

The most important factor relating to the law of search and seizure, and what each officer should seriously consider before he begins any search for or collection of evidence is that WHENEVER POSSIBLE A SEARCH WARRANT SHOULD BE OBTAINED BEFORE SEARCHING FOR OR SEIZING EVIDENCE.

Both state and federal constitutions guarantee to everybody protection against unreasonable searches and seizures. This protection extends to their person, houses, papers, and other property. No search warrant may be issued without probable cause, supported by oath or affirmation, and every warrant must particularly describe the place to be searched and the persons or things to be seized.

The protection given by the Fourth Amendment arose from the unpleasant experiences suffered by colonial Americans when searches by English soldiers were conducted under the authority of "writs of assistance" or "general warrants." These writs and warrants were issued with little restraint, without probable cause, and empowered authorities to conduct searches virtually any place on the mere suspicion that goods subject to seizure might be discovered.

The words of the Fourth Amendment must be interpreted by the courts so that the meaning of the law can be applied to the fact situations of each case presented. Thousands of cases have defined "person," "houses," "probable cause," "search," and other words which appear in the Amendment.

Although persons subjected to unlawful searches and seizures have recourse to civil actions against officials who violate their rights, the most common procedure by which they protect themselves is through the application of the exclusionary evidence rule. The exclusionary rule is simply that evidence obtained by unreasonable searches and seizures will not be admitted upon trial, usually upon objection raised by the defendant at a pre-trial "suppression hearing." The rule is not provided for in the Constitution, rather it was developed by the courts as their solution to the means by which the provision of the Amendment would be enforced, not adopt it. Today, however, it is universally applied in both federal and state courts because of the holding of the Supreme Court of the United States in the case of Mapp v. Ohio in 1961. The purpose to be fulfilled by the rule is that officers will be deterred from illegally searching for or seizing evidence when they know that it cannot be used against the defendant to prove his guilt.

Search Warrants

A search warrant is an order written in the name of the State, signed by a judicial officer in the proper exercise of his authority, directing a sheriff, constable, or other officer to search a specified place for evidence, stolen property or other "fruits" of a crime, or contraband, and to bring the articles enumerated before the court if they are discovered.

The following are criteria or requirements which must be met before a valid search warrant may be issued:

1. **Probable Cause**

    If the facts in the affidavit are sufficient to lead a reasonable and prudent man to believe that a crime has been committed and that the articles described can be found at the place specified, then issuance of a search warrant is justified. Information received by an officer from an undisclosed informant may be used as the basis for a search warrant, but the applicant for the warrant must be able to give the judicial officer substantial reasons to support the probable validity of the information which has been provided. The underlying circumstances upon which the applicant bases his belief must be specified by him. It is not sufficient to merely state, even with fervor, the police officer's belief. The facts of which he is aware which led to the development of that belief must also be stated.

2. **Oath of Affirmation**

    If this requirement is not fulfilled, the evidence obtained will not be admitted. The presumption that the magistrate had sworn the applicant is rebuttable by the defendant, and if no oath was administered the warrant is invalid and the evidence will be lost (excluded).

3. **Particular Description of Place and Things**

    Whatever the wording to describe the place to be searched, the objective to be served is that the officers who are commanded to conduct the search will not, if they follow the description included in the warrant, search the wrong premises and disturb the rights of the innocent. If the warrant does not identify the property to be seized, it will not justify any seizure of that property. Contraband such as prohibited arms, explosive devices, and gambling equipment will ordinarily not be required to be as specifically described as stolen goods, since contraband is sizeable by any officer lawfully observing it. When warrants are obtained for contraband, the best description possible under the circumstances should always be attempted.

4. **Issuing Official**

    The purpose served by requiring warrants is to assure that the innocent will not be disturbed by uncontrolled and unreasonable actions of officials of the executive branch of government. Therefore, the impartial and objective consideration by the judiciary of the probable cause and the reasonableness of the contemplated action is interposed as a restraint. Attempts to bypass this objective, even to accomplish other well-founded purposes such as the efficient issuance of warrants, have generally been found unconstitutional by the courts.

5. **Property Subject to Seizure**

Under early law, only stolen property could be seized under a search warrant. However, types of articles subject to seizure have been greatly expanded. Limitations still exist in some states such as requiring that only stolen or embezzled property (fruits of the crime), articles used to commit the crime (instrumentalities), or articles which are prohibited or controlled by statutes (contraband) may be seized. Such restrictions prevent officers from taking objects which are important as evidence, such as shoes worn by a suspect which could be compared with footprints found at the scene, but which fail to meet the definition of statutory restrictions. The United States Supreme Court in *Warden v. Hoyden* held in 1967, that statutes which permitted search warrants to issue for "mere evidence" are constitutional. It is up to those states which still follow the old rule to change their statutes or court decisions to permit seizure of evidence, but they are not required to do so.

Only those items specified in the warrant may be seized. If other property is seized, it must be under authority other than that provided by the warrant.

6. **Execution Only By Those Ordered**

A search warrant may only be executed by those commanded by it to act, but the person designated may be specifically by either name or class (peace officers, for example). The person designated may be assisted by others, however.

7, **Time Limit**

A search warrant must be executed within a reasonable time or it will fail to meet constitutional requirements. The amount of time which is reasonable varies, of course, according to the circumstances of each case. Most jurisdictions have by statute limited the time in which a search warrant may be executed, and the permissible period varies from a number of hours to more than a week. Some jurisdictions require special judicial authorization for warrants to be served at night

8. **Prior Notice, Demand, and Forcible Entry**

If the local law allows and the warrant is for the seizure of items which can be destroyed quickly or if officers are aware of facts which reasonably lead them to believe notice to occupants would lead to danger of attack, entry may usually be effected without notice. Otherwise they are first required to notify persons within the premises of their identity and right to enter and make a demand that they be permitted to enter. Reasonable and necessary force may be used to effect entry when officers must act quickly to avoid evidence destruction or attack, or if they are denied entry after notice has been given and their demand had been refused. Force may also be used to enter unoccupied premises or when the denial is passive, for example, when occupants remain silent and do not open the door.

Warrantless Searches and Seizures

Three factors have influenced and caused the development of those laws under which warrantless searches are permitted. They are permitted and lawful:

1. By consent
2. When necessity or emergency require immediate action
3. Where no right to protection exists

Consent Searches

A general principle of law is that one can waive any right or privilege to which he is entitled. However, because rights and privileges have arisen from previously experienced problems, court observe very carefully the evidence presented in support of contentions that a defendant consented to a search.

Consent must be voluntary, the prosecution has the burden of proving consent clearly, and some sort of positive action by the person waiving must be shown. For example, unless the person positively states his consent or makes some clearly understood gesture, the consent will not be held to be voluntary.

The search cannot extend beyond that granted by the terms of the consent in either area or time. That is, consent to search a room will not permit other rooms or the whole house to be searched, and the person may stop the search at any time simply by revoking his consent.

The person consenting must have the capacity to do so. A person who has the right to possess premises or things may give consent, but others may not. For example, the occupant of a hotel room may consent to its search but not the management, a parent can consent to a search of a minor child's room but not that of an adult child if the room is exclusively that child's, although permission to search areas used in common by the family is valid; a minor child's consent is unlikely to be held valid, but an adult child can consent to a search of at least jointly used areas; a spouse can consent if the premises are occupied by both spouses; and a person caring for the personal property of another may permit search of it.

Immediate Action Required

The most prevalent situations under which this exception is granted are searches made incident to a lawful arrest. Necessity is the motivating factor in permitting these searches. The two purposes served are to protect the arresting officer from attack and to prevent the person from access to things which would facilitate his escape, and to assure that evidence will not be destroyed by the defendant.

Should any of the following criteria not be met, the evidence discovered will be excluded:

1. The arrest must be lawful.
2. The search must be made for the purposes listed above (protection, security, evidence).
   An arrest for an unlicensed vehicle, to be followed by a citation, may not be the basis for a search for drugs as there is no relationship between the offense and the purpose of the search.
3. The arrest must not be a sham or subterfuge made only to initiate a search not based on reasonable cause.

An arrest warrant sworn out by officers (who merely suspect a burglary by the subject) charging the defendant with spitting on the sidewalk for the purpose of gaining entrance to his residence when they execute it, evidence of the burglary would be excluded.

Both the area searched and the time during which the search will be permitted are limited. Officers may make a reasonable search of areas within the person's reach or the distance through which he might be able to quickly leap in order to obtain a weapon for attack or evidence to destroy. Searching for evidence during an arrest beyond this area is no longer permitted without a search warrant. The search must be made contemporaneously with the arrest. After the subject has been removed from the scene and/or confined in jail, the necessity of immediate action no longer prevails, and the officer must obtain a search warrant to search the area of the arrest. An arrested person may be immediately fully searched, as opposed to a mere pat-down for weapons, incident to an arrest for which he is actually being taken into custody, or the search may be delayed until booking.

Once in jail, an arrestee or his property room effects may be researched without a warrant where the searches are not unreasonably made, i.e., harassment searches.

The right of officers to search a car beyond the reach of the subject being arrested, for example in the closed trunk or even the locked glove compartment,, would have to be based on grounds other than the arrest itself, i.e., on probable cause to search those areas, on consent, or "plain sight," or on a valid inventory.

When probable cause exists and the evidence is contained within a moving (or about to be moved) vehicle, officers may search. There is a significant difference in the necessity for immediate action between searches of buildings and searches of vehicles which may speedily be moved out of the jurisdiction before a search warrant can be obtained. An occupied car on a highway is movable, and the persons within it are alerted to the presence of officers. The evidence may never again be located if courts were to require officers to obtain a warrant to search under these circumstances. To conduct a warrantless search of a "moving" vehicle, the officer should have that amount of information which would cause a court to readily issue a search warrant if there were time to procure one. The officer may make the search without first arresting the person. The search will be upheld under the vehicle exception if the essential requirements of probable cause are shown to have existed prior to the search.

Where No Right to Protection Exists

Seizures of evidence without a search is not a violation of the Fourth Amendment when officers are lawfully present and the article seized is seen by them. Courts do not require officers to leave obvious evidence to be destroyed, but officers must not be trespassers at the time the evidence is observed. Furthermore, if an officer is a trespasser when he does see evidence, he cannot then procure a search warrant on the basis of the information he acquired as a trespasser.

The protection offered by constitutional provisions are to protect persons against the acts of government officers, not private parties. Therefore, if a private person obtains evidence through unlawful entrance or burglary, the evidence may be used against the criminal defendant. Of course, if an officer initiated the private person's action or participated in it, the evidence would be excluded. Searches and seizures are unlawful when they reasonably intrude into areas where the person can reasonably expect privacy, but not outside those areas. Open fields, public streets, and other places of similar description are outside the restrictions of the Fourth Amendment.

Inventories of vehicles which come into the hand of the police through impounding procedures are permitted. The inventory made of the vehicle is for the purpose of making an inventory of its contents to protect the owner rather than a search for evidence of an offense. The officer's intrusion is only justifiable if it is a good faith attempt to protect the property in the car. In effect, the evidence is discovered "accidentally" while the officer is doing what he has a right to do and where he has legitimate cause to be.

POLICE SCIENCE NOTES

POLICIES, PROCEDURES, AND REGULATIONS

Good, effective management techniques applied to any organization require that each person within the agency knows what is expected of him and what to expect of others as they carry out their functions and bring the group effort to life. Professional management is important to police departments, too. All officers and employees should be well informed as to what they are to do, how they are to do it, and the goals to be attained by both their own unit and the department as a whole.

Every person in the organization should know exactly the person who is his superior as well as those who are his subordinates.

Channels should be established through which information flows up and down and through which authority is delegated. These lines of control permit the delegation of authority, the placing of responsibility, the supervision of work, and the coordination of effort. Lines of control should be clearly defined and well understood by all members so that each may know to whom he is responsible and who, in turn, is responsible to him.

Sound and adequate enforcement policies are essential to gaining enforcement objectives and will guide police officers in putting into effect the kind of enforcement program envisioned by the administration. Clear statements of policy will help to resolve doubts in determining administrative intent. Policy development is essential to the success of any organization, and policies should be in writing so that they can be used as the basis on which the departmental operations are constructed.

Policy indicates the general course of direction of an organization, within which the activities of the personnel and units must operate. This establishment of *general* administrative guidelines relates to and complements the main objectives of the organization. For example, the policy concerning the issuance of citations in traffic accident cases might take the following form: "Violations of driving regulations cause traffic accidents, and accidents may be reduced to effective traffic law enforcement. Violators should be issued citations when evidence exists to justify such action." The intent of this policy statement is to inform officers that the policy of the department is to enforce laws. Obviously, this policy is not concerned with the procedures to be followed in preparing each citation, nor does it establish any precise rules. Procedures and rules and regulations must not only follow policy, but must originate from policy.

Established policy, although allowing individual supervisors to think for themselves, limits possible mistakes within manageable bounds. Independent thinking should be encouraged because it develops administrative abilities. Potential executives can be developed only by permitting discretion and initiative on the part of the supervisors. Carefully delineated policy statements allow this latitude.

The term *Policy* is not synonymous with *Procedure*, nor do either of these terms have the same meaning as *Rules and Regulations*. The following definitions are offered to clarify and insure uniformity of terminology:

Policy

Policy consists of principles and values which guide the performance of a department in a particular situation. It is a statement of guiding principles which should be followed in activities which are directed toward the attainment of department objectives. Policy is formulated by analyzing objectives and determining through research those principles which will best guide the department in achieving its objectives. Policy is based upon police ethics and experience, the desires of the community and the mandate of the law.

Policy is articulated to inform the public and department employees of the principles which will be adhered to in the performance of the law enforcement function. Additionally, policy establishes operational standards to assist department employees in the necessary exercise of discretion in discharging their responsibility.

An officer in the performance of his duty is confronted with an infinite variety of complex situations which require police action. Since policy is objective rather than situation oriented, it is broad enough in scope to encompass most situations. Policy, therefore, must be stated in general terms.

Procedure

A procedure is a method of performing an operation or a manner of proceeding on a course of action. It differs from policy in that it directs action in a particular situation to perform a specific task within the guidelines of policy. Both policies and procedures are objective oriented; however, policy establishes limits of action while procedure directs response within those limits.

Rule or Regulation

A rule or regulation is a specific prohibition or requirement which is stated to prevent deviations from policy or procedure. Rules and regulations allow little deviation other than for stated exceptions.

Many departments have been studied by police management consultants, and the results of these surveys are, with few exceptions, predictable. The larger the agency, the better their policies and procedures and the greater the change that they are all in writing and periodically reviewed and changed to fit present circumstances.

Policy and procedure formulation require planning and research. The larger agencies can afford such activities but the smaller ones cannot. The larger the organization is the greater likelihood that there is a formalized planning and research unit with permanent staff personnel.

Of the nearly 40,000 police departments in the United States, 98.9% have less than 100 personnel, and 82.2% have less than five.

There should be written directives applicable to auxiliary officers. At the very minimum these should cover such matters as eligibility for membership, application procedures, use of equipment and the wearing of the uniform, agency organization, disciplinary procedures, powers of arrest, use of force (including carrying of weapons both on and off duty), pursuit driving restrictions, and procedures for separation from the force.

Sworn officers are administered oaths before entering upon their duties. The intention is to impress upon officers that their conduct must be exemplary. Oaths of office for the police and codes of ethics are usually brief, but their every word is of the greatest import.

The departmental oath for auxiliary police may be included in the application for membership in the auxiliary police. The following oath is typical:

> I hereby acknowledge my complete understanding that the standby law enforcement assignment for which I am volunteering carries with it the requirement that I will, without question, obey and execute to the best of my ability the legal orders of those designated to supervise and command my activities; that I am to complete all assigned training courses; and that my violation or disregard of the Rules and Regulations of my organization will be cause for disciplinary action or dismissal. Furthermore, I understand that any false statements intentionally made in my application disqualifies me for membership in the _____ Police Auxiliary.
> Signed:_____
> Date:_____

The community expects better and more moral behavior from the police than they do of both over governmental employees and members of the private sector. These expectations apply both on and off duty, and all officers are subjected to close scrutiny in all their statements and actions. The community demands that those who enforce group standards rigidly abide by them.

Following are basic principles guiding conduct applicable to the police:

Courtesy

Officers are expected to be courteous at all times no matter how great the provocation, even if such would cause others to lose their tempers. This is not to say that they are to be servile. Although it is true that they are servants of the public need, they are not servants of individual members of the community as officers act within their sphere of authority. It is not difficult to be courteous when one learns to be an *objective* enforcer of the law, and this means that personal prejudices and animosities are to be repressed. Officers should be particularly attentive to persons who seek information or assistance and in each case try to put themselves in the "others' shoes"—no officer should act toward persons in any manner other than what he would reasonably expect from them under similar circumstances. It must be constantly borne in mind by policemen that many persons whom they will meet professionally will be under great stress and may act in ways that they will later regret. But the officer who acts unprofessionally will be remembered negatively. The person who provoked the officer will then blame the officer for all that transpired, and the lawbreaker will then have a "patsy" on which to blame his own faults.

Punctuality

Officers should be punctual in their engagements and expeditious in the performance of their duties. Again, the community expects more from them than from others.

Professional Objectivity

The professional officer is just, impartial, and reasonable in his enforcement of the laws he is sworn to uphold. Objective law enforcement never includes overstepping the limits of legal authority and power, and the officer's action or inaction will never be for personal gain or in vengeance.

Protection of Public Funds

Officers are custodians of the public property entrusted to their care and shall not misuse their equipment or otherwise be wasteful of public funds.

Cooperation

Law enforcement is a cooperative effort among the community and other governmental agencies. Full cooperation by policemen should be offered to both private and public groups so that the safety and welfare of the community will be assured.

Communication

The professional officer actively disseminates practical and useful information to others regarding matters of the public safety and welfare. He does not passively wait for others to come to him.

Exemplary Conduct

The professional officer's conduct, both public and private, is such that the public regards him as an example of fidelity, stability and morality.

Governmental Allegiance

Officers should be faithful in the allegiance to our government, loyal to the ethics of their profession, and accept as a sacred obligation their responsibility as citizens to support the

Constitutions of the Nation and their State and to defend our principles of liberty. Departmental rules, violation of which subjects the member to disciplinary action, often include the following:

Respect, Language

Active lack of respect, manifested by abusive language or non-verbal communication directed toward other personnel or members of the public, is prohibited.

Disobedience

The violation of or deliberate delay in the prompt completion of activities directed to be performed by the lawful orders of any superior officer is prohibited.

Confidentiality

Divulgence of any information concerning the plans, actions, internal activities or case materials of the police department without authority is prohibited.

Intoxication

The use at any time of any intoxicating drug or material proscribed by law is prohibited, and reporting for duty while under the influence of the consumption of any intoxicant while on duty is prohibited, although the ingestion of intoxicants necessarily required by the nature of the assigned (usually undercover) duties being performed by the officer may be permitted.

Misconduct

Any breach of the peace, neglect of duty, or misconduct either within or without the jurisdiction which tends to subvert the good order, efficiency, or discipline of the department or the auxiliary force or which reflects discredit upon the department is prohibited.

Misuse of Position

Affiliation with any group which professes to represent the police department or other agency of the criminal justice system while purporting to act as a representative of the police agency, and utilizing or making reference to one's affiliation with the department to sway others for political purposes is prohibited without lawful permission of superiors of the department for professional purpose.

Wearing of Uniform and Use of Equipment

The auxiliary police will wear only prescribed or issued uniform items, utilize only prescribed or issued equipment or weapons, and maintain these items; and any officer failing to meet these requirements shall be subject to disciplinary action.

Off-Duty Weapons

Off-duty auxiliary officers shall neither carry nor utilize any weapon in contravention to the laws applicable to citizens not falling within the statutory exemptions concerning the possession or use of weapons (or, for those agencies which permit by regulation the carrying of off-duty weapons). Off-duty auxiliary officers may carry any weapon permitted by law upon prior approval by and registration with the department.

Any action by an auxiliary police officer that is illegal or contrary to departmental rules and regulations subjects that officer to disciplinary action, including separation from the force.